HERE BEFORE
GIANTS AND LITTLE PEOPLE
— Volume 2 —

- FIRST EDITION -

COPYRIGHT © 2018 BY PETER A. NETZEL

<u>Absolutely all rights reserved</u>.

Tired Man
Productions
L.L.C.

PUBLISHED IN USA BY TIRED MAN PRODUCTIONS, LLC
BILLINGS, MT 59101

TABLE OF CONTENTS

<u>Introduction</u>

Scholars believe that there is a strong possibility that races of tiny people and giants could have existed long ago; and the reason they are no longer found is due to the fact that they became extinct at the hands of enemies, or were wiped out by disease or some other disaster. But, because ancient cultures rely on oral traditions to transfer history, information, and culture to younger generations through story and song, we have knowledge of these exceptional creatures.

The term "folklore" is defined as "the traditional beliefs, customs, and stories of a community, passed through the generations by word of mouth, through song and dance, and in written form. Synonyms for *folklore* are: oral history, tradition, folk tradition; legends, fables, folk tales, folk stories, and old wives' tales. A *myth* is a "traditional story, often concerning the early history of a people, or explaining some natural or social phenomenon, and typically involving supernatural beings or events." *Mythology* is a "collection of myths, especially one belonging to a particular religious or cultural tradition."

We find races of tiny people and giants mentioned in the folklore and mythology in every part of the world, and all through history. So prevalent are stories of Giants and Little People worldwide, that it is likely a person could find folk tales and myths of these beings in every corner of the globe. In addition to spoken and written stories, skulls, skeletons, bones, and tools have been found throughout the world. These relics add supportive evidence to oral traditions and lore, that unusually small or exceptionally large humans existed at one time.

ILLUSTRATION OF ONE OF THE BEST KNOWN TALES OF GIANTS AND LITTLE PEOPLE: GULLIVER'S TRAVELS. GIANT-SIZED GULLIVER IS CAPTURED BY LITTLE PEOPLE, ON THE ISLAND OF LILLIPUT.

Quite a large number of newspaper articles from the 1800s and 1900s, to the present, tell of human skeletons being found throughout the world. The tallest reported was 36 feet. The smallest was just over 3 feet tall.

There is much debate about whether Giants and Little People were real or imagined. There is also debate about whether such humanoids were gods or aliens from another world; or whether Giants and Little People are the product of genetics and evolution.

As an example of the latter, in *Popular Science Monthly,* July 1887, there is a piece called, "Variations in Human Stature" by M. Guyot Daubes, where he discusses the differences in stature of Giants and Little People:

> The study of human stature involves several questions of more important interest than that of mere theory or curiosity. It may aid us in learning whether the human race is really degenerating, as some persons assert, by determining whether our ancestors in heroic and prehistoric times had the superior physical prowess that is often ascribed to them. It should teach us whether there are races of dwarfs and of giants, and what are the distances separating the races that most nearly approach those descriptions.

> We learn from it the exact facts respecting the differences in stature among the people of a single nation, our own, for instance, to which military men attach high value. Other fields of inquiry, of a practical bearing, regard the

causes that influence the stature of populations and races in general, and the growth
of individuals, from infancy up; and the
influence of stature upon the force, agility,
endurance, and physical development of
individuals.

An opinion was current, in the last century,
that our ancestors, at some time in the past,
were the equals or superiors in size to the
largest men now to be found. M. Henrion
presented to the Académie des Inscriptions,
in 1718, a memoir on the variations in the
size of man from the beginning of the world
till the Christian era, in which Adam was
given one hundred and twenty-three feet nine
inches, and Eve one hundred and eighteen
feet nine and three fourths inches.

But after the first pair, the human race, in his
imagination, suffered a regular decrease, so
that Noah was only one hundred feet high,
while Abraham shrank down to twenty-eight
feet, Moses to thirteen feet, the mighty
Hercules to ten feet eight and a half inches,
and Alexander the Great to a bare six feet and
a half. The communication, it is said, was
received with enthusiasm, and was regarded,
at the time, as a "wonderful discovery" and a
"sublime vision."

Possessor of a doctorate in anthropology from Columbia University, Susan B. Martinez, Ph.D., writes in her book, *"The History of the Little People: Their Spiritually Advanced Civilizations Around the World,"* that "....an ancient race of people who were small in stature once inhabited the Earth." Martinez refers to legends and stories from many cultures, such as the "dwarf gods of Mexico and Peru, the Menhune of Hawaii, the Nunnehi of the Cherokee, as well as African Pygmies and the Semang of Malaysia." She draws upon "discoveries of tiny tunnel networks, small coffins, low doorways in mounds, and pygmy-sized huts" as evidence of this ancient race.

No matter their origins, the myths and folk tales centered around Giants and Little People are entertaining reading, while at the same time, giving us a window into the culture of the people and history of the region from where they originate. Oftentimes, Giants and Little People are associated with stories of creation, living in harmony with nature, and morality tales. Many of these legends contain elements of truth and are often based on actual events.

Accounts of Giants and Little People are so numerous throughout the world, that it would be impossible to capture all of the myths and stories in a single book. This book, *HERE BEFORE US, GIANTS & LITTLE PEOPLE,* the second of two volumes, contains an overview and a sampling of details and stories about the Giants and Little People who were here before us.

The popular science fiction television program from the 1960s, *The Twilight Zone,* featured episodes with Giants and Little People as part of the plot line.

Giants & Little People

of

THE

BIBLE

In the Holy Bible, there are mentions of giants. They were called by many names: sometimes by the name of the lands they occupied; other times by name. One of the earliest mentions of giants in Scripture before the Great Flood, is found in Genesis 14. Although Genesis 14:5 does not explain that the Rephaim, Zuzim, Emim, or Amorites were exceptionally tall people—giants.

> In the fourteenth year Chedorlaomer and the kings that were with him came and attacked the *Rephaim* in Ashteroth Karnaim, the *Zuzim* in Ham, the *Emim* in Shaveh Kiriathaim, and the Horites in their mountain of Seir . . . . Then they turned back and came to En Mishpat (that is, Kadesh), and attacked all the country of the Amalekites, and also the *Amorites* who dwelt in Hazezon Tamar (Genesis 14:5–7).

The giants of the Bible were said to be scattered throughout Canaan. The giants Og, Ishbi-benob, Goliath, and others appear in Biblical Scripture. These men were exceptionally tall. Saul, too, must have been a gigantic man; because we are told in

Samuel 9:2 that "from his shoulders and upwards, he was higher than any of the people." (He was a head taller than anyone else.) A race of giants is first mentioned in Genesis 6:1-4. They are the Nephilim:

> "The Nephilim were on the earth in those days, and also afterward, when the sons of God came in to the daughters of men, and they bore children to them. Those were the mighty men who were of old, men of renown."

When the Israelites first approached the Promised Land after the Exodus from Egypt, they were afraid to enter the land because it was filled with "giants," the sons of Anak. Compared to these giants the spies felt like little grasshoppers in comparison:

> So, they gave out to the sons of Israel a report of the land which they had spied out, saying, "The land through which we have gone, in spying it out, is a land that devours its inhabitants; and all the people whom we saw in it are men of great size. There also, we saw the Nephilim (the sons of Anak are part of the Nephilim); and we became like grasshoppers in our own sight, and so we were in their sight."   — Numbers 13:33

Deuteronomy 1:28, contains Moses' recollection of what happened when the spies reported back in terror, describing fearful giants:

> "....whither are we going up? Our brethren have melted our heart, saying, a people greater and taller than we, cities great and fenced to heaven, and also sons of Anakim — we have seen there."

The same event is recounted in Numbers 13:32:

> ....and they bring out an evil account of the land which they have spied unto the sons of Israel, saying, "The land into which we passed over to spy it, is a land eating up its inhabitants; and all the people whom we saw in its midst are men of stature."

According to the website *"Torah: Navigating the Bible,"* http://bible.ort.org/books/torah, says of the Rephaim race of giants:

> In Deuteronomy 2:11 the Rephaim are described as "mighty ones," or "giants." Their land was promised to Abraham (Genesis 15:20), and part of it was given to Lot's descendants (Deuteronomy 2:20). Og, a giant reported to be over ten feet tall, was said to be one of the survivors of the Rephaim (Deuteronomy 3:11; Joshua 12:4, 13:12). Their land was later called Bashan, to the east of the Jordan (Deuteronomy 3:13).

The first reference to the Rephaim is Genesis 14:5, when the Rephaim, Zuzim and Emim people were defeated in a battle with Kedorlaomer and his allies. Deuteronomy 2:20–21 says the Rephaim were strong and tall, like the Anakites. Og, king of Bashan, was described as the last of the Rephaim in his land (Deuteronomy 3:11), and his bed was thirteen feet long and six feet wide.

According to the book of Enoch, the ancient giants were the product of the union of fallen angels and mortal humans. Some angels were sent by God to guard the earth. Some of these "watchers" were seduced by the beauty of the mortal women. The product of the union of fallen angels with the daughters of the earth, were children described as being of gigantic size:

> When men began to multiply on earth and daughters were born to them, the sons of God saw how beautiful the daughters of man were, and so they took for their wives as many of them as they chose. Then the Lord said: "My spirit shall not remain in man forever, since he is but flesh. His days shall comprise one hundred and twenty years." — Genesis 6:1-4

Scripture is not the only source of this story. Famed writer and historian John Milton is best known for writing *"Paradise Lost,"* and *"Paradise Regained."* The latter work contains a description of the fallen angels and their offspring:

> "Before the Flood, Thou with thy lusty crew,
> False-titled sons of God, roaming the earth,
> Cast wanton eyes on the daughters of men,
> And coupled with them, and begot a race."

Common belief is that the Great Flood wiped out the fallen angels and their offspring. The following piece from 1883 discusses the Nephilim and their relation to the Great Flood in Biblical times:

THE COLUMBIAN
Bloomsburg, Pennsylvania
June 8, 1883

ANTEDILUVIAN HISTORY.

AN ATTEMPT TO GET AT THE MEANING OF THE EARLY CHAPTERS OF GENESIS.

THE "GIANTS UPON THE EARTH"

SIGNIFICANT PASSAGES CONCERNING THE CAUSE OF GOD'S ANGER AGAINST MANKIND.

[By JOHN G. FREEZE.]

In the first chapters of Genesis, the narratives of the good and the bad are mingled together in a manner somewhat embarrassing to the general reader; and the difficulty is increased by the division into chapters and verses, which division has been most bunglingly performed. It would be well if the whole chapter system were abandoned, leaving as a convenience, the present distribution into verses, but numbering them from 1, continuing to the end of the respective book, marking the change of subject by the paragraph sign, as is now partially done, and noting the supposed chronology on the margin.

This matter impressed itself forcibly upon my mind lately on an examination of the first six chapters of Genesis, in an endeavor to disentangle the double narrative of the antediluvian history---especially in connection with the meaning of the first, second, and fourth verses of the sixth chapter.

THE NEPHILIM.

Were there on the earth any beings other than the offspring of Adam and Eve? In answer to that question, let us read the first, second, and fourth verses of the sixth chapter of Genesis:

"And it came to pass, when men began to multiply on the face of the earth, and daughters were unto them, that the sons of God saw the daughters of men that they were fair; and they took them wives of all which they chose. There were giants in the earth in those days; and also after that, when the sons of God came in unto the daughters of men, and they bore children unto them, the offspring became mighty men which were of old, men of renown."

Here, then, we have mingling in this compound which we call humanity: first, the daughters of men; second, the sons of God; third, the Nephilim, the giants.

The daughters of men are no other than the descendants of Adam, whether direct or by the line of Cain, for we are to remember that all of both lines were destroyed, except the family of Noah, who were preserved on account of the personal righteousness of Noah. We are also to observe that the word used by the writer of the original for God is "Elohim" and therefore being a proper name of the Deity, these male persons are not supposed to be or considered to be sons of chiefs or princes, but really and actually what they are called, and are some intelligent created beings higher than man and distinct from him. And, finally, that the Nephilim are properly "Fallen Ones" and not giants, if the word is taken as relating simply to stature, and that the word translated "mighty men," "men of renown," is gibborim, and that the gibborim are the offspring of the marriages of the sons of God with the daughters of men.

Who were Nephilim? The word is used, in my judgment, to designate those renegade, degraded, fallen angels or beings, elsewhere styled the sons of God. As if we were to say, "The sons of God married the daughters of Adam;" and in answer to a word of incredulity the further remark is made, "There were fallen ones, Nephilim, in those days."

THE SONS OF GOD.

It seems too plain for argument that these Nephilim, whoever and whatever they were, were the cause of this disturbance. Were they angels, were they other created beings, higher or lower, from heavenly places? Or were they spirits cast out of heaven and who escaped with Satan from hell? The designation seems to be of an order. In Job, those who come in regular course of duty to present themselves before the Lord are the sons of God; and Satan came also in the midst of them. In antediluvian times, the phrase uniformly used in speaking of these earth-visiting heavenly intelligences is "Sons of God." Afterwards, as a mere messenger, "the angel of the Lord appeared unto Hagar," and under the same designation there are other similar manifestations. It is not until Second Samuel 14:20, only about 1,000 years before Christ, that we have the angel in a higher character than a messenger. There it is said: "And my Lord is wise, according to the wisdom of an angel of God, to know all things that are in the earth;" unless we say that Job 4:18 is older: where it is said as a marginal reading "Behold, He put no trust in His servants, nor in His angels in whom he put light."

Wherever an angel has appeared or is spoken of, it is as a male and in the forms of a man; and in the early history of the race, the frequent and friendly appearance of angels as messengers, assistants and guides seems to be almost a matter of course. No surprise is expressed at any manifestations or at any occurrence in which they play a part as if it were unusual or unexpected. Did they always come as God's messengers and only when sent, or were wise to know all things that were in the earth, and did they volunteer to assist and counsel? Were they free to roam through the new creation? And, roaming at will, like as Adam, liable to fall? It may be held so; and that after the flood, this liberty was restrained to special messages. If, then, these angels, fallen from their first estate, coming to the earth as sightseers or as messengers, seduced by the beauty of women, remained on earth, we can faintly imagine how these immortal beings might and would introduce infinite wretchedness, change the nature of all flesh and corrupt and make the imagination of the thoughts of man's heart evil continually.

Hopes of earthly immortality, claims of heavenly descent, boasts of spiritual superiority, dissatisfaction with more human husbands, exciting all the very worst passions of a nature already fallen, would produce a condition of things well described by the sacred writer. And, it was such a state of semi-immortality, of moral degradation and of family discord, running, no doubt, through the whole human race, that made the absolute destruction of the offspring of these unnatural marriages a necessity for the restoration of the descendants of Adam, and even then, with some evil imaginings remaining.

Memorials to primordial giants still exist in Palestine, where there are graves of enormous dimensions, such as the grave of Abel, near Damascus, which is 30 feet long; that of Seth in Anti-Lebanon, which is about the same size; and that of Noah, in Lebanon, which is 70 yards in length. The Egyptians also wrote about giants who lived in the land of Canaan. Such large beings were said to be between 7 and 10 feet tall and mighty men. Usually presented as enemies in ancient books and folklore, giants were either destroyed by God—as in the Great Flood—or in battle with men.

Perhaps the most famous giant of the Bible is Goliath of Gath, champion of the Philistines. We know of him from the story of how David, a humble shepherd boy, slew the huge giant with just a stone. Goliath, according to 1 Samuel 17:4, was "six cubits and a span in height." Assuming the cubit to be the cubit of a man, that would make him nine feet nine inches high. And if a cubit of twenty-one inches is assumed, it would make him about eleven feet five inches high. In the last chapter of Samuel, we are told that Goliath's coat of mail weighed "five thousand shekels of brass," which is about two hundred and eight pounds. "And the staff of his spear was like a weaver's beam;" and his "spear's head weighed six hundred shekels of iron," which is about twenty-five pounds.

Samuel 21:16 describes David's battles with other giants, one of whom had six fingers on each hand and six toes on each foot:

> A giant named Ishbibenob, who was carrying a bronze spear that weighed about 35 kilograms and who was wearing a new sword, thought he could kill David. But Abishai son of Zeruiah came to David's help, attacked the giant, and killed him. Then David's men made David promise that he would never again go out with

them to battle. "You are the hope of Israel, and we don't want to lose you," they said. After this there was a battle with the Philistines at Gob, during which Sibbecai from Hushah killed a giant named Saph. There was another battle with the Philistines at Gob, and Elhanan son of Jair from Bethlehem killed Goliath from Gath, whose spear had a shaft as thick as the bar on a weaver's loom._Then there was another battle at Gath, where there was a giant who loved to fight. He had six fingers on each hand and six toes on each foot. He defied the Israelites, and Jonathan, the son of David's brother Shammah, killed him. These four were descendants of the giants of Gath, and they were killed by David and his men.

—2 Samuel 21:16-22

The Dead Sea Scrolls:
The Book of Giants

Contained in the Dead Sea Scrolls, which are ancient manuscripts found in the Qumran Caves near the Dead Sea, is found *The Book of Giants*. The patriarch Enoch was well known to the ancients. The oldest reference to Enoch is found in The Book of Enoch. The Biblical Book of Genesis also gives his age as 365 years; it says that he "walked with God," and afterward "he was not, because God had taken him." (Gen. 5:24).

Additional, previously unknown or little-known texts about Enoch were discovered at Qumran in 1946. Among these, is *The Book of Giants*. Enoch lived before the Flood; this was a time when human beings lived much longer. Enoch's son Methuselah, died at the age of 969 years. Also, during the time of Enoch, angels and humans interacted freely. Some of the angels begot children with human females. The offspring of these unnatural unions were "giants 450 feet high." The wicked angels and the giants began to oppress the human population around them, and to endeavored to teach all humans to do evil. (1 Enoch 6-16).

And it came to pass, when men began to multiply on the face of the earth, and daughters were born unto them, That the sons of God saw the daughters of men that they were fair; and they took them wives of all which they chose. And the LORD said, "My spirit shall not always strive with man, for that he also is flesh: yet his days shall be an hundred and twenty years." There were giants in the earth in those days; and also after that, when the sons of God came in unto the daughters of men, and they bore children to them, the same became mighty men which were of old, men of renown. (Genesis 6:1-4)

Fragment of *The Book Of Giants*.

The Book of Giants retells part of this story, with details about the exploits of the giants, especially the two children of Shemihaza, Ohya and Hahya. Much of the content of the fragments of these ancient texts concerns the giants' "ominous dreams," Enoch's efforts to interpret them, and his efforts to intercede with God on the giants' behalf. Enoch did not succeed. God intervened and imprisoned the angels until the final judgment. He then destroyed the earth with a great flood.

Little People

There do not seem to be many references to Little People, or dwarfs, in Scripture. There is one reference found in Leviticus 21:17, stating that dwarfs were not permitted to enter the First Temple in Jerusalem to worship:

> Speak to Aaron, saying, "None of your offspring throughout their generations who has a blemish may approach to offer the bread of his God. For no one who has a blemish shall draw near, a man blind or lame, or one who has a mutilated face or a limb too long, or a man who has an injured foot or an injured hand, or a hunchback or a dwarf or a man with a defect in his sight or an itching disease or scabs or crushed testicles. No man of the offspring of Aaron the priest who has a blemish shall come near to offer the Lord's food offerings; since he has a blemish, he shall not come near to offer the bread of his God. He may eat the bread of his God, both of the most holy and of the holy things, but he shall not go through the veil or approach the altar, because he has a blemish, that he may not profane my sanctuaries, for I am the Lord who sanctifies them."

Conversely, in kind of a mixed message in 1 Samuel 16:7, the Lord said to Samuel:

Do not look on his appearance or on the height of his stature, because I have rejected him. For the Lord sees not as man sees: man looks on the outward appearance, but the Lord looks on the heart.

Zacchaeus, a man of very short stature appears in Luke 19:2-4:

And there was a man called by the name of Zacchaeus; he was a chief tax collector and he was rich. Zacchaeus was trying to see who Jesus was, and was unable because of the crowd, for he was small in stature. So, he ran on ahead and climbed up into a sycamore tree in order to see Him, for He was about to pass through that way.

It has been theorized that Jesus was a Little Person. In *"The Genuine Works Of Flavius Josephus, The Jewish Historian,"* Christ is described as being:

...a man of simple appearance, mature age, dark skin, small stature, three cubits high, hunchbacked, with a long face, long nose, and meeting eyebrows, so that they who see him might be affrighted, with scanty hair (but) having a line in the middle of the head after the fashion of the Nazarenes, and with an undeveloped beard.

There are a variety of sources that describe Jesus Christ as being small in stature. The average male of that time stood about 5 ft. 1 inch and weighed on average about 110 pounds. The Acts of John 5:90 contains this description: *"I was afraid and cried out; and he, turning about, appeared as a man of small stature…"*

Within the *Acts of John* are found more details on the appearance of Christ. An example is when he relates his experience of the earthly Jesus:

> And when we left the place, wishing to follow him again, he again appeared to me, bald-headed but with a thick and flowing beard; but to James he appeared as a youth whose beard was just starting. We were perplexed, both of us, as to the meaning of what we had seen. But when we followed him, we both became gradually more perplexed as we thought on the matter. Yet to me there appeared a still more wonderful sight; for I tried to see him as he was; and I never at any time saw his eyes closing but only open.

> And sometimes he appeared to me as a small man and unattractive and then again as one reaching to heaven. Also, there was in him another marvel: when I sat the table, he would take me upon his breast and I held him,

sometimes his breast felt to me to be smooth and tender; and sometimes, hard like stone, so that I was perplexed in myself and said, "What does this mean?"

Another glory I will tell you, brethren. Sometimes when I meant to touch Him, I met a material and solid body; and at other times again when I felt him, the substance was immaterial and bodiless as if it were not existing at all. (88-9; 93)

At another time he took me and James and Peter to the mountain, where he used to pray; and we beheld such a light on him that it is not possible for a man who uses mortal speech to describe what it was like. Again, in a similar way, he led us three up to the mountain saying, "Come with me." And we went again and saw him at a distance praying.

Now I, because he loved me, went to him quietly as though he should not see, and stood looking upon his back. And I saw that he was not dressed in garments, but was seen by us as naked and not at all like a man; his feet were whiter than snow, so that the ground there was lit up by his feet, and his head reached to heaven; so that I was afraid and cried out. He turned and appeared as a man of small stature and took hold of my beard and pulled it and said to me, "John, be not unbelieving, but believing, and not inquisitive."

And I said to him, "What have I done, Lord?"
And I tell you brethren, I suffered such pain
for forty days at the place where he took hold
of my beard, that I said unto him, "Lord, if
your playful tug has given me so much pain,
what if you had given me a beating?" And he
said to me, "Let it be your concern from
henceforth not to tempt him who is not to be
tempted." (90:cf; Matthew 17:1-9)

The image of a short (and unattractive) Jesus is
provided by other sources. In the *Coptic Acts of
Paul and Thecla,* Paul describes him as "a man
small in size, bald-headed with eyebrows meeting,
rather hook-nosed." (v.3) The *Koran* (Fath Al-Bari,
v.6, Trad. 3437) makes note of the small stature
of Jesus in the story of the night that the
prophet Muhammad flies to Jerusalem on a winged
horse to visit the prophets Abraham, Moses, and
Jesus, saying that "Jesus was the smaller of the
three." In *The Acts of Peter,* from the Bible, Jesus
is described as "small and ugly to the ignorant."
Andrew of Crete relates that Christ was bent or
even crooked.

Ephraem the Syrian was a deacon and hymnologist
of the 4th century. A compilation of his writings
was produced in 1847 by J.B. Morris. The book,

entitled *"Selected Works of S. Ephraem the Syrian by Ephraem, Syrus, Saint, 303-373,"* Jesus Christ is described: "God took human form and appeared in the form of three human ells (cubits); he came down to us small of stature."

Another Biblical interpreter, Theodore of Mopsuestia, described the appearance of Christ, saying "Thy appearance, O Christ, was smaller than that of the children of Jacob."

Little People inhabit the interrelated mythology, folklore, and literary history of people worldwide. In spite of such widespread occurrence of dwarflike characters, it seems odd that they are not featured widely within the Bible. The explanation for this is probably because of the pagan roots of legends of dwarfs and elves. The church played a pivotal role in changing Little People from fearless, shape-shifting warriors with magical powers, into cheerful helpers and cute garden gnomes.

Santa helpers, elves, are portrayed as little bearded dwarfs in red caps who are mischievous and playful, helpful and industrious. But their roots go much deeper than their inclusion in fairy tales and popular stories. Elves and dwarfs are part of a much older belief system that predates Christianity.

Dwarfs and elves were fantastical tiny people who lived in wild and uncultivated regions; they were the keepers of the secrets of nature. They possessed magical abilities from being able to change their size at will. They had superhuman strength and healing powers. They were excellent craftsmen, creating swords that nothing could dull or magical charms or jewelry.

According to Wikipedia at Internet address: https://en.wikipedia.org, the primordial giant, Ymir, gave birth to dwarfs. They sprang from his body:

> *Poetic Edda* is the modern attribution for an unnamed collection of Old Norse anonymous poems, all primarily of text from the Icelandic medieval manuscript known as the *Codex Regius*.

> The *Codex Regius* is arguably the most important extant source on Norse mythology and Germanic heroic legends, and from the early 19th century onwards, it has had a powerful influence on later Scandinavian literatures, not only by its stories but also by the visionary force and the dramatic quality of many of the poems.

> Dwarves were originally born out of the decomposing body of Ymir, the primordial giant.

These children of Ymir who created a race in their image were named Móðsognir and Durinn. They were not the only ones, however, since the gods took Ymir's skull to use as the celestial vault, set it atop four columns, under each of which they placed a dwarf. These dwarves bear the names of the four cardinal points: Norðri, Suðri, Austri, Vestri.

The first dwarf turns up in medieval German literature between 1023 and 1050, but other non-literary evidence exists to show that dwarves were present long before this. As a result, it becomes apparent that the medieval romances drew upon folk traditions, among other things.

In this same geographical region, the *Heldenbuch* (Book of Heroes), printed in Strasbourg around 1483, puts a Christian spin on the earlier mythological material when it relates how God peopled the earth that he had just created. God first made dwarves to develop the earth; afterward he created the giants, whose duty it was to protect the dwarves against the then-teeming population of dragons. But the giants turned treacherous and began oppressing the dwarves, at which point God created heroes to restore and keep secure His order.

Another very old text, the thirteenth-century Middle High German translation of the *Magnificat,* says: "God distributed the demons among the entire earth. In the waters and mountains lived the Nixies and the Dwarves, in the forests and swamps the Elves, the Thurses, and other spirits."

We should note that an Icelandic tale from the nineteenth century, *Huldumanna Genesis* (The Origin of the Hidden Men), made dwarves the children of Eve. Because they were unwashed, Eve hid them from the eyes of God, who then decreed: "Whatever should be hid from my sight should also be hid from that of men." These children were therefore invisible: they dwelt in the hills and mountains, in holes, and among the rocks. The magic of dwarfs and elves can be rekindled if we recognize their signs and invite them back into our world.

Giants & Little People

of

ANCIENT

GREECE

&

ROME

The Trojan War was a legendary conflict between the early Greeks and the people of Troy, in western Anatolia (Turkey), that occurred in the 12th or 13th century B.C.

The conflict was touched off when Paris, son of the Trojan king, ran off with Helen, wife of Menelaus of Sparta (one of the city-states of Greece). The brother of Menelaus, Agamemnon, led a Greek expedition against Troy to rescue Helen and get revenge. The Trojan War lasted 10 years. It finally ending when the Greeks pretended to withdraw, leaving behind them a giant wooden horse. A group of warriors was hidden inside the wooden horse. Thinking that the Greeks had gone, the Trojans brought the horse into their city.

By dark of night, the hidden Greeks climbed out of the horse and opened the gates of Troy for their comrades, who then sacked Troy, massacred its men, and carried off its women.

"The Little People" by Susan B. Martinez, Ph.D., contains a description which shows the connection

between Biblical Little People to the time of the Trojan War:

> Yet, the same facts present themselves in other places. The earliest Alaskans, as indigenous tradition and extant artifacts allow, were master engravers/carvers with "fair hair and blue eyes." Tracing these master carvers and painters, we find the Sky People in Hebrew legend as well, the immediate forbears of Noah (Noe) having preserved (antediluvian) knowledge on *engraved* pillars, under the inspiration of Holy Ones or Watchers. These celestial beings were called "I'rin," the name strikingly similar to Oahspe's "I'hin," designating the white-skinned and white- (or yellow-) haired Little People who became extinct 3,500 years ago.
>
> Noah himself, as told in the Book of Enoch, descended from those Holy Ones and was born "white as snow," with hair "white as wool." Radiant, "like a child of the angels," the infant rose from the hand of the midwife, opened his mouth, and praised the Lord of Righteousness. All of which proved quite disturbing to his father who feared the wonder of this strange birth, until his grandfather Enoch explained the *heavenly-earthly* intermixing that took place "in the time of Jared, my father." Sky-People, in Levantine dress.

Noah's son Jaffeth, we have seen, populated parts of Asia after the Deluge and here again is found evidence of those snow-white carvers. Jaffeth (now "Iapetos"), according to Flood legends of the region, escaped to Mt. Ida in a boat of skins. He went on to found the grand city of Troy, whose people, according to Heinrich Schliemann, "had a great taste for art" and produced exquisite *carvings* and inscribed earthenware vessels. Excavating the royal palace, Schliemann also came upon women's bracelets of such small size as to fit a nine-year-old. Other works typical of the Little People, such as the colossal mortuary *mounds* on the Plains of Troy, have been discovered in Asia Minor, where ancient myth recalls the founding Mother as "an exquisite, delicate, milk-white maid."

In the excerpt above, Martinez refers to "Oahspe" *(Oahspe: A New Bible),* which was published in 1882. The book contains "new revelations from the Ambassadors of the angel hosts of heaven prepared and revealed unto man in the name of Jehovah...." According to *Wikipedia,* the book was "produced by an American dentist, John Ballou Newbrough, who reported it to have been written by automatic writing." (Automatic writing, or psychography, is a psychic ability that causes a person to produce written words without consciously writing. The words arise from a subconscious, spiritual or supernatural source.) Giants and Little People appear in the *Oahspe* text:

The Ancient Races of Man

OAHSPE IDENTIFIES THE TRUE RACES OF MAN

The first races of man came about through the one time blending of animal man (Asu also called Adam in ancient legends) with materialized ethereans (angels). Thcsc offspring of this blend of animal (Asu) and angel man were distinguished from each other by the more or less ratio of animal to angel. This was expressed in their physiology, intellectual capacity and spiritual potential. The first intermixing occurred around 76,000 years ago resulting in a race of man that was half animal – half angel. These were called I'hins. They were diminutive, well-shaped humans with shorter arms and longer legs, with the ability to walk upright. They were also capable of speech and could perceive their angel forebears.

This ability to perceive their forebears was the *su'is* sight (ability to see spirits and spiritual things) which was passed on in more or less degree to all of their descendants

SOME ANCIENT RACES OF MAN

Included in the various races of man were a wide range of physical characteristics. The I'hins were small and gracile (slender) with fine features and hair. The Druks were stout with long arms and short legs, The I'huans were tall and copper colored. There were also in-betweens, the Yak being a mix between Druk and I'huan. Moreover, there were differences in each of the races through the ages. At one point, some of the I'hins had become very small; and, at least twice, the Druks had become very large – called giants.

– Oahspe, Synopsis of 16 Cycles; 09/1.22.

Now, for the most part, all the people had become I'hins, small, white and yellow. Nevertheless, there were ground people, with long arms, who were large; but they dwelt by themselves, and their food was of all types of flesh, fish, and creeping things. The ground people were brown and black, and they lived to be two hundred, and even four hundred years old. But there were giants (Druks) in those days and in time after that; and my chosen came to them, and they bore children to them also.

– Oahspe, The Lord's First Book; 11/1.29.

Epic Greek poet, Homer, wrote of giants. In *The Odyssey,* his sequel to *The Iliad,* Homer wrote about gigantic beings, saying: "On the earth there once were giants." The poem's main character is Odysseus; he is king of Ithaca in Greece. The *Odyssey* chronicles his journey home after the fall of Troy.

At one point in his journey, Odysseus and his men enter the cave of the Cyclops, the giant son of Poseidon and the sea nymph, Thoosa. Odysseus blinded the gigantic one-eyed Cyclops by driving a wooden stake into the giant's eye. The captives escaped by hanging underneath the bellies of Cyclops' sheep as they filed out from the cave to pasture. The Cyclops then throws the top half of a mountain at Odysseus as he prays to the fleeing man's father, Poseidon, saying that his son had blinded him. This enrages Poseidon, who then curses Odysseus by delaying his homecoming for many years.

The following passage from *The Odyssey* contains names and ancestry of ancient Giants:

> These beings that are close to the gods include the Phaeacians who lived near Cyclopes,

whose king, Alcinous, is the great-grandson of the king of the giants, Eurymedon, and the grandson of Poseidon. Some of the other characters that Odysseus encounters are Polyphemus who is the Cyclops son of Poseidon, God of Oceans; Circe who is the sorceress daughter of the Sun that turns men into animals; Calypso who is a goddess; and the Laestrygonians, who are cannibalistic giants.

The Laestrygonians in Homer's *Odyssey* are giant cannibals. They eat many of Odysseus' men. By throwing giant rocks the Laestrygonians destroy 11 of Odysseus's fleeing ships.

Time Magazine, ran a story in its October 28, 1946 issued entitled, *Science: Giants of Old.* This piece takes a look at oral and written records; actual bones and skeletons; artifacts and scientific findings that "substantiate the actual existence of those post-glacial mid-sized or smaller sized giants, stating that:

> "They are larger than humans today, but not nearly as large as early Epoch Giants. The records and artifacts suggest current Epoch giant hominids up through the post Colombian era, were the smaller of the giants, standing between 8' to 13' in height, and weighing between 850 and 3200 lbs...."

> "The records indicate that giants from the Last Great Cataclysm were between 16' and 24' tall. Following that cataclysm, giants decreased in size down to 12' to 15' during the later Holocene about 3,500 years ago. One of the survivor groups of larger giants had nearly gone extinct, a remnant tribe living in the Valley of Bashan, in the foothills of Mt. Hermon in Northern Israel, near the Beqaa Valley."

Maximinus Thrax was giant man who once held the office of Roman Emperor. Historian, Augustus, wrote *Historia Augusta,* a collection of biographies of Roman emperors written between 293, the year of the nomination of these Caesars, and 305, the year of Diocletian's retirement. He says that Maximinus was 8½ feet (2.6 m) tall, and incredibly strong—he could pull fully loaded carts by himself. Augustus describes Maximinus Thrax's big feet– twice the size of the average soldier–and his huge hands like this:

> Maximinus was almost eight and a half feet tall; and certain men deposited a shoe of his, that is, one of his royal boots, in a grove which lies between Aquileia and Arcia, because, sooth, they agreed that it was a foot longer than the measure of any foot of man. Whence also is derived the vulgar expression, used for lanky and awkward fellows, of "Maximinus' boot."

> I have put this down lest anyone who reads Cordus should believe that I have overlooked anything which pertained to my subject. He was of such size, so Cordus reports, that men said he was six inches over eight feet in height; and his thumb was so huge that he used his wife's bracelet for a ring. Other stories are reported almost as common talk — that he could drag wagons with his hands and move a laden cart by himself, that if he struck a horse with his fist, he loosened its teeth, or with his heel, broke its legs, that he could crumble tufaceous stone and split saplings, and that he was called, finally, by

some Milo of Croton, by others Hercules, and by others Antaeus.

Maximinus Thrax had a huge appetite and great stamina, according to biographer, Augustus:

> It is agreed, moreover, that often in a single day he drank a Capitoline amphora of wine, and ate forty pounds of meat, or, according to Cordus, no less than sixty. It seems sufficiently agreed, too, that he abstained wholly from vegetables, and almost always from anything cold, save when he had to drink. Often, he would catch his sweat and put it in cups or a small jar, and he could exhibit by this means two or three pints of it.

> Severus, on the birthday of Geta, his younger son, was giving military games, offering various silver prizes, arm-rings, that is, and collars, and girdles. This youth, half barbarian and scarcely yet master of the Latin tongue, speaking almost pure Thracian, publicly besought the Emperor to give him leave to compete, and that with men of no mean rank in the service. Severus, struck with his bodily size, pitted him first against sutlers—all very valorous men, none the less—in order to avoid a rupture of military discipline. Whereupon Maximinus overcame sixteen sutlers at one sweat, and received his sixteen prizes, all rather small and not

military ones, and was commanded to serve in the army.

The second day thereafter, when Severus had proceeded to the parade-ground, he happened to espy Maximinus rioting in his barbarian way among the crowd, and immediately ordered the tribune to take him in hand and school him in Roman discipline. And he, when he perceived that the Emperor was talking about him—for the barbarian suspected that he was known to the Emperor and conspicuous even among many—came up to the Emperor's feet where he sat his horse.

And then Severus, wishing to try how good he was at running, gave his horse free rein and circled about many times, and when at last the aged Emperor had become weary; Maximinus, after many turns, had not stopped running, he said to him, "What say you, my little Thracian? Would you like to wrestle now after your running?"

Maximinus answered, "As you please, Emperor." On this Severus dismounted and ordered the most vigorous and the bravest soldiers to match themselves with him; whereupon he, in his usual fashion, vanquished seven at one sweat, and alone of all, after he had gotten his silver prizes; he was presented by Severus with a collar of gold; he was ordered, moreover, to take a permanent post in the palace as the bodyguard. In this way, he rose in prominence and became famous among the soldiers, well-liked by the tribunes, and admired by his comrades. Maximinus could get anything he wanted from the Emperor, Severus, who helped Thrax to advance in rank

Portrait busts, in the Louvre Museum in Paris, France, as well as coins from his time, show Maximinus Thrax as a large, muscular man with a strong jaw and short hair.

when he was still very young. In height and size and proportions, in his great eyes, and in whiteness of skin he was preeminent among all.

Historian Herodias, a contemporary of Maximinus, wrote about the great size of Maximinus:

He was in any case a man of such frightening appearance and colossal size that there is no obvious comparison to be drawn with any of the best-trained Greek athletes or warrior elite of the barbarians. In any case, he was much larger, heavier and stronger than any others in the Roman Court, including Gladiators, and slave Barbarians. In AD 235 this giant became the most powerful man in the Roman Empire. Maximinus of Thrace (Bulgaria) was a simple shepherd when his impressive size and strength attracted the attention of the Roman emperor in AD 202. Maximinus wrestled 16 of the emperor's burliest soldiers. Then, only slightly winded, he raced the emperor's horse and went on to overcome 7 more hefty legionnaires. The Thracian colossus was inducted into the army on the spot. Maximinus rose through the ranks, proving himself such a beloved leader that he was given supreme command of the imperial army. In AD 235 the army and the Senate proclaimed him Emperor of Rome.

The following letter composed by Maximinus, about his son, Gaius Julius Verus Maximinus (or Maximinus the Younger) is contained within the text of *Historia Augusta:*

And yet — lest we seem to have omitted anything at all — I have set down a letter written by his father Maximinus, when he had now become emperor, in which he says that he had proclaimed his son emperor in order to see, either in painting or actuality, what the younger Maximinus would look like in the purple. The letter itself was of this nature: "I have let my Maximinus be called emperor, not only because of the fondness which a father owes a son, but also that the Roman people and that venerable senate may be able to take an oath that they have never had a more handsome emperor."

After the fashion of the Ptolemies this youth wore a golden cuirass; he had also a silver one. He had a shield, moreover, inlaid with gold and jewels, and also a gold-inlaid spear. He had silver swords made for him, too, and gold ones as well, everything, in fact, which could enhance his beauty — helmets inset with precious stones and cheek-pieces done in the same fashion.

The omens that he would be emperor were these: A snake coiled about his head as he was sleeping. A grape-vine which he planted produced within a year huge clusters of purple grapes, and grew to an astounding size. His shield blazed in the sun. A small lance of his was split by lightning and in such a manner that the whole of it, even through the iron, was cleft and fell into two halves. And from this the soothsayers declared that from the one house there would spring two emperors of the same name, whose reign would be of no long duration. His father's cuirass — many saw it was stained not with rust, as is usual, but all over with a purple color.

These omens, moreover, occurred for the son: When he was sent to a grammarian, a certain kinswoman of his gave him the works of Homer all written in letters of gold on purple. And while he was yet a little boy, he was asked to dinner by Alexander as a compliment to his father, and, being without a dinner-robe, he wore one of Alexander's.

When still an infant, moreover, he mounted up into a carriage of Antoninus Caracalla's that unexpectedly came down the public way, seeing it empty, and sat down; and only with great ado was he routed out by the coachmen. Nor were there lacking then those who told Caracalla to beware of the child. But he said, "It is a far chance that this fellow will succeed me." For at that time he was of the undistinguished crowd and was very young.

The omens of his death were these: When Maximinus and his son were marching against Maximus and Balbinus they were met by a woman with disheveled hair and woeful attire, who cried out, "Maximini, Maximini, Maximini," and said no more, and died. She wished to add, it seemed, "Help me!"

And at their next halting-place hounds, more than twelve of them, howled about his tent, drawing their breath with a sort of sobbing, and at dawn were found dead. Five hundred wolves, likewise, came in a pack into that town whither Maximinus had betaken himself—Emona, many say, others Archimea —at any rate, it was one which was left abandoned by its inhabitants when Maximinus approached.

It is a lengthy business to enumerate all these things; and if anyone desires to know them, let him, as I have often said, read Cordus, who has related them all, to the point of telling idle tales.

Maximinus died at age 65 in 238 A.D., but not of natural causes. During his reign as Roman Emperor, he came to hate Roman aristocrats; it is said that they hated him because he refused to come to Rome. Maximinus became paranoid and brutal. The public turned against him and openly taunted him. Ultimately, his soldiers turned against him. Maximinus was assassinated by his own Praetorian guards as he slept in his tent. Events leading up to the death of Maximinus Thrax are described by historian Augustus, thusly:

For to hide the lowness of his birth he put to death all who had knowledge of it, some of whom, indeed, were friends who had often pitied him for his poverty and made him many presents. And never was there a more savage animal on earth than this man who staked everything on his own strength, as though he could not be killed. Eventually, indeed, when he almost believed himself immortal because of his great size and courage, a certain actor, they say, recited Greek verses in a theatre while he was present, the sense of which in Latin was this—

And he who cannot be slain by one,
is slain by many.
The elephant is huge, and he is slain!
The lion is brave, and he is slain!
The tiger is brave, and he is slain!
Beware of many together, if you fear not one alone.

DENARIUS – Roman Coin of Maximinus

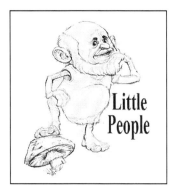

Herodotus was a Greek historian who lived in the fifth century B.C. (484–425 B.C.). He is often referred to as "The Father of History" because of the way that he carefully and methodically studied and organized his research materials and composed histographies. In *"Tales From Herodotus XV, Exploration of Africa,"* he writes:

Pygmies & the Source of the Nile

The Nile is known only as far as four months of sail and road beyond the flow in Egypt. It flows from the west and the setting sun. And beyond that, no one can speak of it with certainty; for that land is a waste, because of its heat. But I have heard the following from some men, Cyrenaeans, who said that they went to a shrine of Ammon and came there into *discourse* with Etearchus, king of the Ammonians; and how from other topics, they came to a discussion concerning the Nile, that no one knew its source.

But Etearchus said that some Nasamonean men once came to him, who said, when they were asked if they had more to say concerning the wilderness of Libya, that there were among them some unruly children born of powerful men, who, when they became men, contrived a number of excesses, one in particular being to choose by lot five of their number that would go see the wilderness of Libya. For along the northern sea of Libya, from Egypt up to the peak of Soloeis, which is the end of Libya, there dwell the Libyans and many tribes of the Libyans, except whatever the Greeks and the Phoenicians hold. And beyond this, Libya teems with wild beasts, and beyond the wild beasts there is sand, fiendishly dry, an empty wasteland.

And so the youths, so the Nasamoneans say, sent out by their fellows, well stocked with water and provisions, went through the inhabited places first; and when they had gone through them, they came upon the beastlands, and from there they went through to the wasteland, making their way against the westerly wind. And having gone through much sandy land for many days, they saw at last trees growing in a plain and they went to it and touched the fruit that was on the trees. And small men came toward those who touched the fruit, smaller than average men, who took them and led them through a very large marsh, and having gone through it, they arrived at a city in which everyone was, with respect to size, like those who led them, and black of skin.

A great river flowed to the city, and it flowed from the west toward the rising sun, and crocodiles could be seen in it. And so, let the story of Etearchus the Ammonian be set forth by me only to this point, except to say that they returned home and they told the Nasamoneans, or so the Cyrenaeans say, and the men to whom they had come were all wizards. And Etearchus surmised that this river was indeed the Nile."

Apart from bones and historical writings about Giants and Little People in our ancient past, there have also been found numerous structures, either gigantic or miniature in size, which are man-made. In many cases, archaeologists have no explanation for who built them or how.

In eastern Iran, there are ruins of an ancient village called Makhunik. Many of the houses there stand only 1.5 to 2 meters tall (4'11" to 6'7") at the site. And, within the small structures, ceilings are as low as 1.4 cm or (4'7"). Archaeologists found many ancient graves containing evidence of Little People. Some of the residents were just one meter in height, which is about 3'4" tall.

EASTER ISLAND GIANTS

STONEHENGE

PERUVIAN TEMPLE

The world is filled with gigantic structures that have been the subject of many theories about their origin, ranging from the belief that giants built them; to the theory that ancient aliens constructed them using advanced technology.

From the Bible's comprehensive listing of 36 tribes of Giants, and details about 22 individual giants who lived in the ancient Holy Land; to the dramatic Greek legends populated with Giants, the stories told by people all over the globe support the verity of the presence of Giants living throughout ancient times.

In addition to oral and Biblical accounts, remains of Giants have been found worldwide throughout history. Buried under stone and earth; sometimes accompanied by gigantic weapons and other artifacts, we have convincing proof that such Giant humans did indeed inhabit our planet.

Remains of giant humans have been found in practically every part of the globe: Tunisia; Pennsylvania; Glen Rose, Texas; Gargayan in the Philippines; Syria; Morocco; Australia; and throughout the Urbasa mountain range in Spain, Java, and China. The list goes on almost endlessly.

In spite of the vast amount of skeletal evidence, bones, unearthed tools and teeth—that are unusually large by normal human standards—it seems that there are many more skeptics than believers among the scientific community.

In fact, these Giant finds, along with discoveries relating to evidence of Little People, have led some theorists to believe that man-kind of antiquity may have come in three distinct sizes: Giants, Humans, and Hobbits. Many folks in the modern world often regard mention of these different-sized human races in ancient texts and folklore as the product of a vivid imagination. This, in spite of the fact that many different cultures record very similar accounts of the three distinct heights of people. As more of the various remains are uncovered throughout the world, maybe disbelievers will be convinced that the "myths" were actually accurate depictions of life in antiquity.

The "Terracotta Army" was discovered in Shandong province of China, in the tomb of Qin Shi Huang. They were put there, presumably, to serve and guard him in the afterlife. There are around 8,000 life-size figures of warriors, each one different, standing in rows in this tomb.

Giants & Little People

of

IRELAND

Irish tradition recounts stories of the brutal, war-like Fomorians, who were a race of Giants that invaded Ireland in ships from Africa in ancient times. Irish folk tales say that these giants demanded children at Halloween time. The Fomorians were finally driven north to the Hebrides Isles off northwest Scotland, and to Tory Island off northwest Ireland, in the deep Atlantic. From there, they preyed on the people of Ulster. The Fomorian giants were said to be endowed with double-rows of teeth, and were endowed with six fingers on each hand and six toes on each foot.

In both Irish and Manx popular folklore, there is the tale of a giant by the name of Fionn mac Cumhaill (sometimes translated in English as McCool or MacCoul). He was a hunter-warrior in Irish mythology. Tales of him occur also in the mythologies of Scotland and the Isle of Man.

In the book, *Manx Fairy Tales,* by Morrison Peel, 1929, Fionn is portrayed as a magical, good-natured giant. The most famous story attached to Fionn tells how, one day, while making a pathway in the sea towards Scotland – The Giant's Causeway – Fionn is told that the giant Benandonner (or, in the Manx version, a buggane or huge ogre) is coming to fight him. Knowing he cannot defeat the colossal Benandonner, Fionn asks his wife Oona to help him. She dresses her husband as a baby, and he hides in a cradle. Then she makes a batch of griddle-cakes, hiding griddle-irons in some of them. When Benandonner arrives, Oona tells him Fionn is out but that he will return shortly.

As Benandonner waits, he tries to intimidate Oona with his immense power, breaking rocks with his little finger. Oona then offers Benandonner a griddle-cake; but when he bites into the iron concealed within, he chips his teeth. Oona scolds him for being weak (saying her husband eats such cakes easily), and feeds one without an iron to the 'baby,' who eats it with no trouble.

In the Irish version, Benandonner is so awed by the power of the baby's teeth and the size of the baby that, at Oona's prompting, he puts his fingers in Fionn's mouth to feel how sharp his teeth are. Fionn bites Benandonner's little finger off. Scared of the prospect of meeting the father of such a strong baby, Benandonner races back to Scotland.

Many geographical features in Ireland are attributed to Fionn mac Cumhaill. Legend has it that he built the Giant's Causeway as stepping-stones to Scotland, so as not to get his feet wet. He also once scooped up part of Ireland to fling it at a rival, but it missed and landed in the Irish Sea — the clump became the Isle of Man and the pebble became Rockall; the void became Lough Neagh.

"The Ironing Stone" at Kylemore Castle is said to be a magical wishing stone put there by giants. Located at Connemara, County Galway, Ireland, if you stand with your back to the stone, make a wish, and throw a small stone back over the Ironing Stone three times, your wish will be granted. Legend has it that this big chunk of granite was dropped here by two baby giants playing with their mother's hot ironing stone. Another version of the tale says that a hot ironing stone was being tossed between two nearby mountains by the two mythical Irish giants, Cu Chulainn and Fionn McCool. When it hit the ground, the iron cooled into this magical stone.

Legend has it that Fionn McCool resided on the distinctive mountain known as "The Diamond." This mountain faces the Kylemore valley. It is known as "The Diamond" because, when the sun shines on the mountain, the exposed quartz in the stone sparkles – like a diamond.

From *Irish Names Of Places* (1910), comes this story by P.W. Joyce recounting the Irish fairy tale of Fionn McCool and the famous "ironing stone":

The Giants & The 'Ironing Stone'

Cú Chulainn and Fionn McCool are two of Ireland's best known mythological heroes. Legend has it these giants often fought each other on the Connemara mountains.

Cú Chulainn lived on the opposite side of the valley on the mountain known as 'Dúchruach' meaning 'Black Stack.' Dúchruach is the mountain which Kylemore Abbey is nestled against. It takes its name from its unusual black stone and stands out from all the other mountains in the area.

The giants, Cú Chulainn and Fionn McCool, were hot tempered and regularly came into conflict with each other. One day, during one of their heated arguments, Cú Chulainn picked up a giant stone and threw it towards Fionn

McCool. The stone narrowly missed Fionn McCool and landed at an unusual angle on the Kylemore estate, where it lies today. The shape of the stone resembles a traditional iron used for ironing clothes.

This stone is known as 'The Ironing Stone.' Local children use it as a wishing stone. If a child stands with their back against the stone, makes a wish and throws a small pebble back over the stone three times, that wish will be granted.

Besides Finn McCool, other giants are given credit for the naming of a particular place. Carnes, or heaps of stones laid over corpses, are found in several parts of Ireland. Such monuments are sometimes called "Dermot or Granny's beds." In the southern counties of Ireland, they are called Giant's Beds. The notion of the "Giant's Bed" is taken from *Keating's History of Ireland*:

The Giant's Bed

The giant legend is one of the most well-known legends in Irish mythology. A large flat rock lies near the Abbey. Local legend holds that it marks the grave of a ferocious giant who terrorized the people of Kylemore, who had to feed him from their own meager provisions. When the giant's appetite had all but decimated the livestock, vegetable gardens, and fish stocks of the valley, he then announced to the locals that they would have to feed him their children! Luckily, before this terrible event happened, a brave young man returned from fighting in France and killed the giant.

To get close enough to deal the fatal blow, he dressed in his mother's shawl and pretended to be an old woman bringing the giant his breakfast. When he was close enough, the brave young man produced his sword and ended the giant and his reign of terror.

A gigantic rock was placed over the giant where he lay to ensure that he would never rise again, from the "Giant's Bed."

~ ~ ~ ~ ~

The Fomorians and Finn McCool are giants found in the ancient mythology of Ireland. In addition to mythological figures, giants are found in Irish fairy tales, like this one:

IRISH FAIRY TALES
Dublin, Ireland; 1906
By Edmond Leamy

The Little White Cat

A long, long time ago, in a valley far away, the giant Trencoss lived in a great castle, surrounded by trees that were always green. The castle had a hundred doors, and every door was guarded by a huge, shaggy hound, with tongue of fire and claws of iron, who tore to pieces anyone who went to the castle without the giant's leave.

Trencoss had made war on the King of the Torrents; and, having killed the king, and slain his people, and burned his palace, he carried off his only daughter, the Princess Eileen, to the castle in the valley. Here he provided her with beautiful rooms, and appointed a hundred dwarfs, dressed in blue and yellow satin, to wait upon her, and harpers to play sweet music for her, and he gave her diamonds without number, brighter than the sun; but he would not allow her to go outside the castle, and told her if she went one step beyond its doors, the hounds, with tongues of fire and claws of iron, would tear her to pieces.

A week after her arrival, war broke out between the giant and the king of the islands, and before he set out for battle, the giant sent for the princess, and informed her that on his return he would make her his wife. When the princess heard this she began to cry, for she would rather die than marry the giant who had slain her father.

"Crying will only spoil your bright eyes, my little princess," said Trencoss, "and you will have to marry me whether you like it or not."

He then bade her go back to her room, and he ordered the dwarfs to give her everything she asked for while he was away, and the harpers to play the sweetest music for her. When the princess gained her room, she cried as if her heart would break. The long day passed slowly, and the night came, but brought no sleep to Eileen. In the grey light of the morning she rose and opened the window, and looked about in every direction to see if there were any chance of escape. But the window was ever so high above the ground, and below were the hungry and ever watchful hounds. With a heavy heart she was about to close the window when she thought she saw the branches of the tree that was nearest to it moving. She looked again, and she saw a little white cat creeping along one of the branches.

"Mew!" cried the cat.

"Poor little pussy," said the princess. "Come to me, pussy."

"Stand back from the window," said the cat, "and I will."

The princess stepped back, and the little white cat jumped into the room. The princess took the little cat on her lap and stroked him with her hand, and the cat raised up its back and began to purr.

"Where do you come from, and what is your name?" asked the princess.

"No matter where I come from or what's my name," said the cat, "I am a friend of yours, and I come to help you."

"I never wanted help worse," said the princess.

"I know that," said the cat; "and now listen to me. When the giant comes back from battle and asks you to marry him, say to him you will marry him."

"But I will never marry him," said the princess.

"Do what I tell you," said the cat. "When he asks you to marry him, say to him you will if his dwarfs will wind for you three balls from the fairy dew that lies on the bushes on a misty morning, as big as these," said the cat, putting his right forefoot into his ear and taking out three balls—one yellow, one red, and one blue.

"They are very small," said the princess. "They are not much bigger than peas, and the dwarfs will not be long at their work."

"Won't they," said the cat. "It will take them a month and a day to make one, so that it will take three months and three days before the balls are wound; but the giant, like you, will think they can be made in a few days, and so he will readily promise to do what you ask. He will soon find out his mistake, but he will keep his word, and will not press you to marry him until the balls are wound."

"When will the giant come back?" asked Eileen.

"He will return tomorrow afternoon," said the cat.

"Will you stay with me until then?" said the princess. "I am very lonely."

"I cannot stay," said the cat. "I have to go away to my palace on the island on which no man ever placed his foot, and where no man but one shall ever come."

"And where is that island?" asked the princess, "and who is the man?"

"The island is in the far-off seas where vessel never sailed; the man you will see before many days are over; and if all goes well, he will one day slay the giant Trencoss, and free you from his power."

"Ah!" sighed the princess, "that can never be, for no weapon can wound the hundred hounds that guard the castle, and no sword can kill the giant Trencoss."

"There is a sword that will kill him," said the cat; "but I must go now. Remember what you are to say to the giant when he comes home, and every morning watch the tree on which you saw me, and if you see in the branches anyone you like better than yourself," said the cat, winking at the princess, "throw him these three balls and leave the rest to me; but take care not to speak a single word to him, for if you do all will be lost."

"Shall I ever see you again?" asked the princess.

"Time will tell," answered the cat, and, without saying so much as good-bye, he jumped through the window on to the tree, and in a second was out of sight.

The morrow afternoon came, and the giant Trencoss returned from battle. Eileen knew of his coming by the furious barking of the hounds, and her heart sank, for she knew that in a few moments she would be summoned to his presence. Indeed, he had hardly entered the castle when he sent for her, and told her to get ready for the wedding. The princess tried to look cheerful, as she answered:

"I will be ready as soon as you wish; but you must first promise me something."

"Ask anything you like, little princess," said Trencoss.

"Well, then," said Eileen, "before I marry you, you must make your dwarfs wind three balls as big as these from the fairy dew that lies on the bushes on a misty morning in summer."

"Is that all?" said Trencoss, laughing. "I shall give the dwarfs orders at once, and by this time tomorrow the balls will be wound, and our wedding can take place in the evening."

"And will you leave me to myself until then?"

"I will," said Trencoss.

"On your honor as a giant?" said Eileen.

"On my honor as a giant," replied Trencoss.

The princess returned to her rooms, and the giant summoned all his dwarfs, and he ordered them to go forth in the dawning of the morn and to gather all the fairy dew lying on the bushes, and to wind three balls—one yellow, one red, and one blue. The next morning, and the next, and the next, the dwarfs went out into the fields and searched all the hedgerows, but they could gather only as much fairy dew as would make a thread as long as a wee girl's eyelash; and so, they had to go out morning after morning, and the giant fumed and threatened, but all to no purpose. He was very angry with the princess, and he was vexed with himself that she was so much cleverer than he was, and, moreover, he saw now that the wedding could not take place as soon as he expected.

When the little white cat went away from the castle he ran as fast as he could up hill and down dale, and never stopped until he came to the Prince of the Silver River. The prince was alone, and very sad and sorrowful he was, for he was thinking of the Princess Eileen, and wondering where she could be.

"Mew," said the cat, as he sprang softly into the room; but the prince did not heed him. "Mew," again said the cat; but again, the prince did not heed him. "Mew," said the cat the third time, and he jumped up on the prince's knee.

"Where do you come from, and what do you want?" asked the prince.

"I come from where you would like to be," said the cat.

"And where is that?" said the prince.

"Oh, where is that, indeed! as if I didn't know what you are thinking of, and of whom you are thinking," said the cat; "and it would be far better for you to try and save her."

"I would give my life a thousand times over for her," said the prince.

"For whom?" said the cat, with a wink. "I named no name, your highness," said he.

"You know very well who she is," said the prince, "if you knew what I was thinking of; but do you know where she is?"

"She is in danger," said the cat. "She is in the castle of the giant Trencoss, in the valley beyond the mountains."

"I will set out there at once," said the prince "and I will challenge the giant to battle, and will slay him."

"Easier said than done," said the cat. "There is no sword made by the hands of man that can kill him, and even if you could kill him, his hundred hounds, with tongues of fire and claws of iron, would tear you to pieces."

"Then, what am I to do?" asked the prince.

"Be said by me," said the cat. "Go to the wood that surrounds the giant's castle, and climb the high tree that's nearest to the window that looks towards the sunset, and shake the branches, and you will see what you will see. Then hold out your hat with the silver plumes, and three balls––one yellow, one red, and one blue—will be thrown into it. And then come back here as fast as you can; but speak no word, for if you utter a single word the hounds will hear you, and you shall be torn to pieces."

Well, the prince set off at once, and after two days' journey he came to the wood around the castle, and he climbed the tree that was nearest to the window that looked towards the sunset, and he shook the branches. As soon as he did so, the window opened, and he saw the Princess Eileen, looking lovelier than ever. He was going to call out her name, but she placed her fingers on her lips, and he remembered what the cat had told him, that he was to speak no word. In silence he held out the hat with the silver plumes, and the princess threw into it the three balls, one after another, and, blowing him a kiss, she shut the window. And well it was she did so, for at that very moment she heard the voice of the giant, who was coming back from hunting.

The prince waited until the giant had entered the castle before he descended the tree. He set off as fast as he could. He went up hill and down dale, and never stopped until he arrived at his own palace, and there waiting for him was the little white cat.

"Have you brought the three balls?" said he.

"I have," said the prince.

"Then follow me," said the cat.

On they went until they left the palace far behind and came to the edge of the sea.

"Now," said the cat, "unravel a thread of the red ball, hold the thread in your right hand, drop the ball into the water, and you shall see what you shall see."

The prince did as he was told, and the ball floated out to sea, unravelling as it went, and it went on until it was out of sight.

"Pull now," said the cat.

The prince pulled, and, as he did, he saw far away something on the sea shining like silver. It came nearer and nearer, and he saw it was a little silver boat. At last it touched the strand.

"Now," said the cat, "step into this boat and it will bear you to the palace on the island on which no man has ever placed his foot—the island in the unknown seas that were never sailed by vessels made of human hands. In that palace there is a sword with a diamond hilt, and by that sword alone the giant Trencoss can be killed. There also are a hundred cakes, and it is only on eating these the hundred hounds can die. But mind what I say to you: if you eat or drink until you reach the palace of the little cat in the island in the unknown seas, you will forget the Princess Eileen."

"I will forget myself first," said the prince, as he stepped into the silver boat, which floated away so quickly that it was soon out of sight of land.

The day passed, and the night fell; and the stars shone down upon the waters; but the boat never stopped. On she went for two whole days and nights, and on the third morning the prince saw an island in the distance, and very glad he was; for he thought it was his journey's end, and he was almost fainting with thirst and hunger. But the day passed, and the island was still before him.

At long last, on the following day, he saw by the first light of the morning that he was quite close to it, and that trees laden with fruit of every kind were bending down over the water. The boat sailed round and round the island, going closer and closer every round, until, at last, the drooping branches almost touched it. The sight of the fruit within his reach made the prince hungrier and thirstier than he was before, and forgetting his promise to the little cat—not to eat anything until he entered the palace in the unknown seas—he caught one of the branches, and, in a moment, was in the tree eating the delicious fruit. While he was doing so the boat floated out to sea and soon was lost to sight; but the prince, having eaten, forgot all about it, and, worse still, forgot all about the princess in the giant's castle. When he had eaten enough he descended the tree, and, turning his back on the sea, set out straight before him. He had not gone far when he heard the sound of music, and soon after he saw a number of maidens playing on silver harps coming towards him. When they saw him they ceased playing, and cried out:

"Welcome! welcome! Prince of the Silver River, welcome to the island of fruits and flowers. Our king and queen saw you coming over the sea, and they sent us to bring you to the palace."

The prince went with them, and at the palace gates the king and queen and their daughter Kathleen received him, and gave him welcome. He hardly saw the king and queen, for his eyes were fixed on the princess Kathleen, who looked more beautiful than a flower. He thought he had never seen anyone so lovely, for, of course, he had forgotten all about poor Eileen pining away in her castle prison in the lonely valley. When the king and queen had given welcome to the prince a great feast was spread, and all the lords and ladies of the court sat down to it, and the prince sat between the queen and the princess Kathleen, and long before the feast was finished, head over ears in love with her. When the feast was ended the queen ordered the ballroom to be made ready, and when night fell the dancing began, and was kept up until the morning star, and the prince danced all night with the princess, falling deeper and deeper in love with her every minute. Between dancing by night and feasting by day weeks went by. All the time poor Eileen in the giant's castle was counting the hours, and all this time the dwarfs were winding the balls, and a ball and a half were already wound. At last the prince asked the king and queen for their daughter in marriage, and they were delighted to be able to say yes, and the day was fixed for the wedding. But on the evening before the day on which it was to take place the prince was in his room, getting ready for a dance, when he felt something rubbing against his leg, and, looking down, who should he see but the little white cat. At the sight of him the prince remembered everything, and sad and sorry he was when he thought of Eileen watching and waiting and counting the days until he returned to save her. But he was very fond of the princess Kathleen, and so he did not know what to do.

"You can't do anything tonight," said the cat, for he knew what the prince was thinking of, "but when morning comes go down to the sea, and look not to the right or the left, and let no living thing touch you, for if you do you shall never leave the island. Drop the second ball into the water, as you did the first, and when the boat comes step in at once. Then you may look behind you, and you shall see what you shall see, and you'll know which you love best, the Princess Eileen or the Princess Kathleen, and you can either go or stay."

The prince didn't sleep a wink that night, and at the first glimpse of the morning he stole from the palace. When he reached the sea, he threw out the ball, and when it had floated out of sight, he saw the little boat sparkling on the horizon like a newly-risen star. The prince had scarcely passed through the palace doors when he was missed, and the king and queen and the princess, and all the lords and ladies of the court, went in search of him, taking the quickest way to the sea. While the maidens with the silver harps played sweetest music, the princess, whose voice was sweeter than any music, called on the prince by his name, and so moved his heart that he was about to look behind, when he remembered how the cat had told him he should not do so until he was in the boat. Just as it touched the shore the princess put out her hand and almost caught the prince's arm, but he stepped into the boat in time to save himself, and it sped away like a receding wave. A loud scream caused the prince to look round suddenly, and when he did he saw no sign of king or queen, or princess, or lords or ladies, but only big green serpents, with red eyes and tongues, that hissed out fire and poison as they writhed in a hundred horrible coils.

The prince, having escaped from the enchanted island, sailed away for three days and three nights, and every night he hoped the coming morning would show him the island he was in search of. He was faint with hunger and beginning to despair, when on the fourth morning he saw in the distance an island that, in the first rays of the sun, gleamed like fire. On coming closer to it he saw that it was clad with trees, so covered with bright red berries that hardly a leaf was to be seen. Soon the boat was almost within a stone's cast of the island, and it began to sail round and round until it was well under the bending branches. The scent of the berries was so sweet that it sharpened the prince's hunger, and he longed to pluck them; but, remembering what had happened to him on the enchanted island, he was afraid to touch them. But the boat kept on sailing round and round, and at last a great wind rose from the sea and shook the branches, and the bright, sweet berries fell into the boat until it was filled with them, and they fell upon the prince's hands, and he took up some to look at them, and as he looked the desire to eat them grew stronger, and he said to himself it would be no harm to taste one; but when he tasted it the flavor was so delicious he swallowed it, and, of course, at once he forgot all about Eileen, and the boat drifted away from him and left him standing in the water.

He climbed on to the island, and having eaten enough of the berries, he set out to see what might be before him, and it was not long until he heard a great noise, and a huge iron ball knocked down one of the trees in front of him, and before he knew where he was a hundred giants came running after it. When they saw the prince they turned towards him, and one of them caught him up in his hand and held him up that all might see him. The prince was nearly squeezed to death, and seeing this the giant put him on the ground again.

"Who are you, my little man?" asked the giant.

"I am a prince," replied the prince.

"Oh, you are a prince, are you?" said the giant. "And what are you good for?" said he.

The prince did not know, for nobody had asked him that question before.

"I know what he's good for," said an old giantess, with one eye in her forehead and one in her chin. "I know what he's good for. He's good to eat."

When the giants heard this, they laughed so loud that the prince was frightened almost to death.

"Why," said one, "he wouldn't make a mouthful."

"Oh, leave him to me," said the giantess, "and I'll fatten him up; and when he is cooked and dressed he will be a nice dainty dish for the king."

The giants, on this, gave the prince into the hands of the old giantess. She took him home with her to the kitchen, and fed him on sugar and spice and all things nice, so that he should be a sweet morsel for the king of the giants when he returned to the island. The poor prince would not eat anything at first, but the giantess held him over the fire until his feet were scorched, and then he said to himself it was better to eat than to be burnt alive.

Well, day after day passed, and the prince grew sadder and sadder, thinking that he would soon be cooked and dressed for the king; but sad as the prince was, he was not half as sad as the Princess Eileen in the giant's castle, watching and waiting for the prince to return and save her.

And the dwarfs had wound two balls, and were winding a third.

At last the prince heard from the old giantess that the king of the giants was to return on the following day, and she said to him:

"As this is the last night you have to live, tell me if you wish for anything, for if you do your wish will be granted."

"I don't wish for anything," said the prince, whose heart was dead within him.

"Well, I'll come back again," said the giantess, and she went away.

The prince sat down in a corner, thinking and thinking, until he heard close to his ear a sound like "purr, purr!" He looked around, and there before him was the little white cat.

"I ought not to come to you," said the cat; "but, indeed, it is not for your sake I come. I come for the sake of the Princess Eileen. Of course, you forgot all about her, and, of course, she is always thinking of you. It's always the way—

"Favored lovers may forget,
Slighted lovers never yet."

The prince blushed with shame when he heard the name of the princess.

"Tis you that ought to blush," said the cat; "but listen to me now, and remember–if you don't obey my directions this time you'll never see me again, and you'll never set your eyes on the Princess Eileen. When the old giantess comes back, tell her you wish, when the morning comes, to go down to the sea to look at it for the last time. When you reach the sea, you will know what to do. But I must go now, as I hear the giantess coming." And the cat jumped out of the window and disappeared.

"Well," said the giantess, when she came in, "is there anything you wish?"

"Is it true I must die tomorrow?" asked the prince.

"It is."

"Then," said he, "I should like to go down to the sea to look at it for the last time."

"You may do that," said the giantess, "if you get up early."

"I'll be up with the lark in the light of the morning," said the prince.

"Very well," said the giantess. Saying "good night," she went away.

The prince thought the night would never pass, but at last it faded away before the grey light of the dawn, and he sped down to the sea. He threw out the third ball, and before long he saw the little boat coming towards him swifter than the wind. He threw himself into it the moment it touched the shore. Swifter than the wind it bore him out to sea, and before he had time to look behind him the island of the giantess was like a faint red speck in the distance. The day passed, and the night fell, and the stars looked down, and the boat sailed on, and just as the sun rose above the sea it pushed its silver prow on the golden strand of an island greener than the leaves in summer. The prince jumped out, and went on and on until he entered a pleasant valley, at the head of which he saw a palace white as snow.

As he approached the central door it opened for him. On entering the hall, he passed into several rooms without meeting with anyone; but, when he reached the principal apartment, he found himself in a circular room, in which were a thousand pillars, and every pillar was of marble, and on every pillar save one, which stood in the center of the room, was a little white cat with black eyes. Ranged round the wall, from one door-jamb to the other, were three rows of precious jewels. The first was a row of brooches of gold and silver, with their pins fixed in the wall and their heads outwards; the second a row of torques of gold and silver; and the third a row of great swords, with hilts of gold and silver. And on many tables was food of all kinds, and drinking horns filled with foaming ale.

While the prince was looking about him the cats kept on jumping from pillar to pillar; but seeing that none of them jumped on to the pillar in the center of the room, he began to wonder why this was so, when, all of a sudden, and before he could guess how it came about, there right before him on the center pillar was the little white cat.

"Don't you know me?" said he.

"I do," said the prince.

"Ah, but you don't know who I am. This is the palace of the Little White Cat, and I am the King of the Cats. But you must be hungry, and the feast is spread."

Well, when the feast was ended, the king of the cats called for the sword that would kill the giant Trencoss, and the hundred cakes for the hundred watch-dogs.

The cats brought the sword and the cakes and laid them before the king.

"Now," said the king, "take these; you have no time to lose. Tomorrow the dwarfs will wind the last ball, and tomorrow the giant will claim the princess for his bride. So, you should go at once;

but before you go take this from me to your little girl."

And the king gave him a brooch lovelier than any on the palace walls.

The king and the prince, followed by the cats, went down to the strand, and when the prince stepped into the boat all the cats "mewed" three times for good luck, and the prince waved his hat three times, and the little boat sped over the waters all through the night as brightly and as swiftly as a shooting star. In the first flush of the morning it touched the strand. The prince jumped out and went on and on, up hill and down dale, until he came to the giant's castle. When the hounds saw him they barked furiously, and bounded towards him to tear him to pieces. The prince flung the cakes to them, and as each hound swallowed his cake he fell dead. The prince then struck his shield three times with the sword which he had brought from the palace of the little white cat.

When the giant heard the sound, he cried out: "Who comes to challenge me on my wedding day?"

The dwarfs went out to see, and, returning, told him it was a prince who challenged him to battle.

The giant, foaming with rage, seized his heaviest iron club, and rushed out to the fight. The fight lasted the whole day, and when the sun went down the giant said:

"We have had enough of fighting for the day. We can begin at sunrise to-morrow."

"Not so," said the prince. "Now or never; win or die."

"Then take this," cried the giant, as he aimed a blow with all his force at the prince's head; but the prince, darting forward like a flash of lightning, drove his sword into the giant's heart, and, with a groan, he fell over the bodies of the poisoned hounds.

When the dwarfs saw the giant dead, they began to cry and tear their hair. But the prince told them they had nothing to fear, and he bade them go and tell the princess Eileen he wished to speak with her. But the princess had watched the battle from her window, and when she saw the giant fall she rushed out to greet the prince, and that very night he and she and all the dwarfs and harpers set out for the Palace of the Silver River, which they reached the next morning, and from that day to this there never has been a gayer wedding than the wedding of the Prince of the Silver River and the Princess Eileen; and though she had diamonds and pearls to spare, the only jewel she wore on her wedding-day was the brooch which the prince had brought her from the Palace of the Little White Cat in the far-off seas.

~ ~ ~ ~ ~

ffin, moves its jaws
rible manner, and
ound. Behind the
d a sexton's spade.
real human bones,
nake.
's sale of lost pro-
heir Broad Street
esides passengers'
-room parcels, and
und in the trains
stock on hand in
also sold in the
onsists of merchan-
for which a claim
n made and paid.
in the unclaimed
y actually receive
bricks, or a grocer
at both may refuse
ge on the consign-
ady may receive a
me social function ;
ged in transit, and
he consignees will
and put in a claim
nts for the amazing
lots " that figure in

the extraordinary
ailway company is
, which is at this
ondon and North-
ny's Broad Street
lograph of which is

and exnioited it in Liver-
pool and Manchester at sixpence a head,
attracting scientific men as well as gaping
sightseers. Business increased, and the
showman induced a man named Kershaw

THE IRISH GIANT AT BROAD STREET GOODS STATION.

THE LOST PROPERTY OFFICE.

This photo of a fossilized Irish giant was taken at a London rail depot, and appeared in the December 1895 issue of *Strand Magazine*.

83

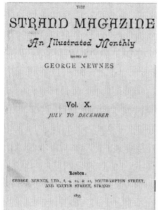

Here is the story printed in the 1895 issue of *Strand Magazine,* which tells of the "fossilized Irish giant" who ended up in North Western Railway Company's Lost Property Office:

Pre-eminent among the extraordinary articles ever held by a railway company is the fossilized Irish giant, which is at this moment lying at the London and North Western Railway Company's Broad Street goods depot, and a photograph of which is attracting sightseers, a showman has reproduced here.

This monstrous figure is reputed to have been dug up by a Mr. Dyer, whilst prospecting for iron ore in Country Antrim, Ireland. The principal measurements are: Entire length, 12 ft. 2 in.; girth of chest, 6 ft. 6 in.; and length of arms, 4 ft. 6 in. There are six toes on the right foot. The gross weight is 2 tons 15 cwt.; so that it took half-a-dozen men and a powerful crane to place this article of lost property in position for *The Strand Magazine* photographic artist.

Briefly, the story is this: Dyer, after showing the giant in Dublin, came to England with his queer find, and exhibited it in Liverpool and

Manchester at sixpence a head, scientific men as well as gaping sightseers. Business increased, and induced a man named Kershaw to purchase a share in the concern. In 1876, Dyer sent his giant from Manchester to London by rail; the sum of £428. 6d. being charged for carriage by the company, but never paid.

Evidently, Kershaw knew nothing of the removal of the "show," for when he discovered it, he followed in hot haste; and, through a firm of London solicitors, moved the Court of Chancery to issue an order restraining the company from parting with the giant, until the action between Dyer and himself to determine the ownership was disposed of. The action was never brought to an issue, and the warehouse charges, even at a nominal figure, will amount to £138 on Christmas Day, 1895. In addition to this large sum, there is the cost of carriage, and about £60 legal expenses which the railway company incurred.

The injunction obtained by Kershaw, which prevents the North Western Railway Company from dealing with the giant is still in force; and the sanction of the Court must be obtained before it can be removed from its resting place at Broad Street Goods Depot, where it remains a weird relic of distant ages in a vast hive of latter-day industry.

Whether or not you believe that the giant mummy in the last story from *Strand Magazine* is a hoax, it is nevertheless an interesting tale.

Actual giants really did live in Ireland. Below is a brief listing and details about some of the Emerald Isle's notable giants.

MEN OF UNCOMMON STATURE

In his *History of Mankind*, anthropologist Dr. James Pritchard wrote:

> "In Ireland men of uncommon stature are often seen, and even a gigantic form and stature occur there much more frequently than in this island: yet all the British Isles derived their stock of inhabitants from the same sources. We can hardly avoid the conclusion that there must be some peculiarity in Ireland which gives rise to these phenomena." "Frederick the Great ascended the throne, he soon afterward disbanded the enormously expensive regiment of giants; and, with the money saved, established in their place four regiments of men of ordinary stature."

FITZGERALD

London's *Daily Post,* in its August 1, 1732, issue, devoted a paragraph to informing its readers that "about the middle of July, an Irishman named

Fitzgerald who was seven feet high, and a lieutenant in the King of Prussia's Guards, came to London."

EDMUND MALONE

In the Philosophical Transactions for 1698, Dr. William Musgrave issued the following report on the Irish giant Edmund Malone: "The measure of some of the parts of this Irish-man, nineteen years of age, shown at Oxford, were communicated to me by Dr. Plot. He was seven feet six inches high, his finger six inches and three quarters long, the length of his span fourteen inches, of his cubit (the distance from the elbow to the finger-tips) two feet two inches, of his arm three feet two inches and a quarter, from the shoulder to the crown of his head eleven inches and three-quarters." Earlier, in 1684, the giant appeared before the Court of Charles II.

The amazed king walked under his outstretched arm, an event that Malone mentioned thereafter in his handbills, as in the following: "The Gyant; or the Miracle of Nature. Being that so much admired young man, aged nineteen years last June, 1684. Born in Ireland, of such a prodigious height and bigness, and every way proportionable, the like hath not been seen since the memory of man: he hath been several times shown at court, and his majesty was pleased to walk under his arm, and he is grown very much since, he now reaches ten foot and a half, fathoms near eight foot, spans fifteen inches; and is believed to be as big as one of the giants in Guildhall. He is to be seen at the sign of the Catherine Wheel in Southwark fair. Vivat Rex."

MURPHY, THE IRISH GIANT

Working on the Liverpool Docks apparently did not appeal much to Murphy, the Irish giant. So, he quit to wait on tables at the hotel. But because he was a man of extraordinary height, Murphy drew large crowds to the hotel. One day he decided he might as well get paid for being a curiosity and began exhibiting himself. In May of 1857, the Emperor and Empress of Austria invited the touring County Down native to appear before them. Before he died of smallpox at Marseilles, at the age of twenty-six, Murphy had amassed a small fortune. He measured almost nine feet and weighed three hundred and thirty-six pounds.

SHAWN NABONTREE

On December 6, 1856, the *Mayo Constitution* carried this obituary: "One of the last of the mythical line of Irish giants, in the person of Shawn Nabontree, died at Connemara, Ireland, on Friday last. He owed his sobriquet to his unusual stature, being a man of extraordinary athletic symmetry, seven feet in height, and weighing over twenty stone [280 pounds]. His family, the Joyces, has been for many years one of the wonders of Connemara. He died at the age of seventy, and has left four stalwart sons."

PATRICK COTTER O'BRIEN

Patrick Cotter O'Brien was a native of Kinsale in the kingdom of Ireland and measured nearly nine feet high. O'Brien's great size sometimes placed him in humorous situations. In an article published in the *Mirror* for 1826, his hairdresser, who lived at Northampton, noted that the giant was a man of mild disposition, but he recalled when "an impertinent visitant excited his choler one day, during his residence here [at Northampton], by illiberal allusions to the land of his birth. The Philistine was sensible of the insult, seized the prig by the collar, held him out at arm's length, and gave him three or four mild agitations."

Another time, O'Brien was riding in his coach, which was about to be robbed. Because of his huge frame, his carriage maker had adapted the coach to his better use. By sinking the foundation some feet, the maker found a way to accommodate his long legs without changing the carriage's appearance very much. So, when the highwayman rode out into the road and stopped the coach he expected nothing out of the ordinary. But as O'Brien put "his head forward to observe the cause that impeded his progress, the highwayman was struck with such a panic, that he clapped spurs to his horse and made a precipitous retreat."

Patrick Cotter O'Brien had himself a special coach made, with a lowered floor that included a box for his feet. It was said that Patrick's height allowed him to walk down the street and light his cigars on the street lamps. Much of the giant's life was spent in Bristol, and he is still referred to as the 'Bristol Giant.'

CHARLES BYRNE

Charles Byrne (1761–1783) or "The Irish Giant," was a man regarded as a curiosity or freak in London in the 1780s. Byrne's exact height is of some conjecture. Reports put Byrne's height at between 8 ft. 2 in. (2.49 m.), and 8 ft. 4 in. (2.54 m.) tall. Skeletal evidence places him at just over 7 ft 7 in (2.31 m.). This giant lad was born in 1761 in the small village of Littlebridge, Ireland, near the border of Derry and Tyrone County. His Irish father and Scottish mother were of normal stature. It is said that Byrne had been conceived on top of a haystack, and that this was the cause of his great height.

By his late teens, Byrne had grown to enormous height. He decided to set off for Britain to seek fame and fortune. Landing first in Scotland, he became an instant success. His celebrity spread as he made his way down northern England, arriving in London in early 1782, aged 21. Here, Charles Byrne entertained paying audiences. His gentle, likeable nature endeared him to the public. By mid-1782, Byrne had inspired a hit London stage show called *Harlequin Teague*, or the Giant's Causeway.

But, unfortunately, Byrne's great height was the result of the growth disorder known today as acromegaly. At age 22, his health declined sharply. At the same time, while drinking in a pub, he was a victim of a pickpocket. This loss of his life savings, which he carried in his pocket, combined with his failing health ultimately ended two months later. Charles Byrne died in June 1783, at the age of 22.

The Hunterian Museum, run by the Royal College of Surgeons of England, obtained the giant's bones and have had them on display to this day. But in June of 2018, Hannah Devlin at *The Guardian*, "reports that the museum — which is currently closed to the public for a three-year refurbishment — has stated its board of trustees will meet to discuss what to do about the controversial bones."

Irish giants are the topic of discussion in numerous old newspapers and magazines. Excerpts of some of these follow:

KALGOORLIE WESTERN ARGUS
Western Australia,
December 17, 1912

GIANTS & DWARFS.

NOTABLE EXAMPLES;
MEMORIES OF THE PAST.

Fraulein Brunnhilde, who recently arrived in England from Berlin, is said to be the tallest girl in the world. She is 7 ft. 11 in. high, 18 years of age, and weighs 20 stone. Yet she would be almost a pygmy compared with other giants and giantesses who have figured in the world's history. Thomas Cornello relates that, at Triolo, a castle in Upper Calabria, in an underground temple, was discovered a skeleton 18 feet long, with head two and one half feet long, each tooth weighing over an ounce. The bones of the skeleton weighed over 3 cwt.

In the 17th century there was exhibited at the sign of the Catherine Wheel, in Southwark Fair, "a Gyant or Miracle of Nature," who was described in the playbills as "that so much admired young man, aged 19 years last June (1681). Born in Ireland, of such a prodigious height and bigness, and every way proportionate, the like that hath not been seen in the memory of man. He has been several times shown at Court, and his Majesty was pleased to walk under his arm. He is grown very much since; he now reaches ten foot and a half, and is believed to be as big as one of the Gyants in Guild Hall." About the same time, there was on exhibition at the Golden Ball, at Charing Cross, "a giant, lately arrived from Holland," being the tallest person ever seen there before; being about eight feet high and between 27 and 28 years of age; the son of a clergyman, who was born in Finland."

One of the sights of Bartholomew Fair in the early part of the 18th century was "a tall Englishman, 8 ft. high, and but eleven years of age." In the first year of the 18th century there were also exhibited at the Sun Tavern in Queen Street, Cheapside, "a wonderful and strange Englishman. who is 7 feet 11 inches in height, being not yet 20 years of age as of November 1701. His limbs are all proportionate to his tallness and years of growth."

NEARLY TWELVE FEET HIGH.

Classical lore has many records of giants. The Greeks described Orestes as being 11-1/2 ft. in height. Pliny says that the tallest man of his age was Gabara, who was 9 ft. 9 inches in height. He was brought from Arabia in the reign of Claudius Maximus, the Emperor, was 8 ft. 6 inches in height, and is said to have worn his wife's bracelet as a ring upon his thumb. Hercules was small compared with these men, as he is said to have been only 7 ft. high. Funnam, a Scot who lived in the time of Eugene II, King of Scotland, measured 11-1/2 feet. Jacob le Marie, in his voyage to the Straits of Magellan, reports that, on December 17, 1615, they found at Port Desire several graves containing skeletons 10 ft. and 11 ft. long. The Chevalier Scory, in his voyage to the Peak of Tenerife, reported the discovery in one of the sepulcher caverns of the mountain, the body of a Guanche 18. ft long, with 80 teeth in the head.

On January 11, 1613, some masons digging near the ruins of Castle of Dauphine, came across a brick tomb 18 ft. below the surface, which was 30 ft. long, 12 ft. wide, and 8 ft. high. Inside the tomb they found an entire human skeleton 25 ft. long, 10 ft. wide across the shoulders, and 5 ft. deep from breastbone to back. Near Mazzarino, in Sicily, in 1516, according to tradition, the accuracy of which seems more than doubtful, was found a giant 30 ft. high, with the head the size of a hogshead; and each of his teeth weighing 5 oz. Near Palermo, in the valley of Mazara, another skeleton of a giant 30 ft. long is said to have been found in 1548, and another of 33 ft. in 1550, but these stories are equally incredible.

FAMOUS LITTLE MEN

On the opposite end of the scale, there have been from time to time exhibited in England, many famous dwarfs. In 1688 and 1689 John Worrenberg, born in Switzerland, in 1659, was "on show" in London. He never exceeded 2 ft. 7 inches in height, but is said to have been "as big and strong in his arms and legs as any full-grown man." He was drowned in 1695 while being carried in his box over a plank from the quay to the ship. The plank broke, and the porter fell with the box into the River Meare.

Jeffery Hudson was born in 1616 at Oakham, Rutland. His parents were both tall, but he never exceeded 18 inches in height. He was taken into the service of the Duke of Buckingham. On one occasion, Hudson was served up at table in a pie dish. He was given to Henrietta Maria, consort to King Charles I, as a servant. In the Civil Wars he was made a Captain of the Horse in the King's service, and accompanied the Queen to France, but was banished from that country for killing the brother of Lord Crofts in a duel. For many years, he was a slave in Barbary, but was redeemed. When he came to England in 1678, he was arrested on suspicion of being concerned in Oates' plot, but was discharged. He died in 1682.

Julia, the niece of Augustus, had a dwarf named Conopas, who was a little over 2 ft. in height, and Andromedo, one of her maids, was the same height. Two of the Roman knights, Marius Maximus and Marcus Tullius, were under 3 ft. in height. John d'Estrix, of Mechlin, who had a very long beard, was under 3 ft. He was a learned man, and spoke at least three languages fluently. He was always carried out by a servant.

~ ~ ~ ~ ~

WARRAGUL GUARDIAN
Warragul, Victoria
August 9, 1889
Bn Dn. ANDREW WILSON.

The production, now and then, of individual animals which vary greatly from their neighbors in size, is, of course, a well-known feature of life. In almost every grade of existence we find such examples of departure from the natural type of the race. The giant on the one hand, and the dwarf on the other, are familiar illustrations of a law (or laws) of development, the exact working of which we do not fully comprehend, but whose scope is probably not far removed from that which takes the conditions of nourishment under its especial charge.

It is true, that there may be much more complicated phases involved in the development of a giant or dwarf than those which regard over-nutrition and overgrowth as the main features of the process. We may have likewise to take into account facts of heredity or inheritance, and of "reversion" or "throwback" to ancestors who may have been either abnormally large or singularly small. Apart from all theories of scientists, however,

96

regarding how giants and dwarfs arise, as they often do, from a natural parentage, the consideration of such anomalies is a highly interesting matter; and we may not be very far wrong in our philosophy in any case, if we simply start by assuming that all such developments are not "freaks of nature" at all, but only phases of life, the laws of whose production we do not as yet understand. To call a giant or a dwarf a "freak of nature" is only to throw a sop to the Cerberus of ignorance.

We live in a world which is regulated by law and not by chance; and the "freak" is a meaningless expression in view of this latter conclusion. The legends about giants are, of course, many. One Henrion, a learned French man, argued in 1718 for the existence in former ages of huge members of the human race. He tells us that Adam was 123 feet 9 inches high. Eve is said to have measured 118 feet 9 inches in height; from which statement it is clear Henrion must have been nothing if not exact!

Noah evidently represented a decreasing state of things, for that patriarch is said to have measured only 27 feet in height. Abraham comes next with a stature of 20 feet; and Moses is next down at 13 feet. Henrion adds that the advent of the Christian era prevented the continuous decrease which had hitherto prevailed, and records his thankfulness that humanity was not permitted to become represented by infinitesimal or microscopic specks.

~ ~ ~ ~ ~

THE GENTLEMAN'S MAGAZINE
Volume 243
July to December, 1877

ON GIANTS

By Andrew Wilson

The ancient and medieval accounts of human giants are intermingled with much that is problematic, and in some cases absolutely fabulous. We are assured, however, that the height of Funnam, a Scotch giant who lived in the time of Pope Eugene, was 11 feet; whilst in 1509, there were discovered at Rouen the remains of the Chevalier Rincon, whose skull was alleged to have been capable of holding a bushel of wheat, whilst the length of his shin bone is stated at 4 feet.

In 1705, the skeleton of a hero named Bucart was disinterred at Valence, the remains measuring some 22 feet in length. These cases of huge development may very appropriately be capped by the Sicilian story of a human skeleton which was gravely maintained to measure 300 feet in length; whilst, with the apparent object of giving additional veracity to the recital, this giant's walking stick was alleged to have also been found, the length of this appendage being given at 30 feet.

The explanation of such fables becomes clear enough, however, when we learn that the bones from which measurements were taken were not those of men at all, but represented the fossil remains of huge quadrupeds and reptiles. Cuvier, the great French naturalist, was one of the first to show forth the absurdities of the common stories about giants; and to prove that fossil elephants and other animals had been really made to do duty for human remains.

In lower life, it is clear, the existence of giant members of species, the ordinary size of which is by no means great, is a fact of zoology. With man, the case is not different, and evidences of human giants are plentiful in the records of anatomists. For example, in the reign of Edward III, Long More, or Mores, an Irish giant, is said to have attained the height of 6 feet 10-1/2 inches. Queen Elizabeth had a Flemish porter who attained the height of 7 feet 6 inches; this height being exceeded by John Middleton, or the "Child of Hale," as he was called, who was born in 1578, and who measured 9 feet 3 inches. C. Munster, a yeoman of the Hanoverian Guard, who died in 1676, attained a height of 7 feet 6 inches; Cajanus, the Swedish giant, who was exhibited in London in 1742, attained a height of 9 feet.

The most celebrated of living giants, are the famous Captain Bates, a native of Kentucky, who attains a height of 8 feet, his wife, born Miss Anna Swan, who was born in Nova Scotia, also measuring 8 feet in height. Chang-wu-gon, the Chinese giant, measured 7 feet 9 inches in stature. Many of our readers will remember the exhibition of the two latter persons a few years ago in London. Chang-wu-gon, the Chinese giant, is also still alive; this tall Celestial measures 7 feet 9 inches in stature.

The details of giant-life exhibit many curious features. Contrary to expectation, and against the spirit of the old legends, our modern giants are, for the most part, the most amiable of tempers. Nature, in this respect, indeed, appears to preserve a wonderful and admirable balance of power in imbuing persons of great physical development with an equable temperament; whilst the dwarfs and pygmies of our race are usually inclined to exhibit a disposition the reverse of benevolent or mild. Probably the only giants of past days concerning details of a thoroughly authentic character have been preserved, are Patrick Cotter, alias Patrick Cotter O'Brien; and Charles Byrne, both individuals hailing from the sister island. There is preserved in the Museum of Trinity College, Dublin, the skeleton of a third Irishman, named Magrath, whose case attained some notoriety in consequence of a Doctor Campbell's statement, in his work entitled *"A Philosophical Survey of Ireland,"* that Magrath's growth was caused by Bishop Berkeley's experiment of feeding the lad. There exists little or no foundation for this statement, which probably arose from the fact that Magrath, having at the age of sixteen attained a stature of over 6 feet, and being poorly fed, presented a fit case for the exercise of the kindly bishop's charity. He, accordingly, caused Magrath to receive a liberal diet for about a month, this treatment restoring the overgrown lad to health.

At his death, Magrath measured 7 feet 8 inches. In the *British Magazine* for 1783, the death of Charles Byrne, one of the giants just mentioned, is duly chronicled. From this source, we learn that Byrne measured exactly 8 feet in height in August, 1780; "whilst in 1782, his stature had gained two inches, and when dead his full length was 8 feet 4 inches."

His death, sad to relate, is alleged to have been caused by excessive drinking "to which," says the writer in the *British Magazine*, "he was always addicted, but more particularly since his late loss of all his property, which he had simply invested in a single bank note of £700."

"In his last moments," continues the narrator, "he requested that his remains might be thrown into the sea, in order that his bones might be removed far out of the reach of the chirurgical fraternity; in consequence of which," we are further informed, "the body was put on board a vessel, conveyed to the Downs, and sunk in 20 fathoms of water."

Byrne died, it is necessary to add, in Cockspur Street, Charing Cross, at the age of twenty-two. The statement that the remains of the giant were buried at sea is quite erroneous. After all, the "chirurgical fraternity," represented by the famous John Hunter, contrived, after much trouble and the expenditure of a considerable sum of money – stated at £500 – to obtain possession of the body; and the visitor to the magnificent Museum in Lincoln's Inn, Fields, may have the pleasure of beholding the skeleton of the once famous Byrne occupying a place of honor in the osteological department. It is interesting to note that Byrne appeared on the stage in 1782, at the Haymarket Theatre in the summer pantomime of *"Harlequin Teague,* or *the Giant's Causeway,"* a title strongly suggestive of Byrne's prominence in the production.

The history of Patrick Cotter, who was born at Kinsale in 1761, shows that giants are by no means exempted from the cares and worries which beset ordinary existence. His parents were poor persons, of ordinary stature; and his father leased him for exhibition to a showman at eighteen years of age, for a period of three years, at the rate of 50 per annum. Arriving at Bristol, Cotter demanded some extra renumeration for himself; and the showman being disinclined to grant his request, Cotter refused to allow himself to be exhibited, with the result of being incarcerated as a debtor. His case, however, being made known to some benevolent person, Cotter was liberated by the contract between his father and the showman being declared to be illegal; and, proceeding thereafter to exhibit on his own account, he realized the sum of 30 in three days.

Cotter adopted the name of O'Brien in order to strengthen the fiction, set forth in the bills, that he was "a lineal descendant of the old puissant King Brien Boreau," and that he possessed, "in person and appearance, all the similitude of that great and grand potentate." His height was stated at "near nine feet," although a memorial tablet in the Trenchard Street Roman Catholic Chapel, Bristol, informs us more truly that his stature only exceeded "eight feet three inches." Cotter died at Clifton on September 8, 1804, having realized a modest competence by exhibiting himself, and having secured, we are told, the respect of the entire community by his well regulated conduct.

Like Charles Byrne, Patrick Cotter was ex-ceedingly anxious that his remains should not fall into the hands of the anatomists, and gave directions that his grave should be built in with bricks and secured with iron bars.

"As we write, the newspapers contain the intelligence of the death of the Buckingham-shire Giant, a person named William Stevens,  who merited his appellation of Giant from his immense weight, rather than from his unusual stature. He died in March, 1877, at the age of 49 years, at the *Five Arrows,* Waddesdon, near Aylesbury. He went to reside at this tavern some 4 years ago, at which time he weighed 18 stones."

The above newspaper account went on to say that, "from that time, his life was spent in eating and drinking, and in exhibiting his increasing weight to interested observers." At his death, he weighed 35 stones, and measured 6 feet 8 inches in height.

Little People

Ireland is filled with ancient ruins and scenic landscapes. The Emerald Isle is also replete with myths and legends passed down from generation to generation.

Thanks to the Irish, every year on March 17, we commemorate St. Patrick, the patron saint of Ireland. Patrick is celebrated for driving all of the snakes from Ireland.

While St. Patrick is probably Ireland's most iconic figure of legend, stories also abound of the Little Folk, a.k.a. fairies. This group contains a number of mythological creatures including gnomes, Sidhe, Will-O'-The-Wisps, elves, sprites, and brownies, etc. Perhaps the most common and well-known of the little people is the Leprechaun. Most everyone has seen this little Irish fellow, especially around St. Patrick's Day.

Origins of the Emerald Isle's wee ones are likely based on legends of one of the ancient tribes of Ireland, the Tuatha De Danann, which means the people of the Goddess Danu. According to the website http://www.ireland-information.com: "The

Tuatha De Danann were one of the great ancient tribes of Ireland. They ruled Ireland from 1897 B.C. to 1700 B.C." and are the "little people of Ireland that gave rise to the leprechaun legend." The Tuatha De Danann landed on the Connacht coastline in a deep cloud of mist. After they emerged from the mist onto land, they burned their boats, planning to settle permanently.

The dominant tribe already in Ireland at that time was the Fir Bolg, who immediately waged war on the tiny invaders. The Tuatha De Danann won; but they allowed the Fir Bolg to remain in Connaught while they ruled the rest of Ireland. These little people were said to be civilized and cultured and they introduced new skills and traditions to the Emerald Isle.

The Tuatha De Danann were, according to Irish mythology, a supernatural race who had come from four cities to the north of Ireland: Falias, Gorias, Murias, and Finias, where they had acquired magical powers and items. These strange drawfs had four great magical treasures with them:

The first talisman was the "Lia Fail" which means *Stone of Destiny* and *Speaking Stone*. This is because the stone was said to scream when a true King of Ireland stood on it. The stone was set on the Hill of Tara and served as the coronation site for the High Kings of Ireland. Also known as the Coronation Stone of Tara, Lia Fail was considered the sacred stone of knowledge which recognized and proclaimed the High King's right to rule. This magical Stone of Fal came from Falias.

The second talisman of the Tuatha De Danann was the "Magic Sword of Nuada" which was a sword that glowed with a white light and inflicted deadly blows when used. "laidheamh Soluis (Irish name for the weapon) means "Sword of Light", or "Shining Sword." According to Cormac mac Airt, a famous High King of Ireland, the sword "shone at night like a candle." Finias had given the little people the Sword of Nuada.

The third talisman was the "slingshot of the Sun God Lugh." This weapon was famed for its accuracy when used, and had come from Gorias.

Lugh was the son of Eithne who was the daughter of Balor of the Evil Eye. It was prophesied that Balor would be slain by his own grandson, so Balor imprisoned Eithne in a high tower so that she would never have a child. But Balor stole a prized cow from Glas Ghoibhneann from Cian, who followed the thief to the island where Eithne was imprisoned. When she saw him, she recognized Glas of Cian from her dreams. He released her from her prison and they became lovers.

She became pregnant by this man, who was the son of Danu and Dian Cécht of the Tuatha De Danann. The child was named Lugh, and he came into possession of the magic light sword and a slingshot that never missed its target.

At this time, there was a race of giants who lived in Ireland, known as the Fomorians, who had arrived two hundred years earlier. This race of giants are sometimes described as having one evil eye. Balor was a Fomorian. There had been conflict between the giants and the little people since their arrival. During the *Second Battle of Mag Tuireadh* against the Fomorians, that King Nuada of the Tuatha De Danann is killed in battle by Balor.

Lugh decides to avenge the death. He faces Balor, who opens his poisonous evil eye that kills all it looks upon. But, Lugh is armed with his magical slingshot. He shoots a stone from it that drives

Balor's eye out the back of his head, killing the Fomorian giant.

The final treasure of the Tuatha De Danann was the "Cauldron of Dagda" which magically contained an endless supply of food. This curious item came from Murias. This "horn of plenty" was named after Dagda, a Tuatha De Danann. He was a chieftain and a druid (Celtic priest) and seen as a father figure to those who knew him. Among his many magical items, was this cauldron, known as the *coire ansic* in the Gaelic language, which means "Cauldron of Plenty." It was so-named because it never ran out of food. Dagda's cauldron was never empty and fed everyone until they were full.

Dating back to the 12th century, the "Lebor Gabala" or "The Book of Invasions" talks about how Ireland came to be populated. The Fomorians, the ancient race of Irish giants, were the only beings left alive on the Irish Isle after the Great Flood. Like the little people, they too had supernatural powers and weapons. Also, some legends say that these giants were party human and partly beast.

Surviving the Great Flood, the Fomorians had Ireland to themselves for a number of years. That is, until the day the great mist rolled in and deposited the race of little people, who arrived with their own magical powers and items. This did not please the current inhabitants, the Fomorians, and conflict ensued.

Sir John Rhys a Welsh scholar, and the first Professor of Celtic at Oxford University, suggested that the Fir Bolg and the Fomorians were one and the same, He also points out that it seems that the Fomorians "represented harmful or destructive powers of nature, while the Tuatha Dé Danann represented the gods of growth and civilization."

These differences in philosophy led to much conflict between the two groups. Battles between the beings are described in the *Battles of Mag Tuireadh* writings.

At first, the little people's king, Nuada, asks that they be given half the island. But the king of the Fir Bolg (a.k.a. Fomorians), Eochaid refuses. The two groups meet at the Pass of Balgatan, and the First Battle of Mag Tuireadh begins. During the battle, Sreng, the greatest warrior of the Fir Bolg, challenges Nuada to hand-to-hand combat.

With one sweep of his sword, Sreng cuts off Nuada's right hand. However, this did not lead to the defeat of the little warriors. They defeated the Fir Bolg and killed their king. According to some accounts, the Fir Bolg flee Ireland.

According to some versions, the Tuatha Dé Danann offer the giants one quarter of Ireland as their own, and the Fir Bolg/Fomorians choose Connacht. But, they seem to disappear from myths after this.

The Tuatha De Danann are said to have ruled until the invasion by the Milesians, the modern day Celts. Legend says that, after the defeat by the Celts, the little people of Danu were allowed to stay in Ireland– but only if they remained underground. Consigned to the underworld, these little people became known as *Aes sidhe* ("the people of the fairy mounds") or more commonly, leprechauns.

Otherworldly dwarf creatures appear in the folklore and myths of countries like Ireland, Scotland and the Isle of Man (also spelled Mann). What follows is a brief listing and description of some of Ireland's Little People:

LEPRECHAUN

Leprechauns are probably the most famous of the fairy folk. Every year, on March 17, St. Patrick's Day, you see a lot of images of tiny bearded men in green coats and hats. Known for causing mischief and hiding pots of gold at the ends of rainbows, the leprechaun gets a lot of attention. Instantly recognizable by their red hair and beards, emerald-green suits, and quick-witted Irish charm, stories of leprechauns have existed for hundreds of years. The word leprechaun is derived from the old Irish word *Lú Chorpain,* meaning small body, and is also associated with the Irish word for shoe maker—*leath bhrógan*—because these Little People are frequently depicted as cobblers.

These magical little creatures are known to possess pots of gold. Leprechauns will avoid contact with humans at all costs, as their gold is highly important to them and they consider mortals to be quite greedy and foolish. If a leprechaun is captured by a mortal, they will offer great wealth in exchange for their freedom. A typical story involving the leprechaun's pot of gold, features a person capturing a leprechaun and demanding to know where his pot of gold is buried. The leprechaun then points out the tree in exchange for freedom, and the captor ties a red handkerchief on the tree, so he might return with a shovel. However, when the man returns later, he discovers that the wily leprechaun has tied red handkerchiefs to all the surrounding trees, thus protecting his gold from discovery!

CLURICHAUN

Illustration by T. C. Croker, from *"Fairy Legends and Traditions of the South of Ireland,"* 1862.

CLURICHAUN

Clurichauns are small red-headed cousins of Leprechauns. Dressed in dapper suits, these sprites are the wild child of Irish folklore. They love to get drunk. Clurichauns are said to love wine even more than gold. If Clurichauns are treated with respect, they will protect your supply of alcohol, but when offended Clurichauns will wreak havoc on your home and spoil your wine. And, they are known to become surly if they have had too much to drink. Clurichauns inhabit wine cellars, and as their ruddy complexion attests, spend most of their time sampling the contents of the hapless publican's or homeowner's alcohol store.

However, if you keep your Clurichaun happy (by keeping your wine cellar well-stocked), he will protect your wine casks from leaks; annoy him, however, and soon all your wine will go bad and chaos will descend. Clurichauns love nothing better than a jolly good party and after a drink or three will often strike up a rousing rendition of an Irish folk song while riding around your house on the pet dog—what could be more charming?

DULLAHAN

The Dullahan is the headless horseman, usually seen riding a black horse; he carries his own head under one arm. The Dullahan is usually male, but there are some female versions. The mouth is said to be in a hideous grin that touches both sides of the head. His eyes are lit up with an evil fire and are darting back and forth, constantly looking for victims. (we often see such grins and glowing eyes on Halloween jack-o'-lantern pumpkins). One of the best known Dullahans appears in Washington Irving's short story, "The Legend of Sleepy Hollow," first published in 1820.

Dullahans are most active in rural areas, and can usually be spotted around midnight on feast days or festivals. This headless rider wears a black cloak. If you see one approaching, you must cover your ears so that you do not hear the name he calls out, in case the name be yours. If a Dullahan is spied at a standstill, you can be sure that there will be a death in the immediate area. The Dullahan can gaze upon the home of a dying person by holding its disembodied head aloft, no matter where that house may be. In this way, it can scan the Irish countryside for miles in every direction, even on the darkest of nights.

GROGOCH

The Grogoch is a half-man, half-fairy aborigine who came from Scotland and settled in Ireland. This fairy is best described as a very small, elderly man with a full coat of thick reddish fur or hair. The Grogoch wears no clothes, but instead sports a coat

of dirt and twigs, which it accumulates on its journeys. Needless to say, these scruffy creatures are not well known for their cleanliness. This half human/half fairy is a helpful fellow, known to help a person do chores like planting and harvesting, or housework. The Grogoch possess the power of invisibility and will only reveal themselves to you if they deem you trustworthy. Their preference for remote, rural dwellings may make them seem unsociable; but they are actually quite the opposite.

If a Grogoch takes a liking to you, it will attach itself to you and follow you home. They are very hard working and, in some cases, try to be so helpful that they get in the way. If you have an unwanted Grogoch in your house, it is best to ask a clergy member to bless the residence. This will drive away the sprite; it will proceed to bother someone else. If they are underfoot outside, offer to pay them. Grogoch get highly offended if offered payment for their assistance and will leave if one persists in paying them. If you want to reward them, they love cream and will down a jug of it in one gulp.

Like most Little People, the Grogoch live in remote areas under rocks, in caves, and hollows. They can some-times be seen relaxing and smoking pipes late at night.

CHANGELING

A Changeling is a child believed to have been secretly substituted by fairies for the parents' real child in infancy. In Irish folklore, the Changeling is sometimes an ugly, stupid, or strange child left by fairies in place of a pretty, charming child. It is rumored that they are ill-tempered and wise beyond their years. You can tell a Changeling baby by the fact that it is ill-tempered and looks wizened in appearance. Most will have very dark eyes and if you look into them you can see wisdom well beyond their age. They may also have physical deformities such as a lame hand or crooked back. They will have grown a complete set of teeth after only approximately two weeks in the human household, and will also exhibit legs as slim as chicken bones, and hands that are coated with a light dusting of hair. Their hands will also become curved and claw-like, eventually resembling the talons of a bird.

116

A Changeling will also grow and develop a lot quicker than a human baby and within a few weeks the Changeling will have a full set of teeth and their legs and arms will be quite bony and thin. A changeling doesn't always appear as a baby—occasionally the Faeries will leave a piece of enchanted wood called a 'stock' in the cradle instead. This stock will appear to grow sick and die right in front of the 'parents' eyes. To amuse themselves, these fairy babies work dark magic in the household; they are happy when a disaster befalls their adopted family. The changelings' new family will never have any good luck while the changeling resides in the family home as the changeling will drain the family of any good fortune that will come their way. A warning, though, to all those people who become parents to a changeling, it must be loved and cared for like it is your own if you ever want to have a chance of seeing your own child again. The threat is that if the changeling is harmed or abandoned in any way, the Faeries will treat your child just as badly or possibly even worse, a risk any parents would not be willing to take.

BANSHEE

The Banshee is a female spirit in Gaelic folklore, whose appearance or wailing warns a family that one of them will soon die. Her scream is believed to be an omen of death. This 'keening' is a warning that there will be an imminent death in the family and as the Irish families blended over time, it is said that each family has its own Banshee! Other Irish mythology stories relating to the Banshee say that she is the ghost of a young girl that suffered a brutal death and her spirit remains to warn family members that a violent death is imminent. It is said that this Banshee appears as an old woman with rotten teeth and long fingernails. She wears rags and has blood red eyes that are so filled with hate that looking directly into them will cause immediate death! This Banshee's mouth is always open as her piercing scream torments the souls of the living.

Historians have traced the first stories of the Banshee to the 8th century which were based on a tradition where women sang a sorrowful song to lament someone's death. These women were known as 'keeners' and since they accepted alcohol as payment, they were said to be sinners and punished by being doomed to become Banshees. It is said that in 1437, King James I of Scotland was approached by an Irish seeress or banshee who foretold his murder at the instigation of the Earl of Atholl. According to the mythology of the Banshee, if she is spotted, she will vanish into a cloud of mist and this action creates a noise similar to that of a bird flapping its wings. Legend says that Banshees don't cause death; they only serve as a warning of it.

BROWNIE

Brownies are 20-36 inches tall, and will remain invisible until they want you to see them. These wee ones are originally from Scotland but have since emigrated along with the Scottish peoples to Ireland and beyond. It is said that each house in Scotland used to have its own Brownie. They are guardians who protect people and property. Brownies fall into the category that protects property. Children especially like Brownies, as they are known to entertain children by telling them stories or teaching them games. Some myths tell of helpful brownies turning into mischievous and troublemaking Boggarts when they are not left some type of appreciation for their work.

WILL-O'-THE-WISP

Will-O'-The-Wisp refers to the ghostly lights sometimes seen at night or twilight over bogs, swamps, or marshes. This phenomenon looks like a flickering lamp, and is sometimes said to recede if approached. Much folklore surrounds the phenomenon of *Ignis Fatuus*, which means "the foolish fire," or "ghost light at night." Appearing as lights seen over boggy and marshy places throughout Ireland and Britain, Will-O'-The-Wisps are said to be spirits of the dead who cannot move on. These bog lights appear to be lanterns or the glowing windows of a house; and, they deliberately cause travelers to veer off the correct path to their doom.

Will-O'-The-Wisps can be seen on land or at sea. Although these lights, flickering in the darkness of the night may be beautiful, a person must not let the Will-O'-The-Wisp's appearance fool them.

Irish storytelling began as an oral tradition. This is why many different variations of the same fairy tale can exist in different parts of Ireland. Native Irish stories and culture easily adapted and mixed with latter day historical Christian figures. This adapting to social changes is how Irish fairy tales survived until the present day. The earliest Irish myths and fairy tales were written down by Irish monks.

From the eighth century on, Irish monks valued traditional Irish folk tales–even though they were based on pagan beliefs–and recorded the tales in writing. The earliest appearance of dwarflike people is to be found in an 8th century  text about the adventures of Fearghas mac Léide; they are called the *Abhaic*.

Since the time of the Medieval monks, Irish fairy tales have been laid down for posterity in a variety of books. Also, there are more modern Irish writers who have been heavily influenced by Irish mythology. Fairy tales containing dwarflike little people are abundant in Irish tradition. The following are some samples of Irish stories in which wee folk appear:

FRANK MARTIN & THE FAIRIES
By William Carleton

Martin was a thin, pale man, when I saw him, of a sickly look, and a constitution naturally feeble. His hair was a light auburn, his beard mostly unshaven, and his hands of a singular delicacy and whiteness, owing, I dare say, as much to the soft and easy nature of his employment as to his infirm health. In everything else he was as sensible, sober, and rational as any other man; but on the topic of fairies, the man's mania was peculiarly strong and immovable. Indeed, I remember that the expression of his eyes was singularly wild and hollow, and his long narrow temples sallow and emaciated.

Now, this man did not lead an unhappy life, nor did the malady he labored under seem to be productive of either pain or terror to him, although one might be apt to imagine otherwise. On the contrary, he and the fairies maintained the most friendly intimacy, and their dialogues—which I fear were woefully one-sided ones—must have been a source of great pleasure to him, for they were conducted with much mirth and laughter, on his part at least.

"Well, Frank, when did you see the fairies?"

"Whist! there's two dozen of them in the shop (the weaving shop) this minute. There's a little old fellow sittin' on the top of the sleighs, an' all to be rocked while I'm weavin.' The sorrow's in them, but they're the greatest little skamers alive, so they are. See, there's another of them at my dressin' noggin. Go out o' that, you shingawn; or, bad cess to me, if you don't; but I'll lave you a mark. Ha! cut, you thief you!"

"Frank, ain't you afeard o' them?"

"Is it me! Arra! What would I be afeard o' them for? Sure, they have no power over me."

"And why have't they, Frank?"

"Because I was baptized against them."

"What do you mean by that?"

"Why, the priest that christened me was told by my father, to put in the proper prayer against the fairies—an' a priest can't refuse it when he's asked—an' he did so. Begorra, it's well for me that he did—let the tallow alone, you little glutton—see, there's a weeny thief o' them aitin' my tallow—because, you see, it was their intention to make me king o' the fairies."

"Is it possible?"

"Devil a lie in it. Sure, you may ax them, an' they'll tell you."

"What size are they, Frank?"

"Oh, little wee fellows, with green coats, an' the purtiest little shoes ever you seen. There's two of them—both old acquaintances o' mine—runnin' along the yarn-beam. That old fellow with the bob wig is called Jim Jam, an' the other chap, with the three-cocked hat, is called Nickey Nick. Nickey plays the pipes. Nickey, give us a tune, or I'll malavogne [beat] you—come now, 'Lough Erne Shore.' Whist, now—listen!"

The poor fellow, though weaving as fast as he could all the time, yet bestowed every possible mark of attention to the music, and seemed to enjoy it as much as if it had been real.

But who can tell whether that which we look upon as a privation may not after all be a fountain of increased happiness, greater, perhaps, than any which we ourselves enjoy? I forget who the poet is who says:

"Mysterious are thy laws; The vision's finer than the view; Her landscape Nature never drew. So fair as Fancy draws."

Many a time, when a mere child, not more than six or seven years of age, have I gone as far as Frank's weaving-shop, in order, with a heart divided between curiosity and fear, to listen to his conversation with the good people. From morning till night his tongue was going almost as incessantly as his shuttle; and it was well known that at night, whenever he awoke out of his sleep, the first thing he did was to put out his hand, and push them, as it were, off his bed.

"Go out o' this, you thieves, you. Go out o' this now, an' let me alone. Nickey, is this any time to be playing the pipes, and me wants to sleep? Go off, now. Troth if yez do, you'll see what I'll give yez tomorrow. Sure, I'll be makin' new dressin's. And if yez behave decently, maybe I'll lave yez the scrapin' o' the pot. There now.

Och! poor things, they're dacent crathurs. Sure, they're all gone, barrin' poor Red-Cap, that doesn't like to lave me." And then the harmless monomaniac would fall back into what we trust was an innocent slumber.

About this time, there was said to have occurred a very remarkable circumstance, which gave poor Frank Thomas a vast deal of importance among the neighbors: A man named Frank Thomas, the same in whose house Mickey M'Rorey held the first dance at which I ever saw him, as detailed in a former sketch; this man, I say, had a child sick, but of what complaint I cannot now remember, nor is it of any importance. One of the gables of Thomas's house was built against, or rather into, a Forth or Rath, called Towny, or properly Tonagh Forth. It was said to be haunted by the fairies, and what gave it a character peculiarly wild in my eyes was, that there were on the southern side of it two or three little green mounds, which were said to be the graves of unchristened children, over which it was con-sidered dangerous and unlucky to pass.

At all events, the season was mid-summer; and one evening about dusk, during the illness of the child, the noise of a hand-saw was heard upon the Forth. This was considered rather strange, and, after a little time, a few of those who were assembled at Frank Thomas's went to see who it could be that was sawing in such a place, or what they could be sawing at so late an hour, for everyone knew that nobody in the whole country about them would dare to cut down the few white-thorns that grew upon the Forth. On going to examine, however, judge of their surprise, when, after surrounding and searching the whole place, they could discover no trace of either saw or sawyer. In fact, with the exception of themselves, there was no one, either natural or supernatural, visible. They then returned to the house, and had scarcely sat down, when it was heard again within ten yards of them.

Another examination of the premises took place, but with equal success. Now, however, while standing on the porch, they heard the sawing in a little hollow, about a hundred and fifty yards below them, which was completely exposed to their view; but they could see nobody. A party of them immediately went down to ascertain, if possible, what this singular noise and invisible labor could mean; but on arriving at the spot, they heard the sawing, to which were now added hammering, and the driving of nails upon the Forth above, whilst those who stood on the Forth continued to hear it in the hollow.

On comparing notes, they resolved to send down to Billy Nelson's for Frank Martin a distance of only about eighty or ninety yards. He was soon on the spot, and without a moment's hesitation solved the enigma.

"Tis the fairies," said he. "I see them, and busy crathurs they are."

"But what are they sawing, Frank?"

"They are makin' a child's coffin," he replied; "they have the body already made, an' they're now nailin' the lid together."

That night the child died, and the story goes that on the second evening afterwards, the carpenter who was called upon to make the coffin brought a table out from Thomas's house to the porch, as a temporary bench; and, it is said, that the sawing and hammering necessary for the completion of his task were precisely the same which had been heard the evening but one before, neither more nor less. I remember the death of the child myself, and the making of its coffin, but I think the story of the supernatural carpenter was not heard in the village for some months after its interment.

Frank had every appearance of a hypochondriac about him. At the time I saw him, he might be about thirty-four years of age, but I do not think, from the debility of his frame and infirm health, that he has been alive for several years. He was an object of considerable interest and curiosity, and often have I been present when he was pointed out to strangers as "the man that could see the good people."

THE FAIRIES

William Allingham

Up the airy mountain,
  Down the rushy glen,
We daren't go a-hunting
  For fear of little men;
Wee folk, good folk,
  Trooping all together;
Green jacket, red cap,
  And white owl's feather!

Down along the rocky shore
  Some make their home,
They live on crispy pancakes
  Of yellow tide-foam;
Some in the reeds
  Of the black mountain lake,
With frogs for their watch-dogs,
  All night awake.

High on the hill-top
  The old King sits;
He is now so old and grey
  He's nigh lost his wits.
With a bridge of white mist
  Columbkill he crosses,
On his stately journeys
  From Slieveleague to Rosses;
Or going up with music
  On cold starry nights,

To sup with the Queen
  Of the gay Northern Lights.

They stole little Bridget
  For seven years long;
When she came down again
  Her friends were all gone.
They took her lightly back,
  Between the night and morrow,
They thought that she was fast asleep,
  But she was dead with sorrow.
They have kept her ever since
  Deep within the lake,
On a bed of flag-leaves,
  Watching till she wake.

By the craggy hillside,
  Through the mosses bare,
They have planted thorn trees
  For pleasure here and there.
Is any man so daring
  As dig them up in spite,
He shall find their sharpest thorns
  In his bed at night.

Up the airy mountain,
  Down the rushy glen,
We daren't go a-hunting
  For fear of little men;
Wee folk, good folk,
  Trooping all together;
Green jacket, red cap,
  And white owl's feather!

THE FAIRY SHOEMAKER

William Allingham

Little cow boy, what have you heard,
Up on the lonely rath's green mound?
Only the plaintive yellow bird
Sighing in sultry fields around,
Chary, chary, chary, chee-ee! —
Only the grasshopper and the bee?—

 "Tip-tap, rip-rap,
Tick-a-tack-too!"
Scarlet leather, sewn together,
This will make a shoe.
Left, right, pull it tight;

Summer days are warm;
Underground in winter,
Laughing at the storm!
Lay your ear close to the hill.
Do you not catch the tiny clamor,
Busy click of an elfin hammer,
Voice of the Leprechaun singing shrill

As he merrily plies his trade?
He's a span
And a quarter in height.
Get him in sight, hold him tight,
And you're a made Man!

II.

You watch your cattle the summer day,
Sup on potatoes, sleep in the hay;
How would you like to roll in your carriage.

Look for a duchess's daughter in marriage?
Seize the Shoemaker then you may!

Big boots a-hunting,
Sandals in the hall,
White for a wedding-feast,
Pink for a ball.
This way, that way,
So we make a shoe;
Getting rich every stitch,
"Tick-tack-too!"

Nine-and-ninety treasure-crocks
This keen miser-fairy hath,
Hid in mountains, woods, and rocks,
Ruin and round-tow'r, cave and rath,
And where the cormorants build;

From times of old
Guarded by him;
Each of them fill'd
Full to the brim
With gold!

III.

I caught him at work one day, myself,
In the castle-ditch, where foxglove grows,
A wrinkled, wizen'd and bearded Elf,
Spectacles stuck on his pointed nose,
Silver buckles to his hose,
Leather apron-shot in his lap--
"Rip-rap, tip-tap,
Tick-tack-too!"

(A grasshopper on my cap!
Away the moth flew!)

Buskins for a fairy prince,
Brogues for his son,
"Pay me well, pay me well,
When the job is done!"

The rogue was mine, beyond a doubt.
I stared at him; he stared at me;
"Servant, Sir!" "Humph!" says he,
And pull'd a snuff-box out.
He took a long pinch, look'd better pleased,

The queer little Leprechaun;
Offer'd the box with a whimsical grace,
Pouf! he flung the dust in my face,
And, as I sneezed,
He was gone!

IRISH FAIRIES IN LITERATURE

The Irish fairy tale tradition has influenced many of the leading figures of English literature. For example, Jonathon Swift wrote Gulliver's Travels while he was living in Ireland. It is likely that Swift he was influenced by the Irish storytelling tradition, which had tales of both giants and little people. W.B. Yeats, the Nobel-laureate, wrote many poems inspired by Irish mythology. Along with friend, Lady Gregory, Yeats was instrumental in recording Irish folklore for posterity. J.R.R. Tolkien, English writer, poet, and university professor, who is best known as the author of the classic works *The Hobbit, The Lord of the Rings*, and *The Silmarillion*, was very familiar with Irish fairy tales. There is more than a hint of the Tuatha de Danaan in his depiction of elves, and his "black riders" are

reminiscent of the Irish Dullahan. And so it seems that, however much we turn to modern forms of entertainment, the  Irish Little People from long ago will continue to live on in various forms.

Giants & Little People

of

ISLE
OF MAN

One of the British Isles, located in the Irish Sea, is the Isle of Man. It is almost equidistant from England, Wales, Ireland, and Scotland. The Manx people are not part of the United Kingdom. Their island is a crown possession (since 1828), and it is self-governing, although under the supervision of the British Home Office.

The folklore of the Isle of Man includes myths of ghosts, goblins, giants, little people, as well as other creatures. The stories have been passed down through the generations.

According to folklore, a giant played a major role in the creation of the Isle of Man. There is a folktale that claims that the Isle of Man was created by Ireland's legendary hero Fionn Mac Cumhaill (Finn McCool). One day, Finn was in pursuit of a Scottish giant. Hoping to prevent the giant's escape by swimming across the sea, McCool scooped up a huge glob of clay and rock from the land mass of the northern Irish coast. He hurled the giant mud ball, but he missed his target and the chunk of earth and rock landed in the Irish Sea, thus creating the Island of Man. The tale goes on to say that the hole Finn McCool gouged out became the Lough Neagh, a large freshwater lake in Northern Ireland. It is the largest lake by area in the British Isles.

There was a famous giant associated with the Isle of Man in the 1800s, who most often went by the name of Colonel Routh Goshen. Also known as the Middlebush Giant, he was billed as the tallest man in the world. Born Arthur James Caley near Sulby, Isle of Man, in 1824, this giant became more commonly known as Colonel Routh Goshen, a stage name. Arthur James Caley was one of twelve children. In his teens, he began to grow very tall; he continued to grow into his twenties.

In May 1851, during a visit to Liverpool, his extraordinary stature attracted much attention; news articles were published about his gigantic size, described at that time as being 7 ft, 6 inches (2.28 m). Shortly afterwards, Caley exhibited himself in Manchester; then London; and later, in Paris, France. Newspapers described his talent, saying things like "Col. Goshen appeared in a condensed version of the *Rough Diamond*, in which he acted the part of Joe. He possesses considerable dramatic ability."

At some point American showman, P.T. Barnum hired Caley for his circus freak show, billing him as Col. Routh Goshen. Publicity sources claim that the giant was born in Egypt; he was also said to be Turkish, Jewish, Arabian, Belgian, and Prussian. His true origins became obscured by the varying biographical ac-

counts that were created to publicize his appearances. Some of his aliases were: Arthur James Caley; Colonel Routh Goshen; The Middlebush Giant; The Arabian Giant; The Palestine Giant; The Sulby Giant; The Manx Giant; and Arthur Crowley.

When he died in 1899, Caley was buried without a tombstone for fear his body would be dug up and put on display. Many years later, however, a tombstone was placed at the gravesite.

Based on the following newspaper samples, it seems like this Manx giant may have lived his life in the tabloids of his time:

BELL'S LIFE

IN SYDNEY &
SPORTING
REVIEWER
New South Wales,
United Kingdom
September 13, 1851

Manx Giant.— The inhabitants of Liverpool were much surprised to see, on Friday, walking up and down our streets, a man of extraordinary dimensions, Arthur Caley, from Sulby, Lezayre, Isle of Man. He is only twenty-three years of age, stands seven feet six inches high, and weighs twenty-one stones. He is a Manx farmer, and has a little property of his own. He arrived in Liverpool by the *King Orry*, Captain Quale, from Douglas. He comes to bid farewell to a number of his friends who are about to emigrate.

THE SALT LAKE HERALD
New South Wales, U.K.
March 9, 1889

COL. ROUTH GOSHEN

He Was One of Barnum's Most Famous Giants.

HIS MATRIMONIAL VENTURES

Some of the Tall Men of History— The Difficulty in Burying Goshen— How He Sat Down Upon a Man.

A certain Russian novelist of great stature, and of Herculean build, once gave vent to a pathetic lament because he was such a big man. He said that he would be willing to make any sacrifice if some convenient genii would transform him into a Lilliputian. Although a man of noble personal beauty and envied by half the officers of the Russian army, he said that he felt as clumsy as Gulliver among the little men. He said that he endeavored to forgot his inches, but he was very absent-minded; he was eternally bumping his head against the tops of doors, which reminded him of what he called his affliction.

He said in touching terms that it was a positive bitterness for him when calling upon some of his aristocratic friends, to be obliged to take one of the small delicate drawing room chairs and contemplate the enormous length of his legs as they stretched away into endless perspective. He said that he often stood at the window of his study and "gazed with anguish at some of the occasionally passing men of small stature, chipper as sparrows in their movements; with bodies as well lined as those of Arabian horses; with no room in their small persons for the development of the morbid dreams and heavy gloominess that oppress the men of big physiques; with the suggestiveness of the lightness of Puck and the rippling mirth of elfin folks; very ideals of creation; masterpieces of Gods handiwork," said this mourning novelist of the land of the czar.

This wail is strange. Big men are as a rule tremendously self-satisfied, and swagger like English dragoons. Their height is a source of lifelong inward complacency; and the small men of, say, 5 feet 4 or 5 feet 6 inches think that they would gladly give several years of their lives to be as tall. Certain scientists claim that men of great stature do not live so long as small men, but this theory has often been disproved. Col.

Routh Goshen, the giant who recently died, was over 70 years old.

SOME HISTORICAL GIANTS

Although the modern scientists have exploded the theory that the men of past centuries were taller than the men of today, there have been many men of wonderful stature, especially during the last two centuries. In the latter part of the 17th century, there lived in Utrecht, a man 8½ feet high, who was born of parents of ordinary stature. Charles Byrne, an Irishman, measured 8 feet 4 inches. He died in 1733 at age 22; and his skeleton, now in the London College of Surgeons, is eight feet long. Edward Malone, also Irish born, in 1682, stood 7 feet 7 inches. Patrick Cotter, still another Hibernian, was 8 feet 7¾ inches high. Pliny tells of an Arabian giant who was over 9 feet high. Barnum has exhibited several giants considerably over 7 feet high.

COL. GOSHEN

Probably the biggest giant ever exhibited in America, was Colonel Routh Goshen, who recently died on his farm in New Jersey. He was with Barnum Circus for many years. His height is variously stated, but he was about eight feet tall. In health, he weighed over 600 pounds; and at the time of his death, he weighed 588 pounds.

His coffin was 8 feet 4 inches in length; and considerable difficulty was found in burying him.

The coffin would not go through the door, so it was left outside near the gate. The body lay indoors on a stage of planks nine feet long. Four men, after much labor, raised the body a little and slipped a broad carpet sling under the waist, fitted at the ends with stout rods, each large enough to be grasped by two men. The arms were tied down and the legs were firmly strapped together with a horses girth in such a way as to offer handles to two men, one on each side. The nine-foot stage with the body on it was then carried outside and placed on the perch at right angles to the coffin.

Here an interesting discussion arose. The New Jersey undertaker wanted to place the stage over the coffin, lift up the body, withdraw the planking, and let the body down into the coffin. The New York undertaker had arranged for eight men to carry the body by the straps and the iron rods to the coffin and lower it. Each presented his argument; the pall bearers and guests who had arrived, gathered round and took part in the discussion. The New York undertaker finally had his way and the body was carried to the coffin and laid in it without mishap. An attempt to remove the sling from under him failed, so the rods were cut off and the carpet was left in the coffin. Then the coffin was hoisted upon boxes and left exposed till after the services. It took eight very strong men to carry the coffin from the undertaker's wagon to the tomb.

Although Barnum advertised Col. Goshen as the "Arabian Giant," he was born on the Isle of Man. He was born a Jew, but he died a Christian. Early in life, he was a ship carpenter and he often wished that he had not abandoned his trade for the show business. He died comparatively well off, as he made a great deal of money exhibiting himself during his lifetime. He retired three or four years ago and has been living on his comfortable farm near Clyde station, New Jersey. He was very popular among his neighbors. And, the women doted on him and visited him frequently.

THE GIANT'S LOVE.

Col. Goshen was twice married, and was divorced both times. The second Mrs. Goshen was a stout, dark complexioned woman of average height. She is a cousin of the fat woman who was the second biggest thing in the Townsend Show that the Colonel traveled with as giant before the war, after he left Barnum's employ. She first met the Colonel twenty years ago in Algonquin, Ill. She was then Miss Mary Welch a 15-year-old girl of Elgin, Ill., with long dark ringlets, big black eyes, and a partiality for tall men. She got into the show free through the professional character of her cousin and used to spend most of the time gazing up in silent wonderment at Col. Goshen's large face and pleasing mustache.

The Colonel, at this time, was the husband of Augusta White, a stout, ruddy-faced German brunette who was the snake charmer of the troupe and who used to make little Mary Welch's eyes bulge in awe as she tossed snakes about on a little platform adjoining the improvised circus ring.

Col. Goshen stayed in Algonquin all that winter and Mary went to see him often. In 1879, when she had grown to be a woman, she again met the big Colonel during a short stay of the show in Chicago; their acquaintance was renewed, and ripened into friendship. The giant was still living with the snake charmer at his farm in New Jersey, but that same year he applied to the Chancellor of the Court of Chancery in Trenton, for a divorce on the ground of his wife's infidelity. His wife made no legal opposition, and a decree of separation was granted.

Early in 1880, Col. Goshen went to New York, where he was joined by Miss Welch, and they were married. After a short wedding tour, the couple settled down on a farm at Middlebush. They lived together until last fall when the Colonel suddenly went west and sent some people to live on the farm who were total strangers to himself, but who were known to Mrs. Goshen. She was taken ill during his absence; and in November, she went back to Elgin to her family to be nursed.

The farm, meantime, remained in the charge of a man named Whittaker and the new boarders.

SUIT FOR DIVORCE.

Not long afterward, however, the Colonel entered suit for divorce from his wife on the ground that she had been intimate with several men. She denied the charges of infidelity and made counter charges against the Colonel of intimacy with three different women. He secured his divorce, however, and lived in unfettered bliss during the last years of his life. When Col. Goshen was suing for a divorce from his last wife, he was not quite so popular among his New Jersey neighbors, Many of them believed that the Colonel was more to blame than his wife. On several occasions they have annoyed him by making insulting remarks. But, as the Colonel was a good-natured man, he took no notice of their taunts. After calling upon his lawyer one day the giant started for his farm. Just as he was entering the front gate, a neighbor named James Gannon drove by. Gannon was a well-built middle-aged man and was an active adherent of Mrs. Goshen in the family trouble. When he saw the Colonel, Gannon stopped his horse and dismounted from the wagon. He walked over to the gate, and in a sarcastic tone of voice remarked, "Ah there, Colonel. You're a fine one, you are!"

"What do you mean?" asked the giant.

"Oh, you're no good," said Gannon. "I don't want anything to do with a man who will turn his wife out of doors and then sue for a divorce. The giant grew somewhat riled and replied, "You tell an untruth! I never turned my wife away. And I don't want any impertinence from you, either."

"Oh, you don't?" said Gannon. "I think I can beat you myself. You're big, but you're no good."

As the Colonel was about to reply, Gannon jumped over the gate and advanced upon him. Gannon struck out for the giant's head and managed to get in a blow on his waist. The colonel was about to retaliate when Gannon drew a knife and made an effort to stab him.

"Stop that, you villain!" cried the giant. Then he grabbed Gannon by the nape of the neck and lifted him clear off the ground with one hand. The giant then took the knife away from Gannon, who struggled fiercely and managed to kick the giant's shins. That was more than the latter could stand and he cuffed Gannon on the head with his open hand.

Then he deliberately threw him upon the ground and quietly sat down upon Gannon, who fainted. A neighbor who was passing rushed to his rescue.

The giant got up and remarked, "I'm a bad man when I'm aroused." Then he retired to his hearthstone. Gannon was revived with much difficulty. He looked like a rubber blanket spread upon the grass. On recovering consciousness, Gannon faintly asked if the giant was also buried under the ruins. When the case was explained to him, he felt his ribs to see if they were all there. He was taken home in a cart. Gannon afterwards said, "The giant is a bad man to fool with. I had no idea he was so heavy. I don't think I shall interfere in his family affairs any more. I thought the house, the barn, and the woodshed had all fallen upon me at the same time."

A museum on the Isle of Man has acquired a curious life-sized metal cast of the hand of Arthur Caley, the "Manx Giant." The cast was donated to the Manx Museum by the widow of the late Dr James Smith Jr, a surgeon and collector of arcade games and carnival memorabilia in America. The artifact is particularly unusual, because it has a small compartment in the top of the hand with an engraved lid on it. Museum staff have speculated that it may once have been a snuff holder for a bar or shop counter.

"Mooinjer veggey" is the name for the Little People of the Isle of Man. They are from two to three feet in height, and are said to be very similar to humans. According to Sophia Morrison in the 1911 book, *Manx Fairy Tales*: "They wear red caps and green jackets and are most often seen on horseback followed by packs of little hounds of all the colours of the rainbow. They are rather inclined to be mischievous and spiteful."

Ms. Morrison goes on to describe Fairy Lore:

> The Island is full of Fairy lore. A good Manxman does not speak of fairies — the word *ferish*, a corruption of the English, did not exist in the Island 200 years ago. He talks of the Little People, or *Mooinjer-Veggey*,[1] or, in a more familiar mood, of "Themselves," Guillyn Veggey,[2] or "Lil Fellas." In contra-distinction to mortals, he calls them Middle World Men, for they are believed to dwell in a world of their own, being neither good enough for Heaven nor bad enough for Hell.

> One may see these Little People in green dresses and red caps, and adorned with Fairy Lace,[3] dancing o' nights in the dark green Fairy Rings upon the grass to the music of the Fairy Fiddle[4] and the chiming of Fairy Bells,[5] which, if some Lil Fella tear his dress upon a drine,[6] may be turned at need into Fairy Thimbles. The Fairy Flowers [7] stand sentinel around,

safe on their slender stalks, for no one dare pluck them or take them home for fear of Fairy Pinches[8] and bad dreams o' night. Other Little People are playing near by on the old Tramman tree,[9] — where the Fairies' Lugs[10] invite them to ride upon the branches. Yet others are dancing on the lonely Niarbyl shore below, some hold their fairy cups in their hands, while their Fairy Bottles of amber wine[11] sparkle coolingly on the waves. Close at hand is heard the sound of Fairy Coopers[12] hard at work making herring barrels in Ooigh-ny-Sieyr, or the Cooper's Cave, at the foot of the precipitous Cronk-yn-Irree-Laa; — if it be in the month of May, happy is the mortal who has heard them, for it is a sign of a good herring season. Ever and anon a chip flies from the cave and immediately turns into a fairy ship. Thus was made the Fairy Fleet,[13] whose tiny riding lights are shining bright in the Bay Mooar. If a fisherman sees the lights he will fish those waters and will be sure of a good catch of herring.

If you stay here till the sun rises, you may see his beams glittering upon the Mermaid's Jewels,[14] and may know that *Ben Varrey* is protecting the shore and that no marauder dare approach. You may see the Mermaid's Hair[15] blown inland by the wind. Should you happen to see this from a boat at sea, you would speak of the protectress of the shore as *Joaney Gorm*,[16] and of the Merman not as Uooinuey! 'arreg, but as Yn Guilley Beg, for it is not lucky to speak of things at sea by their shore names. Even the sea is called *Joaney Gorm* by a fisherman on board his boat. The sun is *Gloyr yn Seihll*,[17] or *Ree yn Laa*,[18] and the moon, *Ben rein ny Hoie*.[19]

Later on in the day, perhaps, rain will fall while the sun is shining — it is the Fairies baking. If ones horse stumbles on the way home, it is because he sees

Fairies. So is the Manxman followed all the day by these little beings!

1. Little Family.
2. Little Boys.
3. Dictyota dichotoma.
4. Egg-case of "gobbag," or dog-fish.
5. Blue-bell.
6. Thorn.
7. Red Campion.
8. Blue marks on the skin.
9. Elder.
10. Ear-shaped fungi.
11. Fucuss nodosus, or knobbed seaweed.
12. Sound of waves in a cave.
13. Phosphorescent effects, the result of emission of light by Protozoa.
14. Sunbeams on the ripples of the wavelets.
15. Sea spume.
16, Blue Joan.
17. Glory of the World.
18. King of the Day.
19. Queen of the Night.

Belief in fairies was widespread on the Isle of Man in its early history; and some people today still believe. The fairies are said to reside in the sides of hills or in ancient burial mounds. The Manx believe that anyone venturing near such places would probably hear lovely fairy music. But, that person must be cautious not to stay long or they might be trapped and captured by the fairies.

These little creatures are only visible to people when they choose to be. Some of these wee ones are good fairies, curing diseases and rescuing people from misfortune. It was an old custom to keep a fire burning in the house during the night, so that the Fairies might come in and enjoy its warmth.

It is said that, on dark, dismal, stormy nights, in the mountain parishes, the people would go to bed earlier in order to allow to the weather-buffeted Fairies the enjoyment of the fire in the home, unwatched. It was also a custom to leave some bread out for the Fairies, and to fill crocks with clean water for them before retiring for the night. This water was never used for any other purpose, but was thrown out in the morning.

Many Manx women refused to spin yarn on Saturday evenings, because this was displeasing to the Mooinjer-Veggey. Also, every time they baked and churned, bit of buttered dough left out for the consumption of visiting Fairies.

But on the Isle of Man, the fairies were not all good; there were also other little people who were mean spirited or evil. Those fairies were known to steal children, abduct adults, or bring bad luck and misfortune. There is a Manx story of the Little People of Fairy Bridge. Legend says that if you cross this bridge, which lies just past Santon Station on the main Douglas-Castletown road, without saying so much as Laa Mie ("good day") to the fairies, you might not have a safe and pleasant visit.

In the work, *Lord Teignmouth's Sketches*, from 1836, there is an account of an instance that points up the fact that Manx fairies will  not suffer any unpleasantry or abuse without retaliating with punishment:

> "A man of Laxey, somewhat intoxicated, met a party of fairies, and began forthwith to abuse and curse them as the devil's imps. They wreaked their vengeance on him by piercing his skin with a shower of gravel. They would not have molested him had he not provoked them by his insults. The catastrophe did not terminate here. The offender sickened that night; his favorite horse died next morning; his cows died also; and in six weeks, he himself was a corpse!
>
> –*Lord Teignmouth's Sketches*, 1836.

It is said that, on April 30th annually, many Man Islanders would fix a wooden cross, bound with sheep's wool, to the inside of their front door to ward off malicious fairies. On this night too was the ceremony of the blowing of the Horns on Peel Hill. This was done to banish evil spirits.

Like other cultures, the Isle of Man has its fairy tales, like the one that follows:

MANX FAIRY TALES
London; 1911

Billy Beg, Tom Beg, & The Fairies

[By Sophia Morrison]

Not far from Dalby, Billy Beg and Tom Beg, two humpback cobblers, lived together on a lonely croft. Billy Beg was sharper and cleverer than Tom Beg, who was always at his command. One day Billy Beg gave Tom a staff, and quoth he, "Tom Beg, go to the mountain and fetch home the white sheep."

Tom Beg took the staff and went to the mountain, but he could not find the white sheep. At last, when he was far from home, and dusk was coming on, he began to think that he had best go back. The night was fine, and stars and a small crescent moon were in the sky. No sound was to be heard but the curlew's sharp whistle. Tom was hastening home, and had almost reached Glen

Rushen, when a grey mist gathered, and he lost his way.

But it was not long before the mist cleared, and Tom Beg found himself in a green glen such as he had never seen before, though he thought he knew every glen within five miles of him, for he was born and reared in the neighborhood. He was marveling and wondering where he could be, when he heard a far-away sound drawing nearer to him.

"Aw," said he to himself, "there's more than myself afoot on the mountains tonight; I'll have company."

The sound grew louder. First, it was like the humming of bees, then like the rushing of Glen Meay waterfall, and last it was like the marching and the murmur of a crowd. It was the fairy host. Of a sudden the glen was full of fine horses and of little people riding on them, with the lights on their red caps shining like the stars above and making the night as bright as day. There was the blowing of horns, the waving of flags, the playing of music, and the barking of many little dogs. Tom Beg thought that he had never seen anything so splendid as all he saw there. In the midst of the drilling and dancing and singing one of them spied Tom, and then Tom saw coming towards him the grandest little man he had ever set eyes upon, dressed in gold and silver, and silk shining like a raven's wing.

"It is a bad time you have chosen to come this way," said the little man, who was the king.

"Yes; but it is not here that I'm wishing to be though," said Tom.

Then said the king, "Are you one of us tonight, Tom?"

"I am surely," said Tom.

"Then," said the king, "it will be your duty to take the password. You must stand at the foot of the glen, and as each regiment goes by, you must take the password: it is *Monday, Tuesday, Wednesday, Thursday, Friday, Saturday.*"

"I'll do that with a heart and a half," said Tom.

At daybreak the fiddlers took up their fiddles; the Fairy army set itself in order; the fiddlers played before them out of the glen; and sweet that music was. Each regiment gave the password to Tom as it went by, "Monday, Tuesday, Wednesday, Thursday, Friday, Saturday" and last of all came the king, and he, too, gave it, "Monday, Tuesday, Wednesday, Thursday, Friday, Saturday."

Then he called in Manx to one of his men, "Take the hump from this fellow's back," and before the words were out of his mouth the hump was whisked off Tom Beg's back and thrown into the hedge.

How proud now was Tom, who so found himself the straightest man in the Isle of Man! He went down the mountain and came home early in the morning with light heart and eager step. Billy Beg wondered greatly when he saw Tom Beg so straight and strong, and when Tom Beg had rested and refreshed himself he told his story how he had met the Fairies who came every night to Glen Rushen to drill.

The next night Billy Beg set off along the mountain road and came at last to the green glen. About midnight he heard the trampling of horses, the lashing of whips, the barking of dogs, and a great hullabaloo, and, behold, the Fairies and their king, their dogs and their horses, all at drill in the glen as Tom Beg had said.

When they saw the humpback they all stopped, and one came forward and very crossly asked his business.

"I am one of Yourselves for the night, and should be glad to do you some service," said Billy Beg.

So, he was set to take the password, "Monday, Tuesday, Wednesday, Thursday, Friday, Saturday." And at daybreak the King said, "It's time for us to be off," and up came regiment after regiment giving Billy Beg the password, "Monday, Tuesday, Wednesday, Thursday, Friday, Saturday."

Last of all came the king with his men. and gave the password also, "Monday, Tuesday, Wednesday, Thursday, Friday, Saturday."

"AND SUNDAY," says Billy Beg, thinking himself clever. Then there was a great outcry.

"Get the hump that was taken off that fellow's back last night and put it on this man's back," said the king, with flashing eyes, pointing to the hump that lay under the hedge.

Before the words were well out of his mouth the hump was clapped onto Billy Beg's back.

"Now," said the King, "be off, and if ever I find you here again, I will clap another hump on to your front!"

And on that, they all marched away with one great shout, and left poor Billy Beg standing where they had found him, with a hump growing on each shoulder. And he came home next day dragging one foot after another, with a wizened face and as cross as two sticks, along with two humps

on his back. And, if those humps have not been taken off, they are there still.

CELTIC FOLKLORE: WELSH & MANX
Oxford; 1901

Four Years In Faery
[By John Rhys]

Like the Welsh fairies, the Manx ones take men away with them and detain them for years. Thus, a Kirk Andreas man was absent from his people for four years, which he spent with the fairies. He could not tell how he returned, but it seemed as if, having been unconscious, he woke up at last in this world.

The other world, however, in which he was for the four years, was not far away, as he could see what his brothers and the rest of the family were doing every day, although they could not see him.

To prove this, he mentioned to them how they were occupied on such and such a day, and, among other things, how they took their corn on a particular day to Ramsey. He reminded them also of their having heard a sudden sharp crack as they were passing by a thorn bush he named, and how they were so startled that one of them would have run back home. He asked them if they remembered that, and they said they did, only too well. He then explained to them the meaning of the noise, namely, that one of the fairies with whom he had been galloping the whole time, was about to let fly an arrow at his brothers. But, as he was going to do this, he (the missing brother) raised a plate and intercepted the arrow: that was the sharp noise they had heard.

Such was the account he had to give of his sojourn in Faery.

~ ~ ~ ~ ~

MANX FAIRY TALES
London; 1911

The Lost Wife of Ballaleece
[By Sophia Morrison]

One time the Farmer of Ballaleece married a beautiful young wife, and they were thinking the world of one another. But before long she disappeared. Some persons said that she was dead and others that she was taken by the Little People. Ballaleece mourned for her with a heavy heart and looked for her from Point of Ayr to the Calf; but in the end, not finding her, he married another wife. This one was not beautiful, but there was some money at her.

Soon after the marriage his first wife appeared to Ballaleece one night, and said to him, "My man, my man, I was taken away by the Little People, and I live with them near to you. I can be set free if you will but do what I tell you."

"Tell me quick," said Ballaleece.

"We'll be riding through Ballaleece barn at midnight on Friday," said she. "We'll be going in on one door and out on another. I'll be riding behind one of the men on horseback. You'll sweep the barn clean, and mind there is not one straw left on the floor. Catch hold of my bridle rein, hold it fast, and I shall be free."

When the night came Ballaleece took a besom and swept the barn floor so clean that not one speck was left on it. Then he waited in the dark. At midnight the barn doors opened wide, sweet music was heard, and in through the open door came a fine company of Little People, in green jackets and red caps, riding fine horses. On the last horse, sitting behind a Little Fellow, Ballaleece saw his first wife as pretty as a picture, and as young as when she left him. He seized hold of her bridle rein, but he was shaken from side to side like a leaf on a tree, and he was not able to hold her.

As she went out through the door she stretched out her right hand and pointed to a bushel in the corner of the barn, and called out in a sad voice, "There's been a straw put under the bushel for that reason you couldn't hold me, and you've done with me forever!"

The second wife had heard what had passed and had hidden the straw, and turned the bushel upside down so that it would not be seen.

The young wife was never heard of any more.

Giants & Little People

of

THE

MIDDLE EAST

&

MEDITERRANEAN

The Mediterranean/Middle East region of the world includes Albania, Algeria, Bahrain, Bosnia, Croatia, Cyprus, Egypt, the Gaza Strip, Greece, Herzegovina, Iraq, Iran, Israel, Italy, Jordan, Kuwait, Lebanon, Libya, Malta, Monaco, Montenegro, Morocco, Oman, Saudi Arabia, Slovenia, Spain, Sudan, Syria, Tunisia, Turkey, the West Bank, and Yemen.

Images and tales of giant fossilized human remains, including entire skeletons of giant races of humans have been circulating on the Internet for a decade or more. Because of the prevalence of photo editing software, these viral "giant" stories which usually include a fantastic photo of a gigantic skeleton or skull; the site of the "major discovery" of a giant skeleton or skeletons being found is often in the Mediterranean or the Middle East. Pictures of giant human skeletons on the web fall into three categories: hoaxes, mis-identification, and scientifically sound. Photoshopped images fall under the first category, hoaxes.

Skeletal remains or bones of dinosaurs, mastodons, mammoths, or other prehistoric creatures are sometimes mistaken as being human. Then, there is the last category of reported discoveries which prove to be scientifically and archaeologically verified remains of giant human beings.

The photographs that follow are said to be hoaxes, and not archeological proof of ancient giants. However, in spite of possibly being misleading and artificially created, such images are startling. They do grab a one's attention and cause a person to do a double take:

This giant skeleton was reportedly discovered in various locations like Iran, Greece, and Arabia.

This image, and the one below, are hoax photos. Internet websites like *Worth1000* (now *DesignCrowd*), hold contests in which entrants show off their skills at manipulating photographs using digital editing software. One of the site's competition categories was "Archaeological Anomalies," in which entrants vied to create the most realistic archaeological hoaxes, like the one above. This website gave the instructions: "Your job is to show a picture of an archaeological discovery that looks so real, had it not appeared at *Worth1000*, people might have done a double take."

"Skull of Goliath Found in Valley of Elah, West of Jerusalem."

"Giant Found in Greece." Digital technology like *Adobe Photoshop* has made the practice of altering photos relatively easy.

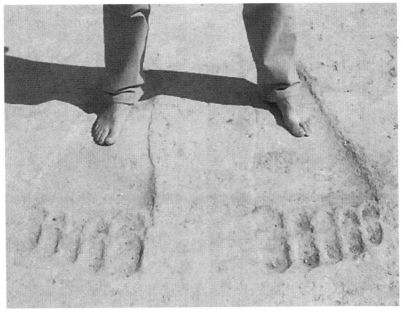

PSEUDOARCHEOLOGY

Along with "faked" photos of ancient giants, there are a number of stories repeated on the Internet which are either completely false, or at the least, highly doubtful. For example, there is the report that, at Agadir in Morocco, giant tools found there are proof that gigantic humans lived there at one time:

> At Agadir in Morocco, reports Peter Kolosimo, the French Captain Lafanechere "discovered a complete arsenal of hunting weapons including five hundred double-edged axes weighing seventeen and a half pounds, which were twenty times as heavy as would be convenient for modern man. To handle the axe at all one would need to have hands of a size appropriate to a giant with a stature of at least 13 feet."

> In 1950, Dr. Louis Burkhalter, former French delegate to the Prehistoric Society, wrote in the *Revue du Musee de Beyrouth*: "I want to make it clear that the existence of gigantic men in the Acheulian age [i.e., between about 75,000 and 150,000 years ago] must be considered a scientifically proven fact." In his paper, *"A Report On Gigantic Implements Found In South Morocco,"* Dr Burkhalter refers to "gigantic" stone tools unearthed at Sasnych [Syria], located five miles from Safitah in the

alluvial ground of Nohr Abrach. These included "bifaces of abnormal dimensions, weighing 2.5 kg. to 3.5 kg." These finds were followed by similar discoveries made by Captain R Lafanechere in south Morocco — biface tools of Acueulean manufacture weighing 4.150 kg., while one specimen was over 8 kg.

The original source for these stories is *Timeless Earth,* a 1968 book by Peter Kolosimo, (pseudonym of Pier Domenico Colosimo), an Italian journalist. He is one of the founders of *pseudoarcheology,* which is defined as "the study of the origins of ancient civilizations using alternative theories and methods not accepted by the traditional scientific community." Kolosimo also popularized ancient astronaut (or ancient alien) theories of contact between extraterrestrial beings and ancient human civilizations, another face of pseudoarcheology, which is also sometimes referred to by skeptics as fringe archaeology, fantastic archaeology, or cult archaeology. Over time, peer pressure from academics has been effective in suppressing the existence of real giants from the pages of history. Professors and other academics ridicule any belief that a race of giant people once co-habited with the other races on Earth. But, the immense amount of data to be found up to this time lends powerful support to the hypothesis that real giants played a role in human history.

So, were the giant tools that have been found in the Mediterranean-Middle East region and elsewhere, made to be used in battle, or maybe ceremoniously by men of giant stature? Your answer will depend upon whether you adhere to accepted science, or are open to entertaining alternative theories of ancient origins. For now, we can only speculate. The discovery of such giant implements do add to the evidence that there may have been real giants in the earth eons ago.

In spite of the skepticism caused by internet hoax images and stories, the scriptural writings of many religions include tales of races of giant men who lived long ago in the lands around the Mediterranean and the Middle East.

The next few newspaper items demonstrate how discoveries of giant skeletons can be mis-identified. For example, the giants described to be over 20 feet long, may be the skeletal remains of prehistoric animals, rather than human giants.

MADERA MERCURY
Madera, California
November 28, 1903

A Skull As Big As A Bushel Basket.

One of the remarkable finds of gigantic human remains of which we have any record, was made at Palermo Sicily, in the year 1516, when an entire skeleton of unheard proportions was unearthed by some marble quarry men. This mammoth remains measured exactly 31 feet from head to foot and 9 ft. 7 in. from point to point of the shoulders. A stone axe buried with this old-time giant may still be seen at Palermo in section "Z" of the St. Isorent Museum. It is made of a bluish looking, fine-grained boulder, and appears to be about 2 ft. 8 in. long by 1 ft. broad, and 9 inches through in the thickest place. A musty, rusty looking tag attached to the relic informs the visitor that it weighs 52 pounds; but the general verdict is that it could not weigh over 30 or 35 pounds.

The skeleton was burned by a mob in the year 1602, during the prevalence of the black death at Palermo, the ignorant, superstitious people believing that it was connected in some mysterious way with the death dealing distemper. The skull of the giant, according to Abbe Ferregus, "was largely excessive of the baskets said to hold the bushel, being fitted above and below with teeth to the number of 64, each of which would have weighed 2 ounces." Cavalier Scory claimed to have found a skull on Tenerife that had 60 teeth.

~ ~ ~ ~ ~

THE COEUR D'ALENE PRESS
Coeur D'Alene, Idaho
October 7, 1905

GIANTS OF THE PAST.

The past was more prolific in the production of giants than the present. In 1830, one of these giants, who was exhibited at Rouen, was ten feet high; and the giant Galabra, brought from Arabia to Rome in the time of Claudius Caesar, was the same height. Pannum, who lived in the time of Eugene II., was eleven and one-half feet in height.

The Chevalier Scory, in his journey to the peak of Tenerife, found in one of the caverns of that mountain, the head of a giant who had sixty teeth and who was not less than eleven feet high. The giant Paragus, slain by Orlando, the nephew of Charlemagne, according to reports, was twenty-eight feet high.

In 1814, near St. Gernad, was found the tomb of the giant Isolent, who was not less than thirty feet high. In 1500, near Rouen was found a skeleton whose head held a bushel of corn, and which was nineteen feet high. In 1623 near the castle in Dauphine, a tomb was found thirty feet long, sixteen feet wide and eight feet high, on which were cut in graystone the words "Kentolochus Rex." The skeleton was found entire and measured twenty-five and one-fourth feet high, ten feet across the shoulders and five feet from breastbone to the back.

But France is not the only country where giant skeletons have been unearthed. Near Palermo, Sicily in 1516, was found the skeleton of a giant thirty feet high; and, in 1559, another forty-four feet high. Near Magrino, on the same island, in 1816 was found the skeleton of a giant of thirty feet whose head was the size of a hogshead and each tooth weighed five ounces.

~ ~ ~ ~ ~

BISMARCK DAILY TRIBUNE
Bismarck, North Dakota
April 4, 1906

THE GIANTS OF OLD

ANCIENT RACES MARVELS OF PHYSICAL DEVELOPMENT.

The Semi-Barbarians of One Thousand Years Ago Were All Remarkably Proportioned Men — The Giants Of Ancient Greece and Rome.

That the human race has degenerated in size as well as longevity is a fact well attested by various authorities. A prominent Washington physician who has made a life study of brain and cerebral developments, says that, on visiting the catacombs of Paris, what struck him most in those vast repositories of the contents of the city's ancient graveyards, was the great size of the skulls in comparison with those of more modern mankind. This superiority of development in the men who lived 1,000 years or more ago the scientist attributes to the open air life then in vogue and the physical sports and exercises indulged in.

There are several races of giants mentioned in the Bible, and the Greek and Roman historians have recorded many examples which serve to show that these specimens of elongated humanity were by no means rare at one period of the world's history. Thus, it is mentioned that the Emperor Maximian was eight feet some inches high. The body of Orestes, according to the Greeks, was eleven and a half feet in height; the giant Galbora, brought from Arabia to Rome under Claudius Caesar, measured near ten feet. The bones of Secondilla and Pusto, keepers of the gardens of Sallust, were but six inches shorter.

The probability is that, outside of cultivated Greece and Rome among the semi-barbarous of the greater part of present day European nations, physical development reached often to more wondrous proportions.

The Chevalier Scory, in his voyage to the peak of Tenerife, says that they found in one of the sepulchral caverns of that mountain, the head of a Guanche which had eighty teeth, and that the body was not less than fifteen feet long. The giant Ferragus, slain by Orlando, nephew of Charlemagne, was eighteen feet high. Revland, a celebrated anatomist who wrote in 1614, says that some years before that time, there was to be seen in the suburbs of St. Germane, the tomb of the giant Isoret, who was twenty feet high.

At Rouen in 1509, in digging in the ditches near the Dominicamo, there was found a stone tomb containing a skeleton whose shin bone reached up to the girdle of the tallest man there, being about four feet long; and, consequently, the body must have been seventeen or eighteen feet high. Upon the tomb was a plate of copper upon which was engraved, "In this tomb lies the noble and puissant lord, the Chevalier Ruon de Valle-mont, and his bones." There is indeed, evidence in the ponderous armor and two-handed swords which remain to us in museums to prove that the knight of the ages of chivalry was a heroic specimen of human architecture.

Platerins, a famous physician, declared that he saw at Lucarne the true human bones of a subject who must have been at least nineteen feet high.

Valance, in Dauphine, boasts of possessing the bones of the giant Bucart, tyrant of the Vivarais, who was slain by an arrow by the Count de Cabillon, his vassal. The Dominicans had a part of his shin bone, with the articulation of the knee, and his figure painted in fresco, with an inscription showing that this giant was twenty-two and one-half feet high and that his bones were found in 1706 near the banks of the Moderi, a little river at the foot of the mountain of Grusol, upon which (tradition says) the giant dwelt.

On Jan. 11, 1688, some masons digging near the ruins of a castle in Dauphine, in a locality which had long been known as the Giant's Field, at the depth of eighteen feet, discovered a brick tomb thirteen feet long, twelve feet wide and eight feet high, on which was a gray stone, with the words "Theotobochus Rex" cut thereon. When the tomb was opened, they found a human skeleton, entire, twenty-five and one-half feet long, ten feet wide across the shoulders and five feet deep from the breastbone to the back. The teeth were each about the size of an ox's foot and his shin bone measured four feet.

Near Margarino, in Sicily, in 1516, was found a giant thirty feet high. His head was the size of a hogshead, and each of his teeth weighed five ounces.

Near Palermo, in the valley of Magara, in Sicily, a skeleton of a giant thirty feet long was found in the year 1548; and another, thirty-three feet high in 1560. Several of the gigantic bones of the latter subject are still preserved by private persons in Italy. The Athenians found thirty-two famous skeletons, one thirty-four and another thirty-six feet in height.

At Totle, in Bohemia, in 758, was found a skeleton the head of which could scarcely be encompassed by the arms of two men together; and whose legs, which are still preserved in the castle of the city, were twenty-six feet long. The celebrated English scientist Sir Hans Sloane, who treated the matter very learnedly, does not doubt the facts above narrated, but thinks the bones were those of elephants, whales, or other animals. But, it has been well remarked that, while elephant bones may be shown for those of giants to superficial observers, this can never be imposed upon distinguished anatomists as have testified in many cases to the mammoth bones being unmistakably human. —*Philadelphia Record.*

Looking past internet hoaxes and exaggerated stories of discoveries related to giant humans found on Earth, there are many believable reports of the actual existence of giants that were here before us. A brief list of some of the giants of record in this portion of the globe, includes:

GREEK HISTORIAN SOLINUS

Gaius Julius Solinus was an early 3rd century historian. He was the author of *De Mirabilibus Mundi* ('The Wonders of the World') which went under the title *Collectanea rerum memorabilium* ('Collection of Curiosities'), and *Polyhistor*. The work describes curiosities in the ancient world, based in part on Pliny's *Natural History* and the *Geography* of Pomponius Mela. The excerpts from *Polyhistor* refer to giants of Solinus' time.

> "Before there were any humans on Pallene, the story goes that a battle was fought between the gods and the giants. Traces of the giants' demise continue to be seen to this day, whenever torrents swell with rain and excessive water breaks their banks and floods the fields. They say that even now in gullies and ravines the people discover bones of immeasurable enormity, like men's carcasses but far bigger."
>
> — Greek historian Solinus, 200 A.D.

178

CAP. III.

OF THE LIKENESS OF SHAPE & FAVOR:
OF THE TALLNESS OF CERTAIN PERSONAGES:
OF THE MEASURE OF A MAN:
OF THE REVERENCE OF THE DEAD.

Now, who so bendeth his mind to consider the causes of likenesses, shall perceive the wonderful disposition of the work of nature. For some time, such likenesses belong to some stock, and descend from issue to issue, into the succession: like as often times young children bear moles, scars, and other marks of their ancestors. As among the Lepids, of whom are of the same line (but not successive; one after another) are found to have been born after one sort, with film over their eyes. As in the famous Poet of Byzance, who, having a mother that was the bastard of an Aethiopian, there was nothing in her resembling her Father, yet did he degenerate again into the likeness of the *Aethiopian* that was his grandfather.

OF THE TALLNESS & PERSONAGES OF MEN
IN OLDEN TIMES.

Now, if we shall more question the personages of men, it will manifestly appear that antiquity has vaunted no lies at all of itself: but that the offspring of our time, being corrupted by succession growing out of kind, has through the years showed decrease of them that are now born, and lost the comeliness of the ancient beauties. Therefore, we conclude that no man can exceed the stature of seven feet because Hercules was no higher than so. Yet, notwithstanding, it was found in the time of Romans under the Emperor Augustus, Pusio, and Secundilla were ten foot high and more; the corpses of whom are yet to be seen in the Charnel House of the Saints.

Afterward, in the reign of Claudius, there was one named Gabbara, brought out of Arabia, that was nine feet and as many inches high. But almost a thousand years before Augustus, there was no such personage seen, neither after the time of Claudius. For what is he in our day yet is not born lesser than his Parents? As for the hugeness of men in the old times, the relics of Orestes do testify; whose bones being found at the Lacedemonians at Tegaea by the information of the Oracle, the fifty and eight Olympians, whom we are assured, were full seven cubits long.

A DEAD BODY OF MONSTROUS BIGNESS.

Also, there are writings registered in remembrance of things done in ancient times, which vouch the assuredness of the truth, wherein it is specified, that in the Candian war, at such time as the rivers more outrageously flowing than fresh waters are wont, had broken up the ground there. After the fall of the said waters, among many clefts in the ground, there was found a body of three and thirty cubits. For desire to see that which, Lucius Flaccus, the Lieutenant, and Metellus himself also, being wonderfully amazed at the strangeness thereof, went thither, and beheld the wonder with their eyes, which they thought a fable to hear reported. I may not let pass the Son of Euthymines of Salymis, who grew three cubits high in Thrace. But he was slow of gate, dull witted, boisterous of voice, too soon ripe, and immediately beset with many diseases. So, he recompensed his hasty growth with unmeasurable punishment of sicknesses. The manner of measuring growth is in two ways. For look how much a man is between the ends of his two longest fingers stretching his arms out. The manner of measuring a man. Is he between the sole of his foot and the crown of his head.

SENONE GIANTS

The Senones were one of the Gallic tribes which invaded northern Italy. They settled on the Adriatic coast around modern Rimini. In the 1934 book by Henri Hubert, entitled *The Rise of the Celts,* Celtic swords that archaeologists recovered "from the second period of La Tene are about 96 inches long." Some of "the latest swords," Hubert adds, "are still longer."

The recovered swords "of course offer mute testimony to the extraordinary size of the Celtic giants who once wielded them.

BATTLE OF ALLIA

In 387 B.C., the Battle of the Allia was fought between the Senones (one of the Gallic tribes) and the Republic of Rome. It started when the Senones invaded northern Italy and the Roman Republic. The battle was fought at the confluence of the rivers Tiber and Allia, about eleven miles north of Rome. According to Herdotus, in *The Histories*, "after a battle, it was the custom at least among the Scythian Celts, for every man to drink the blood from the first man he kills."

Herodotus further explains, "With the heads of their worst enemies, they proceed as follows: once they have sawn off everything below the eyebrows, they carefully clean out the head. If the owner is poor, he will merely stretch calf-leather round it and use it thus. But if he is rich, he will also line the inside with gold and use it as a drinking vessel." So, following the rout of the Romans at the Battle of Allia, the Celts spent the day after severing heads of their victims.

Upon hearing the news of this defeat and aware of the brutality of the Celts, most of the inhabitants of Rome fled the city to escape the terrible Senone giants, who were headed their way. The vengeful giants burned Rome to the ground.

BRENNUS

About 387 B.C., the Celtic chieftain Brennus led three hundred thousand Senone giants across the Apennines into northern Italy. These hordes ravaged Etruscan towns and the surrounding country as they went. This invasion soon led to a war between the giants and Rome. In spite of attempts by the Roman embassy to negotiate a peace between the Etruscans and the Senones. The giant, Brennus, answered the Romans' peace over-ture with a humiliating insult. While weighing out a bushel of gold as a ransom payment to the Senones for their withdrawal, the Romans started an argument over the scales the Senones were using. Thereupon, Brennus threw the weight of his great sword on the scales, with this warning: "Woe to the vanquished!"

AHIMAN

Ahiman was one of three giant brothers whose gigantic height so terrified Caleb and the other men Moses sent to scout out Canaan before a planned attack, that they returned frantic with fear. They had seen Ahiman, Sheshai, and Talmai, rulers of the Anakim nation of Hebron. (Num. 13:22). When the spies returned from exploring the Promised Land, they gave a frightening report of "people great and tall" whom they identified as the sons of Anak (Deuteronomy 9:2). The Israelites, seized with fear and believing themselves to be mere "grass-hoppers....in their sight" (Numbers 13:33), rebelled against God (Deuteronomy 1:26-28) and refused to enter the land God had promised them. Ahiman and his brothers could trace their lineage to Arba, "the greatest man among the Anakim" (Joshua 14:15). The name "Anakim" translates to "long-necked," or "tall." The Hebrews thought that the Anakim were descendants of the Nephilim, the powerful race of giants who dominated the pre-Flood world (Genesis 6:4; Numbers 13:33).

LAHMI

Lahmi was the brother of Goliath. He was just as massive in size as his brother, who was said to be nine feet tall. Lahmi is said to have had six fingers on each hand and six toes on each foot—a physical characteristic also mentioned about giants in other cultures. Among several biblical passages that mention the existence of giants, Samuel 21:20 refers to Lahmi and this extra-digit phenomenon: "In still another battle, which took place at Gath, there was a huge man with six fingers on each hand and six toes on each foot—twenty-four in all."

ISRAEL/SYRIA:

King David and his men had many encounters with giants on the battlefield in ancient times. Goliath, the famous giant slain by King David, was about 12 feet (3.66 meters) tall. He was one of the last giants, the Anakim. Another one from the same region, was Og. These giants were said to be the offspring of the sons of God and the daughters of men (Genesis 6:4). Goliath, according to the Bible, had six fingers and six toes.

CALABRIA'S COLOSSUS

The *Journal Litteraire of the Abbé Nazari* reports that the skeleton of a huge giant exhumed in Calabria, Italy, measured "eighteen Roman feet." The fellow's teeth, adds the journal, "weighed at least an ounce each." Strabo, a Greek geographer and historian whose *Geography* is described as "the only extant work covering the peoples and countries known to both Greeks and Romans during the reign of Augustus (27 B.C.–14 A.D.)" Strabo's *Geography* says this about giants:

> On the isthmus of Pallene there is a city on the peninsula, formerly called Potidæa, founded by the Corinthians, but afterwards it was called Cassandria, from king Cassander, who restored it after it was demolished. It was formerly called Phlegra, and was inhabited by the fabulous giants, an impious and lawless race. Some consider this to be a mere fable, but others, with greater probability on their side, see implied in it the existence of a barbarous and lawless race of people who once occupied the country.

SIX DIGITS IN SUMER-IRAQ

Sumer is the earliest known civilization in the historical region of southern Mesopotamia, modern-day southern Iraq. The Sumerian culture might be the oldest in the world, where civilization was born. Sumerian statues and engravings often depict their gods and kings with six fingers, a trait attributed to giants. Sumerian gods taught the people mathematics based on the six-digits system. Is this because giants existed there? And they had six fingers? The Sumerian believed that their gods came from stars, the Pleiades. Numerous Sumerian seals depict them as men of gigantic stature. They are often taller than members of their courts, even when seated on thrones. Numerous seals show them standing, towering over those standing near them.

ASPEN EVENING CHRONICLE

ASPEN, COLORADO   **MAY 6, 1892**

A number of skeletons of prehistoric men and women have been unearthed during the last twenty years in grottos on the Mediterranean coast not far from Nice. One of them is that of a man whose estimated height is seven feet nine inches; while another, is the skeleton of a woman six feet three inches tall. The fact that, in all discoveries of this character, the remains have been of an unusual height would indicate a physical development in the human race which is not reached today.

According to the *Jewish Encyclopaedia*, (1901), Jericho was once known as the "City of the Giants" due to being a city where Nephilim giants lived. The city walls and masonry were of gigantic and exceptional construction. Archaeologist Sir Charles Marston, in *"Jericho, Sir Charles Marston's Expediton of 1930,"* theorized that "now has been revealed undoubted evidence that the walls of Jericho were razed by an earthquake. This was when Joshua's forces rushed into the city." A few of Jericho's giants escaped.

Procopius, in *De Bello Vandalico* says: "Those who survived, were led by a certain Ifrikish ibn Kais to Africa; and having killed the king of that country, settled there...." two marble pillars were to be seen in the Numidan town Tigisis, with a Phoenician inscription: "We are those who fled from Joshua, the robber, the son of Nun."

Elsewhere in the text by Procopius, *De Bello Vandalico* appear more references to giants:

THE VALLEY OF THE REPHAIM, or THE VALLEY OF THE GIANTS

Here, odd remains can be found of several ancient cities that seem to have housed giant people. These were the same fortified cities that the Hebrews had to take by force, cities such as Ashod (Joshua 11:22). The ancient Egyptian *Execration Texts* refer to Ashod as "the City of Giants." These texts date to the Twelfth Dynasty, about 1900 B.C., and were written on order of the Pharaoh. They show that the Egyptians had huge Anakim in their territory. Written on clay pottery presently in the Berlin Germany Museum, the names of many of the Anakim tribal leaders are recorded.

Further representations of the Anakim in Egypt, are the Temple of Abu, Simbel, the royal tombs of Biban-el-Molukat in Karnak, and the tomb of Oimenpthah I. All display images of giant blond men with white skin.

Heiroglyphics in Oimenepthah I's tomb tell us of a particular giant called Tanmahu or Talmia. The Bible tells us of Talmia's brother, Ahiman, who the ancient Jewish traditions say was the most feared of all the Nephilim. He would taunt passers by, demanding "Whose brother will fight with me?"

Near Gaza, the town of Beit Jibrim still stands today. Its name means "House of the Giants." There is a complex underground city here, part natural cave, and part manmade. Pick marks are visible on the walls of the 60 or so separate chambers whose ceilings reach enormous heights.

Along the Syrian coast is the city of Ras Sharma, once known as Ugarit, where, in 1928, ancient volumes were found describing life in that ancient city. Besides religion, history, and the local economy, the texts frequently mention the Rephaim giants.

The city of Amon was spoken by the Prophet Amos 600 years later; he described its inhabitants as "tall as the cedars and strong as the oaks." (Amos 2:9)

The chief city of the Anakim giants was Kiriath Arba, later renamed by the Hebrews, Hebron. Arba was the mightiest of giants. (Joshua 14, 15, 21, 11)

Archaeologists report that the remains of the city of Gezer "Bear out the unusually tall stature of individuals in ancient Palestine (*The Wycliffe Bible Encyclopaedia, Vol. 1*) According to archaeological expert, R.H. Hall, in his book *The Ancient History of the Near East,* "Recent excavations of the Palestine Exploration Fund at Gezer and various other ressearches have shown that that "the Anakim or Rephaim, 'Giants' of tradition, built the megalithic monuments, the dolmens and menhirs, of Moab and eastern Palestine. Tothem, Graham states that the stone work of time was "inexplicably perfect...stone doors are still hanging on their hinges...all betoken the workmanship of a race endowed with powers far exceeding those of ordinary men...and give credibility to the supposition that we have in them the dwellings of a giant race....we were forced to the conclusion that its original inhabitants, the people who had constructed those cities, were not only a mighty nation, but individuals of greater strength than ourselves." Professor J.L. Porter agrees in his book *The Giant Cities of Bashan* where he also discusses the giant's incredible abilities and skills as stone masons.

All these cities were surrounded by imposing defenseive walls, they "were large and fortified" (Joshua 14:12). "The cities are large, with walls up to the sky (Deut. 1:28). Meaning that these ancient giants were not only strong enough to heave, manipulate and lift the massive stones found making up these walls, but they were accomplished masons. The evidence clearly shows that among the first and greatest of the masons were the giants. The dolmens and manhirs they constructed were the ritual locations, the high places mentioned in Leviticus 26:30, required to summon and work with the Watchers, their own fathers. Fields of these stone objects are still to be seen across northern Jordan. Do the Freemasons today practice similar rituals?

Despite all their stone works, as word spread of the powerful invading Hebrew armies, the giants must have grown fearful. It was through God that the smaller human armies of the Chosen People had their strength. Isaiah 17:9 tells that the Amorites and Hittites, giants also, did not fight against the Hebrews; instead they fled their fortified cities. After hearing of their neighbors, fellow giants, were being massacred in city after city, they decided to go further north and hide.

Next, is a listing of some of the many Giants from the Mediterranean-Middle East region of the world:

Reports of Giants in the Middle East:

- Abishai, Giant Killer
- Abraham & the Giants
- Acmon, Early Ruler
- Ahiman
- Amorites
- Anab's Giants
- Argob's 60 Cities of the Giants
- Ariels
- Arioch, Giant King
- Ashdod's Giants
- Ashteroth Karnaim's Giants
- Avvim
- Bashan's Giants
- Beit Jibrim
- Beth-Paleth's Giants
- Birsha
- Canaan's Anakim
- Corinthian Giants
- David vs. Goliath
- Debir's Giants
- Edom's Giants
- Eleazar the Giant
- Elhanan
- Emim

- Execration Texts
- Gabbaras
- Gath Giants
- Gaza Giants
- Gibborim
- Gibeonites
- Goliath
- Gomarian Giants
- Ham's Giants
- Hebron's Giants
- Horim, or Horites
- Ifrikish ibn Kais
- Ishbi-benob
- Israel's Wars w/Giants
- Jericho's Giants
- Jonathan
- Josephus on Giants
- Kiriath Arba
- Lahmi
- Mercury the Giant
- Nephilim
- Offerus
- Perizzites
- Phlegra's Giants
- Rapha
- Ras Shamra Texts
- Rephaim Giants
- Sacae Giants
- Shamhazai
- Shaveh
- Kiriathaim's Giants
- Sheshai
- Sibecai
- Sihon's & Og's Overthrow
- Sinuhe vs. Retenu
- Sippai
- Sodom & Gomorrah Giants
- Talmai
- Uzim
- Zamzummin
- Zuzim

Little People

In addition to Giants, there is also evidence that stories of chance encounters with Little People may not be just fairy tales or perhaps the result of a hallucination brought on by too much to drink. Such reports have come from the lands of the Mediterranean region. Classical authors like Homer, Aristotle, Juvenal, Pliny, and Herodotus write of races of Little People, pygmy races. Aristotle was a firm believer in the existence of small people.

CALIZI DWARFS OF THRACE

Pliny, in *Natural History,* refers to the Calizi dwarfs of Thrace and regions around the Black Sea. He observed the great variances in human height. In *The Seventh Book Of History of Natives: Chap. XVI,* of *Natural History* Pliny writes:

> In the reign of the deified Augustus, there was a couple called Pusio and Secundilla who were half a [Roman] foot taller [approx. 9' 10" tall] and their bodies were preserved as curiosities in the Sallustian gardens. In the reign of the same emperor, the smallest man was a dwarf called Conopas, who was two [Roman] feet and a palm [approx. 26" tall] in height.

Elsewhere in Pliny's work is this:

While the same *Augustus* sat as president, his niece *Iulia* had a little dwarfish fellow not above two foot and a hand breadth high, called *Conopas*, whom she set great store by and made much of: as also another she-dwarf named *Andromeda*, who sometime had been the slave of *Iulia* the princess, and by her made free. *M. Varro* reporteth, that *Manius Maximus*, and *M. Tullius*, were but two cubits high, and yet they were gentlemen and knights of Rome. And, in truth, we ourselves have seen their bodies how they lie embalmed and chested, which testifieth to no less. It is well known that there be some that naturally are never but a foot and a half high; others again somewhat longer: and to this height they came in three years, which is the full course of their age, and then they die.

We read, moreover, in the Chronicles, that in Salamis one *Euthimenes* had a son, who in three years grew to be three cubits high; but he was, in his gate, slow and heavy, and in his wit was dull and blockish. In this time, under-grown he was, and his voice changed to be great. At three years' end, he died suddenly of a general cramp or contraction of all the parts of his body.

It is not long since I saw myself the like in all respects (saving that under-growing aforesaid) in a son of one *Cornelius Tacitus* a Roman knight, and a procurator or general receiver and treasurer for the State in Gallia Belgica. Such humans the Greeks call *Ectrapelos*: we in Latin have no name for them.

KALLIKANTZAROS,

There are stories of *Kallikantzaros,* mischievous Greek goblins or gnomes, the size of small children; these Little People are said to ride tiny horses. These Greek elves appear during the Twelve Days of Christmas, (from the end of December until Epiphany, January 6.) In Greek folklore, the kalli-kantzaroi, disappear on the sixth of January, Epiphany, when Greek priests, go through all the houses, blessing them with holy water.

ETRURIAN DWARFS

They had such traits as enormous, bulging eyes, protruding eyebrow ridges, and sloping foreheads. Author Thomas Campbell, in his 1829 work, *Letters on the History of Literature: Addressed to the Students at the University of Glasgow* mentions one of them:

> Rules for interpreting the will of Heaven by lightning and otherwise, reached the Etruscans through the kindness of Tages, a wise subterranean dwarf; and from each area, they came to Rome. The dwarf Tages revealed the precepts of human wisdom of the Aruspices. One day, when a peasant was driving his plow in the fields of Tarquinii, a hideous dwarf with

the face of a child under his white hair, Tages, came out of a furrow. All Etruria flocked thither. The dwarf spoke for a long time; the Etruscans collected his words, and the books of Tages, the basis of Etruscan discipline, were for each area what the laws of Manu had been for India and the Pentateuch for the Hebrews.

In the work, *History of Rome, and of the Roman People, From Its Origin to the Invasion of the Barbarians,* by Victor Duruy, 1886, more details of the region's dwarfs are found:

The most ancient of the Mediterranean nations seems to have belonged to the mysterious race, whom one finds at the commencement of so many histories, though there is nothing left of it but its name and its indestructible buildings. After having carried its industry and activity into Greece and its islands, into Macedonia and Italy, and perhaps into Spain, the race disappeared, pursued according to the ancient legends, by the celestial powers and suffering endless misfortunes.

At the commencement of historic times, nothing but uncertain remains of that great people are found, as we discover in the bosom of the earth, the mutilated remains of their primitive creations. It is a whole buried world of civilization arrested then culminated by the victorious tribes destroying it. The powers of the priests of the dwarf society directed, at their will, the clouds and tempests; they summoned the snow and the hail; by their magic power, they changed the form of objects; they were acquainted with fatal charms; they fascinated men and plants by their glance; on animals and on trees they poured the deadly water of the Styx; they knew how to heal, and how to compose subtle poisons. Thus, they had been dispossessed to the extremities of the earth. These industrious dwarfs and formidable magicians, were a nation who knew the earliest arts and had advanced knowledge of science. But, because of their diminutive physical nature, they were subdued and cursed after their defeat by warlike tribes who looked upon work as servile labor and made slaves of the little peoples of the ancient world.

MESOPOTAMIAN DWARFS

Mesopotamian dwarfs in such characters as King Oberon, the Fay found along the road from Syria to Baghdad. He was only 3 feet high, and had an angelic face, though his body was quote "humpy," and his behavior mischievous. Oberon likes to snare wayfarers.

Babylonian herders are depicted as dwarfs. At Khafeje (Sumer), the first temple of Sin had chambers of diminutive proportions, and their pit houses had doorways no taller than 5 feet.

Populations with short stature are reported in Turkey, and in nearby Israel. Regional folklore contains tales of a race of smaller-than-normal people that once lived in Turkey's Taurus Mountains. This is corroborated by Pliny the Elder's report of "a race of pygmies living in the region of Phrygia and Asia Minor." Aristotle, too, places Little people in Asia Minor at Caria.

When Heinrich Schliemann uncovered the fabled city of Troy (Hissarlik, Turkey, today), among the artifacts found was a woman's bracelet of such small size as to fit a child. There are unusual mounds on the plains of Troy that may be one more sign of the long-ago Little People.

DACTYLS

The Dactyls are found in areas of Greece and the Aegean. Female Dactyls are called *Hekaterides*. This group of Little People are skilled at working with metal and said to be adept at the arts of magic and healing. In some legends, Dactyls are said to have taught humans the craft of metalworking, the science of mathematics, and the use of an alphabet.

Phrygian Dactyls

Phrygian Dactyls are one of the oldest dwarf tribes in the Mediterranean region. They are described as rustic earth spirits that lived around Mount Ida in Phrygia. They are claimed to have invented the art of metalworking and even to have discovered iron.

Kabeiroi Dactyls

Kabeiroi are an offshoot of the Mr. Ida tribe who settled at Lemnos, Samothrace, and Thebes. They are superb craftsmen, and said to be descended from the god Hephaestus (the god of fire, metalworking, stone masonry, forges, and the art of sculpture. He was the son of Zeus and Hera and married to Aphrodite.) Kabeiroi are also associated with the sea and sailors. In some accounts, these Little People are described as rowdy wine-drinkers.

Rhodian Dactyls

Rhodian dactyls are the dark side of this group. They are said to be dangerous underworld smiths and magicians; they are sometimes called *Telkhines*.

~ ~ ~ ~ ~

Fast forwarding to more modern literature, there is a fantasy story entitled "The Little People," written by Robert E. Howard, around 1928. In this tale a brother must rescue his sister who is abducted by cave dwelling dwarfs. The brother refers to the dwarfs as "subterranean Picts" and "Mediter-raneans." A similar race of Little People appear in

Howard's 1930 fantasy tale, *"People of the Dark,"* published in *Strange Tales Of Mystery and Terror,* June 1932. Excerpts from this follow:

> I came to Dagon's Cave to kill Richard Brent. I went down the dusky avenues made by the towering trees, and my mood well-matched the primitive grimness of the scene. The approach to Dagon's Cave is always dark, for the mighty branches and thick leaves shut out the sun, and now the somberness of my own soul made the shadows seem more ominous and gloomy than was natural. Not far away I heard the slow wash of the waves against the tall cliffs, but the sea itself was out of sight, masked by the dense oak forest. The darkness and the stark gloom of my surroundings gripped my shadowed soul as I passed beneath the ancient branches—as I came out into a narrow glade and saw the mouth of the ancient cavern before me. I paused, scanning the cavern's exterior and the dim reaches of the silent oaks. The man I hated had not come before me! I was in time to carry out my grim intent. For a moment my resolution faltered, then like a wave there surged over me the fragrance of Eleanor Bland, a vision of wavy golden hair and deep gray eyes, changing and mystic as the sea. I clenched my hands until the knuckles showed white, and instinctively touched the wicked snub-nosed revolver whose weight sagged my coat pocket.
>
> But for Richard Brent, I felt certain I had already won this woman, desire for whom made my waking hours a torment and my sleep a torture. Whom did she love? She would not say; I did not believe she knew. Let one of us go away, I thought, and she would turn to the other. And I was going to simplify matters for her—

and for myself. By chance I had overheard my blond English rival remark that he intended coming to lonely Dagon's Cave on an idle exploring outing—alone.

I am not by nature criminal. I was born and raised in a hard country, and have lived most of my life on the raw edges of the world, where a man took what he wanted, if he could, and mercy was a virtue little known. But it was a torment that racked me day and night that sent me out to take the life of Richard Brent. I have lived hard, and violently, perhaps. When love overtook me, it also was fierce and violent. Perhaps I was not wholly sane, what with my love for Eleanor Bland and my hatred for Richard Brent. Under any other circumstances, I would have been glad to call him friend—a fine, rangy, upstanding young fellow, clear-eyed and strong. But he stood in the way of my desire and he must die.

I stepped into the dimness of the cavern and halted. I had never before visited Dagon's Cave, yet a vague sense of misplaced familiarity troubled me as I gazed on the high arching roof, the even stone walls and the dusty floor. I shrugged my shoulders, unable to place the elusive feeling; doubtless it was evoked by a similarity to caverns in the mountain country of the American Southwest where I was born and spent my childhood.

And yet I knew that I had never seen a cave like this one, whose regular aspect gave rise to myths that it was not a natural cavern, but had been hewn from the solid rock ages ago by the tiny hands of the mysterious Little People, the prehistoric beings of British legend. The whole countryside thereabouts was a haunt for ancient folk lore.

The country folk were predominantly Celtic; here the Saxon invaders had never prevailed, and the legends reached back, in that long-settled countryside, further than anywhere else in England—back beyond the coming of the Saxons, aye, and incredibly beyond that distant age, beyond the coming of the Romans, to those unbelievably ancient days when the native Britons warred with black-haired Irish pirates.

The Little People, of course, had their part in the lore. Legend said that this cavern was one of their last strongholds against the conquering Celts, and hinted at lost tunnels, long fallen in or blocked up, connecting the cave with a network of subterranean corridors which honeycombed the hills. With these chance meditations vying idly in my mind with grimmer speculations, I passed through the outer chamber of the cavern and entered a narrow tunnel, which, I knew by former descriptions, connected with a larger room.

It was dark in the tunnel, but not too dark for me to make out the vague, half-defaced outlines of mysterious etchings on the stone walls. I ventured to switch on my electric torch and examine them more closely. Even in their dimness I was repelled by their abnormal and revolting character. Surely no men cast in human mold as we know it, scratched those grotesque obscenities.

The Little People—I wondered if those anthropologists were correct in their theory of a squat Mongoloid aboriginal race, so low in the scale of evolution as to be scarcely human, yet possessing a distinct, though repulsive, culture of their own. They had vanished before the invading races, theory said, forming the base of all Aryan legends of trolls, elves, dwarfs and witches. Living in caves from the start, these aborigines had retreated farther and farther into the caverns of the hills, before the conquerors, vanishing at last entirely, though folklore fancy pictures their descendants still dwelling in the lost chasms far beneath the hills, loathsome survivors of an outworn age.

I snapped off the torch and passed through the tunnel, to come out into a sort of doorway which seemed entirely too symmetrical to have been the work of nature. I was looking into a vast dim cavern, at a somewhat lower level than the outer chamber, and again I shuddered with a strange alien sense of familiarity. A short flight of steps led down from the tunnel to the floor of the cavern—tiny steps, too small for normal human feet, carved into the solid stone. Their edges were greatly worn away, as if by ages of use. I started the descent—my foot slipped suddenly. I instinctively knew what was coming—it was all in part with that strange feeling of familiarity—but I could not catch myself. I fell headlong down the steps and struck the stone floor with a crash that blotted out my senses...

Later in this story, is this passage:

I cannot describe the grim, gloomy effect of those dark, low-roofed corridors far below the earth. Over all hung an overpowering sense of unspeakable antiquity. Why had the little people carved out these mysterious crypts, and in which black age? Were these caverns their last refuge from the onrushing tides of humanity, or their castles since time immemorial? I shook my head in bewilderment; the bestiality of the Children I had seen, yet somehow they had been able to carve these tunnels and chambers that might balk modern engineers. Even supposing they had but completed a task begun by nature, still it was a stupendous work for a race of dwarfish aborigines.

203

Giants & Little People

of

NORTH

AMERICA

With the advent of the global computer network that provides a limitless variety of information, called the internet, there can be found countless reports of Giants in all parts of the globe. Thanks to this world wide web of information, combined with a huge number of books and other publications on the subject of Giants in North America, it would be an almost impossible task to summarize all of the reports of Giants in North America into one chapter of this book. So, what follows is a much-abbreviated sampling of reports of discoveries of gigantic human remains on the North American continent:

EARLY SPANISH EXPLORERS

In 1519, Spanish explorer Alonzo Álvarez de Pineda was mapping the coastline of the Gulf Coast, marking the various rivers, bays, landmarks, and potential ports, and declaring them the property of the king of Spain. Not far from where the river empties into the Gulf of Mexico he "found a large town, and on both sides of its banks, for a distance of six leagues up its course, some forty native villages." He also noted that, other than giants, the tribes also had a race of tiny pygmies. Pineda described the tribes that settled near the Mississippi river as: "A race of giants, from ten to eleven palms in height and a race of pigmies only five or six palms high." (unit of measure that ranges from 7 to 10 inches; so the giants were at least 6 feet 7 inches to 8 feet tall). On his return from Tampico to the Mississippi, Pineda unknowingly sailed right past a tribe of equally huge Texas Indians.

CRITTENTON, ARIZONA

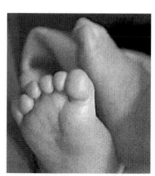

In 1891, a sarcophagus was un-covered eight feet below the surface. It contained a granite mummy case, which had once held a human more than 12 feet tall that had 6 toes on each foot, according to the carving on the case. The body had been buried so many eons ago, that it had turned to dust.

Baby born with 6 toes in Florida in 2009.

GRAND CANYON, ARIZONA

The October 2, 1896, *Los Angeles Times* contained an article written by Dr. Samuel Hubbard, archaeologist and nephew of the first president of the National Geographic Society, and later director of the Oakland Museum. He had just returned from a Grand Canyon expedition that had begun the previous year. He reported that he had discovered the "remains of a 20-foot-tall human giant." His account was widely reprinted in newspapers across the country from 1896 to 1903.

Below, is the reprint of this article, from the *Christian Work: Illustrated Family Newspaper, Volume 71,* August 15, 1901:

EARLY AMERICAN GIANTS

Does anybody believe that there ever has been a race of giants in the world? Does anybody believe that a race of gigantic men, who were from twelve to twenty feet high, ever lived in these United States of America? And yet the proof that such a race of people did live in this country is to be found in the Grand Canyon of the Colorado River in northern Arizona.

This proof is contained in a pair of findings. First, there are huge footprints in the red sandstone, that appear to have been made by the moccasined feet of gigantic men whose tracks measured twenty in. in length, and who stepped five feet at a stride.

Secondly, is the presence of the petrified body of such a man, also in the red sandstone of the Grand Canyon district. This body was that of a living, breathing man, but after death the flesh was replaced by lime or silica, held in solution in the water. There is ample evidence that nature was able to perform this feat, as the petrifying process is being carried on in the canyon to this day.

The third fact is that there is and was a strong and almost universal tradition among the ancient people of Mexico and Peru that such a race of giants lived in their country.

Perhaps it is almost too much to call this proof, but it is at least corroborative testimony.

Last June, I visited the Grand Canyon as a tourist, taking the Atlantic and Pacific Railroad to Flagstaff, thence by stage seventy miles to the Hance trail on the brink of the gorge. There I met Mr. Hull, who was acting as guide into the canyon, and who was a pioneer of northern Arizona. He told me the following story, and, with apologies for my credulity, I believe him:

Three years ago, he and a companion named Jim Lavelle had been prospecting in this part of the country. They found a ledge which they thought was valuable, and had started out of the canyon with samples of the ore, expecting to return in a few days. One of the Indians was with them. Mr. Hull speaks the Indian language fluently, and the Indians have a great admiration for him. The Indian said, "Have you ever seen the big Indian up here?" volunteering to show it. They followed him up a foot trail which led through a crevice in the red wall, thence on to the bench-like formation above, but still in the midst of the red sandstone.

They came to a place where a projecting rock formed a shelter over a sloping table-like slab of stone which was covered with a white incrustation of lime. Outstretched on this slab was the body °f a gigantic man turned into stone. The *body* was entirely nude and lay face downward. They estimated his height to be eighteen or twenty feet. The left arm was out at full length, while the right arm was doubled under his head. The left leg was perfect, but the foot was jammed into a crack in the slab. The right leg was broken off just below the knee, and the broken part was missing. They looked at it ten or fifteen minutes, and then continued their journey, intending to return and make a more complete investigation. Plans changed, and they failed to return.

Mr. Hull told the story to several people, but they either disbelieved him or discouraged him, so it happened that he had never been back there, and that he had never tried to do anything with his discovery. He also told me that reliable Indians had described to him tracks of both men and animals in the solid rock not far from this body, and in the same formation. These he had never seen, but he had no doubt of their existence.

This was startling information, but I had been In a measure

prepared for it. In the first place, it always seemed reasonable to me that the prehistoric, primeval hunting savages should have been of large stature. Gregory tells us that there was a period in the history of the world called the Tertiary or Mammalian Age that was peculiarly favorable to animal life. It is the age

The image contains:

Los Angeles Times

Los Angeles, California   October 2, 1896

GIANTS' FOOTPRINTS

CHICAGOESQUE TRACKS IN THE OLD RED SANDSTONE

Alleged Proof That Men Twenty Feet Tall Lived in the Grand Canyon of the Colorado.

(CONTRIBUTED BY SAMUEL HUBBARD)

of the mammoth, the great cave bear, the cave lion, the woolly rhinoceros, the primeval ox, the great Irish elk, the gigantic sloths and other familiar animals that were far larger then, than now. Was man to be left out entirely amid all this list of giants?

In the work of nature, every cell must be perfect in order to create a perfect organism. Can a perfect society be created out of imperfect individuals? And the gates of opportunity be opened along every path of life?

Later, in 1923, in Arizona's Grand Canyon, Samuel Hubbard discovered the bodies of two petrified human beings 15 and 18 feet in height. According to Hubbard, one of them was buried under a recent rock fall, which required several days' work to remove. The other was in a crevice of extremely difficult accessibility; but Hubbard was able to take photographs of it.

CATALINA ISLAND, CALIFORNIA

Sometime in the late 19th century, giants with double rows of teeth, red hair, and skulls 3 to 6 times the size of normal humans were discovered on Catalina Island in California.

In 1896, a 15-year-old boy named Ralph Glidden, who had moved to Catalina Island that year, accidentally became quite interested in the various Indian artifacts and burial sites found scattered about the Channel Islands. As he was looking for pearls on San Nicolas Island one day, Glidden stubbed his toe on a human skull. This chance event set off a lifelong quest by the amateur archeologist to know more. He went on to organize numerous excavations to uncover ancient burial sites on the islands between the years of 1919 and 1928. Glidden reportedly uncovered hundreds of secret burial sites around the island; a myriad of Indian artifacts and relics; and thousands of ancient Native remains. Among all of the discoveries made by Glidden, were the remains of a race of giants who had once inhabited the island.

He announced that, during his excavations, he had come across several skeletons across the island that were far larger than normal humans, measuring an alleged 7 to 9 feet tall. The claim generated widespread media interest; in the November 10, 1929, issue of the *The Ogden Standard-Examiner*, it was written:

> He (Glidden) claims overwhelming proof that a fair skinned, fair haired, highly intelligent race of great stature lived on Catalina Island, off the southwestern coast of California, perhaps three thousand years ago, and that his excavation of a huge cache of skeletons, domestic utensils, urns, wampum, etc., is quite out of the ordinary class of Indian discoveries.
>
> A skeleton of a young girl, evidently of high rank, within a large funeral urn, was surrounded by those of sixty-four children. And, on various parts of the island, more than three thousand other skeletons were found, practically all the males averaging around seven feet in height, one being 7 feet 8 inches from the top of his head to the ankle, and another being 9 feet 2 inches tall.

Glidden's would not be the only claim of amazing giant finds among the Channel Islands. In 1913, a German named Dr. A.W. Furstenan had found the skeleton of an 8-foot tall human on Catalina Island. It was found among other artifacts, including a flat stone with unidentifiable symbols on it. Found in Avalon Bay in hard black sand, reportedly, this skeleton mostly disintegrated when it was brought to the surface and exposed to air. All that was left intact was the skull, jawbone, and a foot. There was also a later report, in 1959, of a dig on nearby Santa Rosa Island, where several 7-foot-tall skeletons were unearthed. These giants had skulls painted red, double rows of teeth, and 6 fingers and toes. Double rows of teeth were a common feature among the human remains found in the Channel Islands. Yet another of the Channel Islands, San Nicolas Island, also produced numerous finds of larger than average human remains.

DEATH VALLEY, CALIFORNIA

In 1947, in Death Valley, California, the skeletons of nine-foot-tall humans were found. A story in the August 5, 1947 edition of the *San Diego Union,* recounts the story of explorers who unearthed the mummified remains of strangely costumed giants which dated to around 80,000 years ago, near the Arizona-Nevada-California line. The *Union* reported that "Howard E. Hill of Los Angeles was recounting the work of Dr. F. Bruce Russell, a retired Cincinnati physician who had originally located the first of several tunnels near Death Valley in 1931, but had not been able to return to the area until 1947. With the help of Dr. Daniel S. Bovee, who with Hill's father had once helped open up New Mexico's cliff dwellings, Russell had recovered the remains of several men of 8 to 9 feet in height." Hill continued, "These giants are clothed in garments consisting of a medium length jacket and trouser extending slightly below the knees. The texture of the material is said to resemble gray dyed sheepskin, but obviously it was taken from an animal unknown today." He said the explorers believe that what they found was the burial place of the tribe's hierarchy. "Hieroglyphics," he added, "bear a resemblance to what is known of those from the lost continent of Atlantis. They are chiseled, he added, on carefully polished granite."

LOMPOCK RANCHO, CALIFORNIA

Soldiers digging a pit for a powder magazine at Lompock Rancho, California in 1833, unearthed a male skeleton 11 ft. 9 in. tall, with double rows of upper and lower teeth. The skeleton had been covered with boulders that had unknown writing on them; it was surrounded by carved shells, huge stone axes, and other artifacts with unintelligible symbols. The remains were secretly re-buried because local Native Americans became upset about them disturbing the burial site.

LOMPOC JOURNAL
Lompoc, California
July 18, 1908

Find Bones of Giants.

Santa Monica. —What is believed to be the burial ground of the giant race which inhabited these shores before the discovery of California by Cabrillo was found last week by campers. On the beach of Malibu ranch, where they camped, the party observed a skull protruding out of the ocean's shelving bank of sand and gravel. Digging a few minutes they unearthed fourteen more skulls and a number of complete skeletons, all more than seven and several over eight feet long. A large collection of heavy stone mortars, pestles, utensils of various kinds and arrow points were dug up nearby.

SANTA ROSA ISLAND, CALIFORNIA

In the early 1800s, skeletons found off the California coast on Santa Rosa Island, were of gigantic size and contained double rows of teeth. The skeletons were found at a Native American Indian cemetery that contained abalone shells dated to be more than 7.000 years old. According to the book by Hubert Howe Bancroft, *"The Native Races of the Pacific States of North America"* (a five-volume description of indigenous ethnic groups), a Mr. Taylor from San Buenaventura stayed at Santa Rosa Island in 1861. While exploring, he often came across skeletons of Indians in caves, many of them quite large, and with double rows of teeth. Santa Rosa Island is the second largest of the Channel Islands of California, and is about about 150 km. (104 miles) northwest of Catalina Island.

YOSEMITE VALLEY, CALIFORNIA

The "Martindale Mummies" were discovered in 1885 in California's Yosemite Valley. In 1885, a group of miners led by G.F. Martindale noticed a wall of stones on a rock face that did not appear to be of natural origin.

As they removed the rock wall, they came upon another stone wall that was described as being done by someone skilled in masonry. They described the joints between the rocks as being a uniform 1/8 of an inch in thickness. "As pretty as any wall on any building I have ever seen," is how one of the miners described it.

Inside the tomb, they found the mummified remains of a woman that measured 6 ft. 8 in. tall, holding an infant, lying on a carved ledge in the cave. The tall corpse was wrapped in what appeared to be animal skins. It was when the miners removed parts of the skins that they found a child being held to the woman's breast.

Indigenous to the Yosemite region when whites arrived were the Ahwahneechee tribe, whose folklore relates a story of giants called Oo-el-en who came into the Yosemite Valley many years before the white man. The Oo-el-en, like the Si-Te-Cah of nearby Nevada, were cannibalistic giants; they ate the meat of other Native tribes they came across. Oo-el-en would catch the adults and cut them into small pieces, and then hang the flesh in the sun to dry into jerky. The Ahwahneechees legend says that they finally killed the giants and burned their bodies. (The last of the Ahwahnee-chee died in the 1940s.)

Unfortunately, after being removed, these mummies did not receive the best treatment. There are conflicting reports that say that in the 1940s, a man named Smith said he purchased the mummies from a Mrs. Miller in Kansas; he then leased them to a person named, Fleming who owned a traveling carnival and used the mummies as a sideshow. The whereabouts of the mummies was unknown from 1948 to 1968, when they resurfaced at a warehouse in Texas where they were reclaimed by the Smith family.

In 1992, a physician and paleontologist in Ada, Oklahoma, by the name of Dr. Cartmell, purchased the mummies. Suspicious about some of the anatomy, he used radiological equipment to analyze them. He determined that the specimens he had purchased were a manufactured hoax. The upshot of this is that the original mummies were real human beings. But, somewhere along the way, the ancient remains begun to disintegrate; and that, at some point, some showman had recreated a replica of the mother and child mummies for use in freak shows.

In the 1960s, *Ripley's Believe It Or Not Museum* acquired the 6 ft. 8 in. mummies of a mother holding her child. These remains were originally found in a cave in the Yosemite Valley back in 1885.

SAN BERNARDINO SUN

San Bernardino, California   May 24, 1925

Coconino County, Arizona.— Hava Supai Canyon is near the Grand Canyon's South Rim, ninety miles Northwest of Flagstaff. There is a frieze-like band of rock carvings here depicting many extinct American animals as well as a dinosaur like creature resembling a Tyrannosaurus Rex. The Tyrannosaurus is standing on its hind legs. The creature is supporting itself on its great tail as well as its legs. In October and November 1924 the Doheny archaeological expedition led by Samuel Hubbard, curator of Archeology at the Oakland Museum, Charles W. Gilmore, curator of vertebrate paleontology at the United States National Museum, discovered a rock painting in northern Arizona. The image resembles the figure of a standing Tyrannosaurus. The image is millions of years old. The expedition was funded by the oil magnate E.L. Doheny. Hubbard and Doheny had visited this area before. Another petroglyph discovered by Harold T. Wilkins, depicts a Mammoth attacking a man that must have been a giant, at least ten feet tall. The local Indians stated that the drawings had been made by giants of long ago. There are also depictions of the North American Rhinoceros and a Mammoth fighting a human who would have to be ten feet tall if drawn to scale. They are 20 feet above the canyon floor indicating that they might have been created when the canyon was shallower. The pictographs were made by chipping away at desert varnish or black scale on the surface of the red sandstone. The oxidic scale is very slow to form and is already over the pictographs. Most of the petroglyphs are exposed to the weather with no indications of caves or overhanging protective rock ledges. The red sandstone that the area is composed of contains a trace of iron. Over time, this iron content forms a thin black scale on the surface of the stone called desert varnish. By taking a sharp implement such as a piece of flint and cutting through this black surface the red sandstone is revealed. This picture is virtually imperishable and only weather can remove it. There are also dinosaur tracks and fossils in the canyon. The remains of a giant human and a mammoth have also been found here in undisturbed strata thirty million years old, 30,000,000 BC.

THE TOPEKA STATE JOURNAL
Topeka, Kansas
June 23, 1899

ANCIENT MUMMY.

STATE HISTORICAL SOCIETY HAS A BORROWED INDIAN.

A mummified specimen of what was probably once an Indian is being displayed at the rooms of the State Historical Society in the west wing of the State House. The specimen is the property of G.F. Martindale of Scranton, who has been traveling over the country exhibiting it. The specimen is a ghastly sight and is not the most entrancing thing one could look upon in the State House. It is apparently the body of an Indian woman clasping upon her breast, a babe. Both bodies are in a perfect state of preservation so far as the form is concerned, but it has the appearance of having been dried. It is covered by a fabric, apparently, also mummified. The owner says it was found by prospectors in the Yosemite Valley in California. Martindale says the Smithsonian Institute has been attempting to purchase the specimen, but the fact that it does not possess an authentic history, is prohibitive.

~ ~ ~ ~ ~

EVENING STAR
Washington D.C.
August 21, 1921

FIND GIANT SKELETON

WHILE EXCAVATING AT WESTERNPORT, MARYLAND, BONES ARE DISCOVERED.

WESTERNPORT. Md., August 20.—While excavating for a building in the rear of the Morrison property here yesterday, William A. Eiller, a contractor, unearthed parts of a giant skeleton. The find was under a flat stone that weighed about a half ton. The body had evidently been placed in a shallow excavation and this stone put over it. The stone itself had been buried several feet by earth and rocks that had slipped down off the cliff above, but when placed there had evidently been about level with the surrounding ground. The top and front of the skull are in a fairly good state of preservation. The walls of the skull are thick and the cheek bones high, indicating that of an Indian. There is a large double tooth in the upper jaw near the front.

ALTON, ILLINOIS

"The tallest person in recorded history for whom there is irrefutable evidence." This distinction belonged to American giant, Robert Wadlow, of Alton, Illinois.

Robert Wadlow (right) had several nicknames: The Gentle Giant; The Tallest Man Who Ever Lived; The Gentleman Giant; The Boy Giant; The Alton Giant; and The Illinois Giant, are some of them. He is seen in this photo standing next to his 6-foot-tall father. The young man of such long stature, had but a short life. He died in 1940, at the age of 22, from an infection.

Robert Pershing Wadlow was born at Alton, Illinois, in 1918. His entire life was spent there. Born on February 22, 1918, weighing 8 pounds, 6 ounces, Robert Wadlow attracted a lot of attention because, at six months of age, he had grown to weigh 30 pounds. Then, at 18 months, Wadlow weighed 62 pounds. The gigantic lad grew to the full height of 8 feet 11 inches, making him "the tallest person in history," according to the *Guinness Book of World Records*. At the time of his death in 1940, Wadlow weighed 490 lbs. He continued to grow at quite an astounding rate, reaching 6 feet 2 inches and 195 pounds by the time he was eight years old. Robert Wadlow died in his sleep in 1940, at age 22. On July 15, 1940, Robert Wadlow

THE PITTSBURGH PRESS
Pittsburgh, Pennsylvania
October 28, 1928

Robert Wadlow (left) and Jack Grissom, playmates at Alton, Ill. are both 10 years old. Robert is six feet, six inches tall and weigh 211 pounds. Jack is four feet, tw inches tall—about normal for boy of his age.

died in his sleep. He was 8 feet, 11.1 inches tall. His casket weighed 1,000 pounds.

DUNLEITH, ILLINOIS

Within the Twelfth Annual Report of the Bureau of Ethnology, submitted to the Smithsonian Institution in 1891, by J.W. Powell, giant skeletons were found in ancient burial mounds around Dunleith, Illinois:

Illinois: Joe Daviess County.

Members of the Bureau of Ethnology of the Smithsonian Institution discovered a large skeleton between 7 and 8 feet tall. Overlooking the city of East Dubuque (Dunleith) is a line of bluffs whose grassy slopes and summits are dotted over with ancient mounds of unusual symmetry, some of them above the usual size for this section of the country. No. 5, the largest of the group was carefully examined. Two feet below the surface, near the apex, was a skeleton, doubtless an intrusive Indian burial. Near the original surface of the ground, several feet north of the center, were the much decayed skeletons of some 6 or 8 persons, of every size, from the infant to the adult. They were placed horizontally at full length, with the heads toward the south. A few perforated shells and some rude stone skinners and scrapers were found with them. Near the original surface, 10 or 12 feet from the center, on the lower side, lying at full length upon its back, was one of the largest skeletons discovered by the Bureau agents, the length as proved by actual measurement being between 7 and 8 feet. It was all clearly traceable, but crumbled to pieces immediately after removal from the hard earth in which it was encased.

LAKE COUNTY, ILLINOIS

In 1835, mound excavations in Lake County, Illinois, revealed skeletons ranging between 7 and 8 feet tall. *The Historical Encyclopedia of Illinois & History of Lake County,* edited by Newton Bateman and Paul Selby and published in 1902, contains the following reference to the 1835 Lake County giant skeletons:

Excavations...have revealed the crumbling bones of a mighty race. Samuel Miller, who has resided in the county since 1835, is authority for the statement that one skeleton which he assisted in unearthing, was a trifle more than eight feet in length, the skull being correspondingly large, while many other skeletons measured at least seven feet....

LOGAN COUNTY, ILLINOIS

Another mound excavation in Logan County, Illinois, in 1886 produced a number of large skeletons. The artifacts found with the human remains showed higher degree of advancement than the native population of the region had attained.

Illinois: Logan County.

It must be admitted that whatever the uses of these mounds— whether as dwellings or burial places—these silent monuments were built, and the race who built them vanished from the face of the earth, ages before the Indians occupied the land; but, their date must probably forever baffle human skill and ingenuity. It is sometimes difficult to distinguish the places of sepulture raised by the Mound-Builders from the more modern graves of the Indians. The tombs of the former were, in general, larger than those of the latter, and were used as receptacles for a greater number of bodies; and contained relics of art, evincing a higher degree of civilization than that attained by the Indians. The ancient earthworks of the Mound-Builders have occasionally been appropriated as burial places by the Indians, but the skeletons of the latter may be distinguished from the osteological remains of the former by their greater stature.

PIKE COUNTY, ILLINOIS

In 1894, mound excavators in Pike County, Illinois, unearthed large skeletons. The *12th Annual Report of the Bureau of Ethnology to the Secretary of the Smithsonian Institution 1890-1891* (published in 1894), contains details:

Illinois: Pike County.

On the spur of the ridge upon which the Welch mounds of Brown county, hereafter noticed, are situated, and about midway between them and Chambersburg, in Pike county, is a group of circular mounds, possibly the work of another people than those who built the effigies. They are mainly on the farm of Mr. W. A. Hume, who assisted in opening eight of them, of which but two are specially noticed here. The first was 5 feet high and but 2.5 in diameter, of true conical form. It was composed of the usual hard "burial earth" throughout, with nothing of interest at the bottom; but near the top, scarcely covered with earth, was found the skeleton of an adult, doubtless an Indian intrusive burial. The other, situated on the joint of a commanding bluff, was also conical in form, 50 feet in diameter and 8 feet high. The outer layer consisted of sandy soil, 2 feet thick, filled with slightly decayed skeletons, probably Indians of intrusive burials. The earth of the main portion of this mound was a very fine yellowish sand which shoveled like ashes and was everywhere, to the depth of from 2 to 4 feet, as full of human skeletons as could well be stowed away in it, even to two and three tiers. Among these were a number of bones not together as skeletons, but mingled in confusion and probably from scaffolds or other localities. Excepting one, which was rather more than 7 feet long, these skeletons appeared to be of medium size and many of them much decayed.

Mound 42, standing in the ravine, measured 27 feet in diameter and 4 feet high. The construction was found to be similar to that of No. 1; first, the thin layer of vegetable mold; then sandy loam and the clay core; but here was a pit in the original soil, rectangular in form, 3 feet long, 2 feet wide, and 1 in depth, the sides and ends flaring. In this mound there had been three intrusive and two original burials. Two skeletons of the former were in the southwest part, at the depth of 2 feet; the third in the center at the depth of 4 feet, a cut having been made in the top of the core to receive it. The material of the layer over it had a disturbed appearance; indicating that these were intrusive burials. Two other skeletons were found on the bottom of the pit, bundled as usual. The bones of these two are larger than those of any of the other skeletons of this group. Near each gateway, inside, is a mound.

Nos. 10 and 11. These were formerly of about the same shape and size, each being 8 or 9 feet high. No. 11 is now 35 by 40 feet at the base and 4 feet high. In the center, 3 feet below the surface, was a vault 8 feet long and 3 feet wide. In the bottom of this, among the decayed fragments of bark wrappings, lay a skeleton fully 7 feet long, extended at full length on the back, head west.

BREWERSVILLE, INDIANA

A 9 foot 8 inch skeleton was excavated from a mound near Brewersville, Indiana in 1879:

INDIANAPOLIS NEWS
Jennings County, Indiana
November 11, 1967

Remains Of Vanished Giants Found In State

One of the strangest contributions ever to come to hand tells of the existence in what is now Indiana, long before statehood and even before the Indians came here, of a mysterious giant mound-builders race whose men were more than nine feet tall. What's more the contributor of this odd information, Helen W. Ochs of Columbus, Ind., wrote that evidence of their one-time existence here still remains near Brewersville, Jennings County. She quoted from the geological report many years ago on Jennings County, by W.W. Borden, that the remains of the largest work of those mound-builders in that country were to be seen on the bluffs 75 to 100 feet above Sand Creek in Sand Creek Township. The report added:

"It is a stone mound 71 feet in diameter, showing at this time a height of three to five feet above the surrounding surface. The exterior walls appear to be made of stones placed on edge, but the central portion did not show any regular arrangement of the stones."

Mrs. Ochs said the first discovery of human skeletal remains in that mound was made in 1865 when a farmer, getting stone for a spring house, dug into "a sort of tomb" in which he found the skeleton of a small child. She quoted George M. Robison, his son, as saying the top of the mound was not less than 30 feet above the level of the surrounding ground. He added:

> "I well remember that several large forest trees were growing on the top. One was a white oak not less than three feet in diameter at the base."

Discovery of the child's skeleton aroused much curiosity, causing several people to dig into the top of the mound and resulting in the finding of several other skeletons. Mrs. Ochs added:

> "Some of them were bound with perfectly-preserved bands of cedar wrapped around their chest while others were charred, perhaps in observance of a religious rite. Weapons found with the skeletons were unlike those used by Indians."

She quoted Robison further as saying that no intelligent investigative work was conducted there until 1879, 14 years after the discovery of the mound. He continued:

> "The state geologist brought a couple of men here, one from Cincinnati and one from New York, and with Dr. Charles Green of North Vernon, they made quite an extensive examination. Among other things found was the skeleton of a man, it was intact, or rather, I might say, the bones were not scattered. It measured nine feet, eight inches."

> "There was sort of necklace of mica lying around the neck and down across the breast. At the feet stood a sort of 'image' made of burned clay with pieces of flint rock imbedded in it."

Robison kept that image and some of the bones. Mrs. Ochs said that as late as 1937 bones of that giant were in a basket in the office of the Kellar Mill along Sand Creek about a mile below the mound's site:

> "Kenneth Kellar, grandson of Robison, remembers that basket of bones. He said the bones were lost when the 1937 flood washed out the office."

Robinson who told of seeing the huge skeleton exhumed added that, according to the men of science who were there, they were the remains of a white race that had inhabited that part of the country before the advent of the red man. He said there were no signs of anything like pottery, no signs of metal working of any kind, just simply the bones of a "dead and gone race of human beings that we today know practically nothing about. We know not whence they came or where they went."

Mrs. Ochs said that the giant-like race had worked hard to entomb its dead. The rocks in the mound had been placed end to end with no attempt to plaster or seal them together. She continued:

"Evidence that this mound was dug into, has washed out until the one-time graves now are smooth indentations in the leaf-covered ground."

She said that Edith Hale, a retired schoolteacher; Beulah Kellar Lowe, granddaughter, and Kenneth Kellar, the grandson of Robison, remembered the bones and image described by Robison. "This, I feel, substantiates the findings under discussion," Mrs. Ochs concluded.

KOSSUTH CENTER, IOWA

Seven gigantic mummies were discovered near Kossuth Center, Iowa, by Marvin Rainwater, a local farmer. He had been digging a well on his property when he struck a deposit of very hard stone, about 9 feet down. The stone impediment measured over 4 feet wide in every direction. Rainwater noticed that the stone was not the common limestone found in the area, and it appeared to be smooth and polished. He got some neighbors to help excavate further. They discovered that there were several irregularly cut slabs, covering a wide area, each measuring 8 ft. by 10 ft. They were fitted so tightly that a knife blade could not be put between them. Mr. Rainwater knew he had found something very unusual, so he contacted Georg Von Podebrad College and they dispatched a team of archaeologists, anthropologists, and geologists to the site.

The unusual stone was the same type used by Egyptians to build their massive monuments, not native to Iowa. The stone slabs were revealed to be in a perfect square, measuring 188 feet on each side. It took many months to completely uncover the huge structure, which turned out to be a pyramid, similar to the one at Marietta, Ohio. When the scientists of the Rainwater site opened a small, arched entryway, seven huge figures were found seated cross-legged, around a large, deep fire pit. These mummies were of some giant humanoid race, ten feet tall, with red hair. Closer examination revealed double rows of teeth in upper and lower jaws; the foreheads were low and sloping, with prominent brows. One explanation for these mummies were the legends of the Paiute tribe of Native Americans, who tell of a race of redheaded giants who were their mortal enemies centuries ago. Called the Si-Te-Cahs, it was said that the tribe had been driven from Nevada. Another interesting detail is that, the Kossuth County Historical Society is home to three robes made entirely from very long strands of red hair.

TWICE-A-WEEK PLAIN DEALER
Cresco, Iowa
June 2, 1908

Giant Skeleton Is Found.

Lebanon, Ohio.—When digging into a gravel bank on his farm near Stubbtown, this county, John Watkins discovered the burial ground of Miami Indians. The skeleton of a huge woman was unearthed. It measured seven feet and five inches in length. About her neck were ropes of pearls and in her tomb other articles of value. Much excitement was aroused among the farmers in the vicinity, and further excavations brought to light many other skeletons of this extinct race. Some were found in sitting positions and some on their faces. Watkins will try to interest the State Archaeological Society in his find.

Richmond Palladium

February 18, 1846   Richmond, Iowa

The giant human bones that were lately found, 50 feet underground in Williamson County, Tennessee, have been put
together. Nearly all perfect, they are ready for exhibition. The
skeleton measures sixteen feet in length

HOLLY CREEK, KENTUCKY

*In 1965, a man named Kenneth White dug a "perfectly
preserved skeleton" from under a large rock ledge along
Holly Creek, which runs through Wolfe and Breathitt Counties
in Kentucky. When measured, the skeleton came in at 8 feet,
9 inches in length. This intriguing tale can be found in a 1984
book written by Michael Paul Henson, entitled, Tragedy at
Devil's Hollow and other Haunting Tales from Kentucky. In it,
Henson relates how he actually examined a giant body dug out
from under a large rock ledge along Holly Creek in east-central
Kentucky in 1965:*

> *In 1965 Kenneth White built several stalls for his cattle
> under a large, overhanging rock ledge near his home on
> Holly Creek in eastern-central Kentucky. During the
> process of cleaning out an accumulation of leaves, dirt
> and debris under the cliff, he had found a perfectly
> preserved skeleton which he thought might prove to be an
> Indian. The position of the skeleton indicated the body had
> been buried facing east. He found nothing buried with the
> skeleton.*

> *White asked me to examine it with him. All of the bones
> were well preserved, including the fingers and toes. As we
> reassembled the skeleton, my first reaction was curiosity,
> which soon turned to amazement. The assembled skeleton
> measured 8 feet, 9 inches in length. The arms were
> extremely long and the hands were large. By comparison,
> the feet were very small. The skull raised even more*

questions. It measured 30 inches in circumference. The eye and nose sockets were slits rather than cavities, and the area where the jawbone hinges to the skull was solid bone. It would seem that the person could not have opened his mouth. I have never heard of another person or skeleton which fits such a description.

The bones were covered with a powdery white substance which disappeared which touched. No weapons, clothing remains or tools were found with the skeleton which had been buried at least five feet underground. According to archaeologists, this would indicate that it had been there for over 300 years.

We assumed the skeleton to be the remains of an extraordinarily large, deformed Indian. Our assumption was based on the discovery of 20 years previously of a 60-pound, double-edged granite Indian war ax and a flint knife with a 20-inch blade which had been plowed up in the same area by a farmer named Terry. These relics were kept by Terry family for a few years before being lost. White later reburied the bones, and to my knowledge, no scientific examination was ever made of them.

Several questions concerning this skeleton remain unanswered. If this person was buried with clothing, weapons, or tools, what happened to them? What was the white powdery substance covering the bones? Did the substance keep the bones from decaying, and if so, why did it not protect the flesh from decomposition? Could the skeleton have been stripped of all body tissue before burial, such as the ancient Hawaiians are known to have done? There was no dark soil around the skeleton. This is normally present when a body decays and has been buried for several years. If I did not know it was impossible, I would swear, from the condition of the skeleton, that the body had been prepared for burial and placed under the cliff only a few days before my friend dug it up.

Authors Note: Certainly, the evidence for a true race of giant Amerindians is lacking, but there are certainly other possible explanations for a large bipedal human-like skeleton being found in North America. There are several other recorded instances of this same type of skeleton being found elsewhere in Kentucky, Pennsylvania, Wisconsin and Arizona. The skeleton in Pennsylvania had six inch horns in its skull.

Henson and the farmer assumed the skeleton to be a large, deformed member of a Native American tribe who had burial grounds in the region. Because Kenneth White re-buried the bones, instead of taking them to experts for examination, no more is known of this unusual discovery. Michael P. Henson died in 1995; no further notes of his on this fascinating story have surfaced.

BEMIDJI DAILY PIONEER

Bemidji, Minnesota   October 3, 1916

LARGE SKELETON FOUND IN MINNESOTA

Some large mounds have been found in this territory. In some places a number of pieces of pottery have been unearthed. It will be remembered that when the dam at International Falls was under construction several hundred pieces of tempered copper were unearthed from a depth of 15 feet. The articles consisted of fish hooks, knives, spears, and arrows. The art of tempering copper, which was known by these early mound builders, is now a lost art. An unusually large skeleton was also unearthed and thought to have been a woman. Physicians who have examined the skeleton declare that it represented a type of early prehistoric persons who were seven feet tall or more and who possessed an especially large lower jaw. They drew this conclusion because the skeleton found was that of a person of very large stature. The jaw bone was wide and its construction is said to be a special gift of nature to the early man in order that he could masticate the coarser foods which then made up his subsistence. The skull is very large. The well rounded forehead gives evidence of considerable development of intelligence of the natives of Rainy Lake territory. The skeleton will be sent to the Minnesota Historical Society.

The statues of Paul Bunyan and Babe the Blue Ox stand along the shore of Lake Bemidji, Minnesota. They are the first examples of the "Roadside Colossus," which was an important type of advertising in the early days of the automobile. Paul Bunyan is 18 feet high; Babe stands about 10 feet tall. "Big as a mountain and strong as a grizzly bear...." describes folk hero Paul Bunyan, "the greatest lumberjack to swagger through the North American forests." In 1937, *Time Magazine*, featured a centerfold spread of Paul and Babe. The camera giant, Kodak, reports that these statues are the second most photographed giant sculptures in the U.S., just behind Mount Rushmore.

The Jolly Green Giant (right) has a State Park named for him in Blue Earth, MN.

BECKLEY FARM, LAKE KORONIS, MINNESOTA

According to a piece in the *St. Paul Globe,* August 12, 1896, "a hatchet-shaped stone object was plowed up on the farm of Home Beckley, near Lake Koronis, Minn. It weighed about 3 pounds. In the immediate vicinity from time to time, numerous stone arrow-heads have been found; and in a mound not far from Mr. Beckley's farm, the skeleton of a huge man was exhumed."

The Aborigines of Minnesota: A Report Based on the Collections of Jacob V. Brower, and on the Field Surveys and Notes of Alfred J. Hill and Theodore H. Lewis, Minnesota Historical Society, 1911, contains multiple reports of gigantic skeletons found in Minnesota:

> Grant County, near Graham's Lake, human bones, in an earthen pot 13 inches in diameter and about the same in height, arrow-heads, drill, elliptical flings, mussel shells,

> In addition, at Moose Island and Pine City, bones of other giants were discovered. At Moose Island Lake, human bones of men of large stature were found.

> At Pine City are two lone mounds. Mr. Upham says, in his geological report on Pine County: "At Pine City, a mound about 12 ft. high, was leveled down on the land used for the lumber yard of the steam sawmill. It was some 20 rods south of Snake River; and a quarter of a mile west from Cross Lake on land 10 ft. or 15 ft. above the river. Captain Sod, a Chippewa about 100 years old, says that, after a battle with the Sioux some of them were buried in this mound, one being a very large man. This was an intrusive burial, the mound having been built at some much-earlier date. In its removal, several skeletons were exhumed, some being found in erect position; and one of gigantic size."

CLEARWATER, MINNESOTA

When ancient burial mounds were explored in 1888 in Clearwater, Minnesota, the skeletons of 7 giants were found. According to news article from the June 29, 1888 issue of the *St. Paul Pioneer Press,* these skeletons had two complete sets–double rows–of teeth. An Illinois publication, *True Republican,* featured a piece on the Clearwater giants in its August 29, 1888, issue: "A Minnesota farmer near Clearwater, Minnesota, while digging a cellar, came upon seven skeletons in good condition. They were found in a sort of mound, and the bodies had been buried heads downward. The skeletons were from seven to eight feet in height." It is thought that the bodies were buried 200 years ago.

THE TANEY COUNTY REPUBLICAN
Forsyth, Missouri
February 25, 1904:

Giant Skeleton Found.

Workman engaged in digging gravel at Winnemucca, Nevada, the other day, uncovered at a depth of about 12 feet, a lot of bones. They turned out to be part of the skeleton of a gigantic human being. Dr. Samuels examined them and pronounced them to be bones of a man who must have been nearly 11 feet in height. The metacarpal bones measure four and a half inches in length, and are large in proportion. A part of the ulna was found; in its complete form, it would have been between 17 and 18 inch in length. The remainder of the skeleton is being searched for.

WARREN, MINNESOTA

Ten skeletons "of both sexes and of gigantic size" were taken from a Mound at Warren, Minnesota, in 1883. (*St. Paul Pioneer Press,* May 23, 1883)

> The following is condensed from the *Pioneer Press*, May 23, 1882: Mound located near Warren, Marshall County, examined by Hon. J.P. Nelson, was located on the Pembina trail, was 60 ft. by 12 ft. On examination, it was found to contain near the center, the bones of more than ten persons, male and female; and, mingled with them, the bones of badgers, horses, and dogs. The skull was the only specimen that did not crumble on exposure to the air. Their size indicated gigantic stature for their owners.

MARIETTA DAILY LEADER

Marietta, Ohio   **December 2, 1900**

FINDS BONES OF GIANT RACE.

Skeletons of Prehistoric Men, Ten Feet Tall, Dug Up In Missouri.

The fossils of three human beings, evidently prehistoric giants, were found near Monteseno, Missouri, the other day by C.H. Beehler, a farmer, at the depth of 40 feet. The size of the skulls indicates that the bodies must have been at least ten feet high; and the bones, resembling those of a human skeleton, seem to bear out this theory.

Beehler has quite a collection of fossil relics which he has found at various times in this vicinity, which is alive with them. He is confident that he has discovered the missing link, and intends to submit his find to the professors of Washington University in St. Louis to see if they sustain his theory.

Fossils of mastodons and animals extinct for centuries, have been found in this vicinity by people who were plowing or digging wells. It seems to be a regular graveyard for 40 miles around for prehistoric bones which indicate the enormous size of the animals which once roamed the land.

KANSAS CITY, MISSOURI

W.H.R. Lykins wrote in his book, *The History of Pettis County, Missouri: Including an Authentic History of Sedalia, Other Towns and Townships,* 1882, about skulls discovered "of great size and thickness" in mounds near Kansas City, Missouri in 1877. They were in groups of three and five together, at different points for 5 miles up and down the river. Some were built entirely of earth, and some had a rough stone chamber or vault inside; all were covered with earth on the outside to form similar shaped mounds. Mr. W.H.R. Lykins of Kansas City, described the exploration of some of these mounds:

> We did not notice any very market peculiarity as to these bones except their great size and thickness, in the great prominence of the super ciliary ridges. The teeth were worn down to a smooth and even surface. The next one we opened was a stone mound. On clearing off the top of this we came upon a stone wall enclosing an area about 8 feet, with a narrow opening for a doorway or entrance on the south side. The bones were crumbly about 8 feet, with a narrow opening for a doorway or entrance on the south side. The wall of this enclosure was about 2 feet; the inside was smooth and com-pactly built in the corners as correctly squared as if constructed by a practiced workmen. No mortar had been used. At a depth of about 2 feet from the top of the wall we found a layer of five skeletons lying with their feet toward the south. None of the other walls examined were so skillfully laid as this one. The bones were crumbly, and only a few fragments were preserved by coating them well with varnish as quickly as possible after they were exposed to the air. One stone enclosure was found full of ashes, charcoal and burned human bones in the stones and earth of which the mound was composed all show the effects of fire. Hence it is presumed that this was either a cremation furnace or else an altar for human sacrifices – most probably the latter. Some fragments of pottery were found in the vicinity.

Illinois State Journal

Springfield, Illinois   **May 21, 1850**

A GIANT OF THE OLDEN TIME

A human skeleton of unusual size was discovered the other day at Harsimus, New Jersey. It was found about nine feet below the surface, imbedded in several bushels of oyster shells, much larger than any found in the neighboring waters. The remains are doubtless those of an Indian of immense stature. When living, he must have been over eight feet high. The skull measures fifteen inches from the root of the nose over the top, to the base of the occipital bond, and is two feet in circumference. It contains a full set of excellent teeth (except one) even, sound, and white .

THE WYANDOT PIONEER
Sandusky, Ohio
November 29, 1861

A BIG MAN OR A BIG LIE.

Alleged Skeleton of a Prehistoric Man Twelve Feet High.

St. Joseph, Mo.—August 14.—Hon. J. H. Hainly, a well known and reliable citizen of Barnard, Missouri, writes to the *Gazette* the particulars of the discovery of a giant skeleton four miles south-west of that place. A farmer named John W. Hannon found the bones protruding from the bank of a ravine that has been cut by the action of the rains during the past years. Mr. Hannon worked several days in unearthing the skeleton, which proved to be that of a human being whose height was twelve feet. The head through the temples was twelve inches. From the lower part of the skull at the back to the top was fifteen inches and the circumference forty inches. The ribs were nearly four feet long and three and a fourth inches wide. The thigh bones were thirty inches long, and the entire foot eighteen inches in length. The skeleton lay on its face twenty feet below the surface of the ground, and the toes were imbedded in the earth, indicating that the body either fell or was placed there.

We often get asked: "where are the bones?" and we reply: "ask the Smithsonian and the Native Americans."

There is a legitimate answer to the question of what did the Smithsonian do with all of the giant skeletons. The internet is loaded with conspiracy theories that put forth the idea that museums simply destroyed giant skeletons in order to cover up the fact that giants really did exist. If you keep reading, you will find that museums did not enter into a conspiracy to cover up the belief in Giants. In fact, the Smithsonian, like many other similar institutions were simply following the law. Relevant excerpts from an article by Irvin Molotsky and printed as a *Special To The New York Times;* which originally appeared in *Anthro Notes - National Museum of Natural History Bulletin for Teachers, Vol. 17 No. 1/2 Winter/Spring 1995,* follow:

Smithsonian to Give Up Indian Remains

Repatriation Legislation

Through the efforts of the AIAD and the widespread media attention it attracted, the repatriation issue slowly bubbled to the surface of public consciousness and eventually captured the attention of several sympathetic lawmakers. The first piece of legislation to treat this issue was the National Museum of the American Indian (NMAI) Act, which was passed by Congress in 1989. The principal functions of this Act were to authorize the transfer of the Heye Foundation's Museum of the American Indian collections from New York to the Smithsonian Institution. This magnificent collection of Native American artifacts from all over the western hemisphere was to form the basis of the new National Museum of the American Indian. The NMAI Act also required the Smithsonian to inventory and assess the cultural origins of collections potentially affiliated with Native American and Native Hawaiian peoples. Human remains and funerary objects for which cultural affiliation could be established were to be offered for return the appropriate tribal group. The idea that there must be a demonstrable relationship of cultural affiliation between the remains or objects in question and the tribal group to whom they would be offered for return was the cornerstone of this repatriation legislation.

The Native American Graves Protection and Repatriation Act (NAGPRA) was passed the following year, in 1990. This law expanded the repatriation mandate beyond human remains and funerary objects to include the categories of sacred objects and cultural patrimony. It also extended the applicability of this mandate to all federally funded museums, institutions, and agencies.

September 13, 1989 Headline in *The New York Times*.

The Smithsonian Institution agreed today to return the skeletal remains of thousands of American Indians to their tribes for reburial in their homelands, resolving a dispute that pitted the research needs of scientists against the anguish of Indians who say their ancestors have been desecrated. The agreement was a compromise involving the Smithsonian, Congress, and leaders of Indian organizations. All expressed the hope that the Smithsonian's action would prompt other museums to take similar steps. "Obviously, what the Smithsonian does affects other museums," said Ian Brown, assistant director of the Peabody Museum at Harvard University. "A lot of museums are going through a shake-up, trying to come up with a policy on this on their own, including us." David Hurst Thomas, curator of anthropology at the American Museum of Natural History in New York City, said his museum had been conducting such a program quietly for the last year. 'Wonderful and Inevitable' Robert McAdams,

Secretary of the Smithsonian, said the institution would "begin to return the remains when we can identify tribal descendants."

EUREKA, NEVADA

In 1877, in Eureka, Nevada, prospectors found a human leg bone and knee cap sticking out of solid rock. Doctors examined the remains and determined they were from a human being, and one that stood over 12 feet tall. The rock in which the bones were found was dated geologically to the Jurassic Period, over 185 million years old.

LOVELOCK, NEVADA

In 1911, several red-haired mummies, ranging from 6 ft. 6 in. to 8 ft. tall, were found in a cave at Lovelock, Nevada. In February and June of 1931, large skeletons were found in the Humboldt Lake bed near Lovelock, Nevada. The first of these 2 skeletons found, measured 8 ½ feet tall. The second skeleton was almost 10 ft. long. The skeletons were wrapped in a gum-covered fabric similar to Egyptian mummies. (*Review-Miner,* June 19, 1931). In 1939, 7 ft. 7 in. skeleton was found on the Friedman ranch near Lovelock, Nevada. (*Review-Miner,* September 29, 1939).

WHITE SANDS, NEW MEXICO

In 1932, Ellis Wright found human footprints in the gypsum rock at White Sands, New Mexico. This discovery was later backed up by Fred Arthur, Supervisor of the Lincoln National Park, and others, who reported each footprint to be 22 inches long and 8 to 10 inches wide.

ALLEGHANY COUNTY NEW YORK

From the *History of Allegany County, New York*, in 1850 a report that very large human bones were uncovered during excavation for the railroad.

BUFFALO, NEW YORK

1792 Buffalo, New York: Turner's History of the Holland Purchase reports that 7 and 8 foot skeletons were found at an earthen fort in Orleans county with broad flat topped skulls.

NEW YORK

In 1851, a skull, rib bone, and shin bone were found in New York. The length of the bones indicated the height of the person to be over 8 feet tall.

RUTMAN & RODMAN, NEW YORK

In the mid-1800s, J.N. DeHart found vertebrae described as "larger than those of the present type in Wisconsin mounds in 1876."

WESTERN NEW YORK

1849, New York: From *Illustrations of the Ancient Monuments of Western New York* comes the report that an elliptical mound near the Conewango Valley held eight big skeletons. A thigh bone was found to be 28" long. Exquisite stone points, enamelwork, and jewelry were found. Also discovered in the area were a number of other large skeletons one almost 9 feet in height.

JUNIATA SENTINEL AND REPUBLICAN
Mifflintown, Juniata County, Pennsylvania
June 3, 1874

Ancient Americans.

The workmen engaged in opening a way for the projected railroad between Weldon and Garrysburgh, N.C. struck, about a mile from the former place, in a bank beside the river, a catacomb of skeletons, supposed to be those of Indians of a remote age, a lost and forgotten race. Workers dug from the river's bank a vast heap of skeletons, packed closely together, tier on tier, and intermingled with the human bones, were a lot of sharp stone arrows, rude mortars, and pipe-bowls. The bodies exhumed were of a strange and remarkable formation. The skulls were nearly an inch in thickness; the teeth were as large as those of a horse and were filed sharp as those of cannibals, the enamel perfectly preserved. The bones were of wonderful length and strength, the entire skeleton being probably as great as eight or nine feet. Near their heads were sharp stone arrows, some mortars in which their corn was crushed, and the bowls of pipes, apparently of soft soapstone. The bodies were found closely packed together, laid tier on tier, as it seemed. There was no discernable ingress or egress to the mound. The mystery is who these giants were, to what race they belonged, to what era, and how they came to be buried there. To these inquiries no answer has yet been made; and meantime, the ruthless spade continues to cleave skull and body asunder, throwing up in mangled masses the bones of this heroic tribe. It is hoped that some effort will be made to preserve authentic and accurate accounts of these discoveries, and to throw some light if possible, on the lost tribe whose bones are thus rudely disturbed from their sleep in the earth's bosom.

ASHTABULA, OHIO

1878, Ashtabula County, Ohio: While excavating the ground for graves, bones were exhumed, which seemed to have belonged to a race of giants. A skull and jaw were found, which were of such size that the skull would fit easily over a large man's head like a loose fitting helmet, even with the jaw in place. The number of these graves has been estimated to be between two and three thousand.

Sketch of tablet found at Brush Creek Township, Ohio, near the remains of several 9 ft. tall humans, in 1879.

BRUSH CREEK, OHIO

In 1879, in Brush Creek Township, a large mound contained the skeletal remains of humans that measured up to nine feet tall. A large stone tablet etched with unusual inscriptions that are similar to Greek writing, was also found near the giants.

CHESTERVILLE, OHIO

1829, Chesterville, Ohio: In digging away a mound where a hotel was to be built, a large human skeleton was found, but no measurements were made. It is related that the jawbone was found to fit easily over that of a citizen of the village. The local physicians examined the cranium and found it proportionately large, with more teeth than the white race of today. The skeleton was taken to Mansfield, and has been lost sight of entirely.

CONNEAUT, OHIO

1800, Conneaut, Ohio: Among the normal size skeletons found in the remains of mounds were found gigantic bones. Some of the skulls and jaws were large enough to fit over the head and face of a normal man.

LAKE ERIE ISLANDS, OHIO

1898, Lake Erie Islands, Ohio: Eight skeletons were found near the United States Coast Guard lighthouse, one measuring over seven feet in height.

MARION, OHIO

1883 Marion County, Ohio: During general construction projects in the area, giant human skeletons were unearthed.

MEDINA, OHIO

1881 Ohio, Medina County: A jawbone of great size belonging to a human being was discovered, which contained eight jaw-teeth in each side, of enormous size; and the teeth stood transversely in the jawbone. It would pass over any man's face with entire ease.

OHIO VALLEY

1825 Ohio Valley: David Cusick, a Tuscarora by birth, wrote that among the legends of the ancient people of the stock, there was a powerful tribe called *Ronnongwetowanca*. They were giants, and had a "considerable habitation." When the Great Spirit made the people, some of them became giants.

After a time, and having endured the outrages of these giants, it is said that the people banded together, and through the final force of about 800 warriors, successfully annihilated the abhorrent *Ronnongwetowanca*. After that, it was said that there were no giants anywhere. This was supposed to have happened around 2,500 winters before Columbus discovered America, around 1000 BC.

Skeleton of Mound Builder, 7 ft. in length, Serpent Mound, Peebles, Ohio.

PROCTORVILLE, OHIO

1892 Ohio Proctorville: From the *Ironton Register*, "Where Proctorville now stands was one day part of a well paved city, but I think the greater part of it is now in the Ohio river [sic]. Only a few mounds, there; one of which was near the C. Wilgus mansion and contained a skeleton of a very large person, all double teeth, and sound, in a jaw bone that would go over the jaw with the flesh on."

SENECA, OHIO

1872 Ohio, Seneca Township: When the "Bates" mound was opened the remains of three skeletons, whose size would indicate they measured in life, at least, eight feet in height, were found. A remarkable feature of these remains was they had double teeth in front as well as in back of mouth and in both upper and lower jaws.

SEVILLE, OHIO

1873 Ohio, Seville: An Ohio Bicentennial Commission historical marker serves as a reminder that the Giants of Seville, Captain Martin Van Buren Bates and his wife, Anna Swan Bates, lived in the village of Seville in Medina County. Anna stood 7 feet 11 1/2 inches tall and weighed 413 pounds. Martin was 7 feet 9 inches tall and weighed 480 pounds.

TOLEDO, OHIO

Near Toledo, Ohio, in 1895, excavation of a Mound turned up 20 skeletons. They were seated and facing east; beside each, was a large bow with "curiously wrought hier-oglyphic figures." The jaws and teeth were "twice as large as those of present-day people." *Chicago Record,* October 24, 1895; cited by Ron G. Dobbins, *NEARA Journal, Vol. 13*, Fall 1978).

VERMILLION, OHIO

1858 Ohio, Vermillion Township: Skeletons of a race of beings much larger than the local inhabitants were discovered.

ZANESVILLE, OHIO

An article in the publication, *American Antiquarian, Vol. 3;* 1880, tells of mound excavations being done that year near Zanesville, Ohio. According to Dr. Everhart "A skeleton which is reported to have been of enormous dimensions" was found in a clay coffin, with a sandstone slab containing hieroglyphics. In a later publication, *History of Muskingum County, Ohio, With Illustrations & Biographical Sketches of Prominent Men & Pioneers* by J.R. Everhart and A.A. Graham, 1882, is printed the following letter detailing giants found in Ohio mounds:

Brush Creek Township

March 3, 1880

To Mr. Everhart, A.M., Historian

Dear Sir:

On December 1, 1879, we assembled with a large number of people for the purpose of excavating into and examining the contents of an ancient mound, located on the farm of Mr. J. M. Baughman, in Brush Creek Township, Muskingum County, Ohio. The mound is situated on the summit of a hill, rising 15½ feet above the bed of the stream called Brush Creek. It is about 64 feet in width by about 90 feet in length, having an altitude of 11 feet 3 inches; is nearly flat on top. On the mound were found the stumps of sixteen trees, ranging in size from 8 inches to 2 feet in diameter. We began the investigations by digging a trench four feet wide from the east side. When the depth of eight feet had been reached, we found a human skeleton, deeply charred, in close proximity to a stake six feet in length and four inches in thickness, also deeply charred, standing in an upright position. We found there a cranium, vertebrae, pelvis, and metacarpal bones near; while the femurs and fibula extended horizontally from the stake.

At this juncture work was abandoned, on account of the lateness of the hour, until Monday, December 8th, when it was resumed by opening the mound from the northwest. When at the depth of seven and a half feet in the north trench, came upon two enormous skeletons, male and female, lying one above the other, faces together, and heads toward the west. The male, by actual measurement, proved to be nine feet six inches ; the female eight feet nine inches in length. At about the same depth in the west trench we found two more skeletons, lying two feet apart, faces upward, and heads to the east. These, it is believed, were fully as large as those already measured, but the condition in which they were found rendered exact measurement impossible.

On December 22, we began digging at the southeast portion of the mound, and had not proceeded more than three feet when we discovered an altar, built of sand-rock. The altar was six feet in width and twelve feet in length, and was filled with clay, and of about the same shape that the mound originally was. On the top, which was composed of two flat flag-rocks, forming an area of about two feet in width and six in length, was found wood-ashes and charcoal to the amount of five or six bushels. Immediately behind, or west of the altar, were found three skeletons, deeply charred, and covered with ashes, lying faces upward, heads toward the south, measuring, respectively: eight feet ten, nine feet two, and nine feet four inches in length. In another grave a female skeleton eight feet long, and a male skeleton nine feet four inches long — the female lowermost, and the face downward, and the male on top, face upward, behind the site of the altar.

After proceeding about four feet, we found, within three feet of the top of the mound, and five feet above the natural surface, a coffin or burial case, made of a peculiar kind of yellow clay, the like of which we have not found in the township; consequently, we believe it was brought from a distance. Within the casket were confined the remains of a female eight feet in length, an infant three and a half feet in length, the skull of which was scarcely thicker than the blade of an ordinary case-knife. The skull of the female would average in thickness about one-eighth of an inch, measured eighteen and three-fourth inches from the supra-orbital ridge to the external occipital protuberance; was remarkably smooth; perfectly formed.

Within the enclosure was a figure or image of an infant but sixteen inches in length, made of the yellow clay of which the casket was formed; also, a roll of peculiar black substance encased in the yellow clay, twelve inches in length by four inches in diameter, which crumbled to dust when exposed to the air. We also found what appears to have been the handle and part of the side of a huge vase ; it was nicely glazed, almost black in color, and burned very hard. From within a few inches of the coffin was taken a sand-rock, having a surface of twelve by fourteen inches (which had also passed through the fire), upon which were engraved the following described hieroglyphics: [Here a space was left in the notebook for the representation of the inscription found upon the stone; but, for the sake of a true representation, we determined to have photographs made, and make one a part of this report.]

Proceeding north about four feet from where we found the coffin, and within six inches of the top of the mound, we discovered a huge skeleton lying on its face, with the head toward the west. Mr. J. M. Baughman came upon this one accidentally, and, as it fell to pieces, he thinks no one could tell how long it was, but those who saw it unanimously declared it to be the largest of any yet discovered. We have found eleven human skeletons in all, seven of which have been subjected to fire; and, what is remarkable, we have not found a tooth in all the excavations.

The above report contains nothing but facts briefly told, and knowing that the public has been humbugged and imposed upon by archaeologists, we wish to fortify our own statements by giving the following testimonial:

We, the undersigned citizens of Brush Creek township, having been present and taken part in the above excavations, do certify that the statements herewith set forth are true and correct, and in no particular has the writer deviated from the facts in the case.

Signed & Notarized:

Thomas D. Showers	John Worstal	Marshall Cooper
J. M. Baughman	S.S. Baughman	John E. McCoy

THE BILLINGS GAZETTE

Billings, Montana   **August 30, 1907**

PYGMY SKELETON DUG UP.

Prehistoric Cemetery Discovered by South Dakota R. R. Graders.

Oacoma, S.D., Aug. 29.—A remarkable prehistoric burying ground has been cut into by railroad graders near here, and the remains of what appears to be a pygmy race have been discovered. The old burying ground is now a great deposit of gravel, and it is in this that the bones are found. Some 50 skeletons have so far been unearthed. These are all of a race of dwarfs about four feet high. Physicians have pronounced them to be the remains of adults, not children. The bodies were buried standing or sitting. One of the skeletons, however, is that of a giant more than eight feet high. Near the giant's skeleton was found a number of copper implements, as well as several of bone. In one of the graves, were two copper idols about eight inches tall.

UNEARTH SKELETON OF GIANT

Bones of Supposed Mound Builder Those of Man Eight or Nine Feet High.

Dr. W. J. Holland, curator of the Carnegie museum, Pittsburgh, and his assistant, Dr. Peterson, a few days ago opened up a mound of the ancient race that inhabited this section and secured the skeleton of a man who when in the flesh was between eight and nine feet in height, says a Greensburg (Pa.) dispatch to the Philadelphia Inquirer.

This mound, which was originally about 100 feet long and more than 12 feet high, has been somewhat worn down by time. It is on the J. R. Secrist farm in South Huntington township. This farm has been in the Secrist name for more than a century.

The most interesting feature in the recent excavation was the mummified torso of the human body, which the experts figured was laid to rest at least 400 years ago. Portions of the bones dug up and the bones in the legs, Prof. Peterson declares, are those of a person between eight and nine feet in height. The scientist figures that this skeleton was the framework of a person of the prehistoric race that inhabited this section before the American Indians.

The torso and the portions of the big skeleton were shipped to the Carnegie museum. Drs. Holland and Peterson supervised the explorations on the Secrist mound with the greatest of care. The curators believe the man whose skeleton they secured belonged to the mound builder class.

The sun., December 08, 1893,

GASTERVILLE, PENNSYLVANIA

According to a piece in *American Antiquarian, Vol. 7,* 1885, a large Mound near Gasterville, Pennsylvania, contained a vault in which a skeleton measuring 7 ft. 2 in. was buried. Unusual inscriptions were carved on the walls of the vault.

ROANE COUNTY, TENNESSEE

1890 Roane County, Tennessee: A giant skeleton was discovered that measured over 7 feet tall.

SPARTA, TENNESSEE

In 1828, several newspapers reported the discovery of a burial ground in Sparta, Tennessee. When the graves—which were only two feet deep–were opened, they contained tiny stone coffins, which held the remains of very small humans. The tallest of these was 19 inches. The corpses were placed with their heads to the East; their backs appeared to be burned.

WHITE & WILLIAMSON COUNTY, TENNESSEE

In his 1823 book, *The Natural and Aboriginal History of Tennessee,* author John Haywood describes multiple instances of very tall skeletons and other human bones found throughout Tennessee. On the next page, is an excerpt from John Hayward's work, describing an array of incredible finds:

First, then—*Of their Size.*

This is ascertained by the length and dimensions of the skeletons which are found in East and West Tennessee. These will prove demonstratively, that the ancient inhabitants of this country, either the primitive or secondary settlers, were of gigantic stature, compared with the present races of Indians.

On the farm of Mr. John Miller, of White county, are a number of small graves, and also many large ones, the bones in which show that the bodies to which they belonged, when alive, must have been seven feet high and upwards.

About the year 1814, Mr. Lawrence found, in Scarborough's cave, which is on the Calf-killer river, a branch of the Cany Fork, about 12 or 15 miles from Sparta, in a little room in the cave, many human bones of a monstrous size. He took a jaw bone and applied it to his own face, and when his chin touched the concave of the chin bone, the hinder ends of the jaw bone did not touch the skin of his face on either side. He took a thigh bone, and applied the upper end of it to his own hip joint, and the lower end reached four inches below the knee joint. Mr. Andrew Bryan saw a grave opened about 4 miles northwardly from Sparta, on the Calf-killer fork. He took a thigh bone, and raising up his knee, he applied the knee joint of the bone to the extreme length of his own knee, and the upper end of the bone passed out behind him as far as the full width of his body. Mr. Lawrence is about 5 feet, 10 inches, high; and Mr. Bryan about 5 feet, 9. Mr. Sharp Whitley was in a cave near the place, where Mr. Bryan saw the graves opened. In it were many of these bones. The sculls lie plentifully in it, and all the other bones of the human body; all in proportion, and of monstrous size. Human bones were taken out of a mound on Tennessee river, below Kingston, which Mr. Brown saw measured, by Mr. Simms. The thigh bones of those skeletons, when applied to Mr. Simms's thigh, were an inch and a half longer than his, from the point of his hip to his knee: supposing the whole frame to have been in the same proportion, the body it belonged to must have been seven feet high or upwards. Many bones in the mounds there, are of equal size. Suppose a man seven or eight feet high, that is from 18 inches to 2 feet taller than men of the common size; suppose the body broader in the same proportion, also his arms and legs; would he not be entitled to the name of giant?

Excerpt from:

The Natural & Aboriginal History of Tennessee; Up To The First Settlements Therein By The White People, In The Year 1768

by John Haywood

Published: 1823

Excerpt

oontinued:

———

The Natural

& Aboriginal

History of

Tennessee;

Up To

The First

Settlements

Therein

By The

White

People,

In The

Year 1768

———

by John

Haywood

———

Published:

1823

Col. William Sheppard, late of North-Carolina, in the year 1807, dug up, on the plantation of Col. Joel Lewis, 2 miles from Nashville. the jaw bones of a man. which easily covered the whole chin and jaw of Col. Lewis, a man of large size. Some years afterwards, Mr. Cassady dug up a skeleton from under a small mound near the large one at Bledsoe's lick, in Sumner county, which measured little short of seven feet in length. Human bones have been dug up at the plantation where Judge Overton now lives, in Davidson county, four miles southwestwardly from Nashville, in making a cellar. These bones were of extraordinary size. The under jaw bone of one skeleton very easily slipped over the jaw of Mr. Childress, a stout man, full fleshed, very robust and considerably over the common size. These bones were dug up within the traces of ancient walls, in the form of a square of two or three hundred yards in length, situated near an excellent, never failing spring of pure and well tasted water. The spring was enclosed within the walls. A great number of skeletons was found within the enclosure, a few feet below the surface of the earth. On the outer side were the traces of an old ditch and rampart, thrown up on the inside. Some small mounds were also within the enclosure.

At the plantation of Mr. William Sheppard, in the county of Giles, seven and a half miles north of Pulaski, on the east side of the creek, is a cave, with several rooms. The first 15 feet wide, and 27 long; 4 feet deep; the upper part of solid and even rock. Into this cave was a passage, which had been so artfully covered, that it escaped detection till lately. A flat stone, three feet wide and four feet long, rested upon the ground, and inclining against the cave, closed part of the mouth. At the end of this, and on the side of the mouth left open, is another stone rolled, which filling this also, closed the whole mouth. When these rocks were removed, and the cave opened, on the inside of the cave were found several bones—the jaw bone of a child, the arm bone of a man, the sculls and thigh bones of men. The whole bottom of the cave was covered with flat stones of a bluish hue, being closely joined together, and of different forms and sizes. They formed the floor of the cave. Upon the floor the bones were laid. The hat of Mr. Egbert Sheppard, seven inches wide and eight inches long, but just covered and slipped over one of the sculls.

At the mouth of Obed's river, on the point between it and the Cumberland river, which is high ground, certain persons, in digging, struck, a little below the surface, four stones standing upright, and so placed in relation to each other, as to form a square or box, which enclosed a skeleton, placed on its feet in an erect posture. The scull was large enough to go over the head of a man of common size. The thigh bones applied to those of a man of ordinary stature, reached from the joint of his hip to the calf of his leg.

About ten miles from Sparta, in White county, a *conical* mound was lately opened, and in the centre of it was found a skeleton eight feet (*See DD.*) in length. With it was found a stone of the flint kind, very hard, with two flat sides, having in the centre circular hollows exactly accommodated to the balls of the thumb and fore finger. This stone was an inch and a half in diameter, the form exactly circular. It was about one third of an inch thick, and made smooth and flat, for rolling, like a grindstone, to the form of which, indeed, the whole stone was assimilated. When placed upon the floor, it would roll for a considerable time without falling. The whole surface was smooth and well polished, and must have been cut and made smooth by some hard metallic instrument. No doubt it was buried with the deceased, because for some reason he had set a great value on it in his life time, and had excelled in some accomplishment to which it related.

This skeleton belonged to a human body of the same race, education and notions with those who lived on the Volga, Tonais and Obey. The same unknown cause which, in the course of 2000 years, has reduced the size of the ancient Scythians and their tribes, the Gauls, and Germans, and Sarmatians, has produced the same effects here. The descendants of these giants, both in the old and new world, agree with each other in bulk, as their ancestors did with each other, which proves a uniform cause operating equally both in the old and new world. The decrease in bulk seems to have kept pace everywhere with the increase of warm temperature, and with the abbreviation of longevity. The giants of Hebron and Gath, and those of Laconia and Italy, whose large skeletons to this day attest that there they formerly dwelt, compared with those now found in West Tennessee, demonstrate that a change of climate, or of some other cause, has worked a remarkable change in the human system; and with respect to the mammoth, the megalonix, and other animals, has either extinguished or driven them into other and far distant latitudes.

Excerpt continued:

————

The Natural & Aboriginal History of Tennessee; Up To The First Settlements Therein By The White People, In The Year 1768

————

by John Haywood

————

Published: 1823

MANTI, UTAH

In Utah, near the town of Manti, in 1955, a man by the name of John Brewer discovered stone stairs carved on the floor of a cave. After gaining access and exploring further, Brewer discovered a chamber where he found large coffins which contained mummies of large stature. They had red and blond hair. Along with the giants, Brewer found arrowheads, jewelry, and pottery. He also found stone boxes holding metal plates, some made of gold; some of copper; all covered with bark and wood. The plates were inscribed with some indecipherable ancient text. John Brewer, accompanied by his son, found other caves with more artifacts, but no more mummies. He showed his finds to a friend, Dr. Robert Heinerman, who had a Ph.D. in anthropology. *Ancient Historical Research Foundation* carbon dates the boxes that Brewer discovered, from 5 B.C. to 390 B.C.

Secret Chambers in the Rockies
by Jared G. Barton
(From Ancient American Magazine; Volume 4, Issue #28)

Sometime after the turn of the last century, young George Keller and a lad named Lone Eagle were playing among the foothills of the Rocky Mountains above the farm owned by George's father near Manti, Utah. The Kellers were the descendants of freed black slaves, who migrated to the American southwest following the Civil War. Coming to a massive overhang, the Indian boy pointed to a hole in the mountain side and explained, "This is a special place, the Cave of the Great Spirit. My father says it is the holy place of a people who are dead, and that a great chief protects those who are buried there. My father was shown this place by his father when he was a kid. You are the only person other than our people who knows about this place. You must promise not to tell anyone of our secret! Follow me and I will show you inside."

The friends explored the site together, and from the cave floor, George picked up a few flint heads to play with in his room back home. Over the years, he kept his promise and never told anyone about the chamber guarded by the spirit of a great Indian chief. Lone Eagle eventually moved away; and George worked on the Keller farm. He lived in a hillside shed above the farm, not far from the cave of his boyhood experience, to the east. But he rarely visited the site again and took no further interest in it until he met John Brewer, many years later.

Brewer lived with his wife in the small town of Moroni, Utah, where he did odd jobs for farmers in the area. For recreation, he collected Indian arrowheads, and eventually assembled an impressive collection. In early spring, 1955, his numerous artifacts were displayed at the Sanpete County fair, held annually at Manti. While discussing his finds with friends at a local cafe, he was approached by a now elderly negro, George Keller, who told Brewer about a secret cave where many more arrowheads were to be found.

As Brewer recorded in his personal journal for May 10, "I went and looked for the place but I couldn't find it so I went and asked him (Keller) again where it was; but all that I could get was a laugh from him. I thought that he was pulling a fast one on me, so I let it go at that."

Nine days later, "I went out to the Keller place and offered him some wine with the promise that he would show me the place he had told me about a while back. He said that he would not only show me the place but that we would go in! No wonder I couldn't find it; I was on the wrong hill. I went into the cave and found 30 arrowheads right off. I went back to the truck and thanked the man. I then asked how he came to know of the cave and he said that he and an Indian boy played there as an old hideaway."

Nearly twenty years later, I was personally introduced to John Brewer, and he told me about his discovery of the Manti cave in an area behind Temple Hill. We met at Provo, Utah, in the company of Dr. Paul R. Cheesman, head of Book of Mormon Studies in the Department of Religion at Brigham Young University. Brewer impressed me as a soft-spoken, kindly man, but without much worldly experience. He told us about his encounter with old George Keller and the difficulties he experienced while locating the secluded cave. In his search for more arrowheads at the site, he was surprised to find a set of stone steps carved into the cave floor. Clearing away some debris, he claimed the steps led to an entrance of a "tomb."

Entering this chamber, he saw ten stone boxes. He opened five of them; they all contained small, metal plates inscribed with an unknown script. Nearby lay two large stone coffins. Opening them both, he found they contained mummified human remains. One body allegedly had red hair with skin still attached to its bones, while the other was blond. The mummies were excessively large; he guessed some nine feet in length. Brewer made a sketch of the tomb, in which he claimed to have carefully catalogued the position of each plate and box. In removing the coffin lids, he noticed that the mummies were covered with a straw "like cloth." He removed the straw only from the heads of the mummies to reveal their crown and breastplates. Shields and a sword were among other artifacts scattered about the tomb.

As proof, he showed us about sixty metal plates of various sizes and shapes. They all featured characters of a written language unknown to anyone present. At least a few of the plates, preserved by Brewer under a glass picture frame, appeared to be made of gold. Another set, possibly bronze, was encircled by a metal band some five inches square. They were bound by a small metal ring opposite the band.

The next month our meeting with Brewer took place in early March, so he agreed to take Dr. Cheesman and a team from Brigham Young University to the tomb in the near future, as soon as the snow melted. Later, Mr. Peterson said he thought Brewer "was telling the truth and most likely did not have the capacity to perpetuate such an elaborate hoax." Indeed, that was our general impression of the man, but we still wondered if Brewer would actually make good his offer to take Dr. Cheesman to the tomb. Spring and summer came and went in the Sanpete Valley, and Brewer made no effort to contact Dr. Cheesman.

But word of the inscribed tablets had already become controversial, as gossip about his mysterious discovery spread throughout Manti. Respected BYU professors Dr. Hugh Nibley and Dr. Ray Matheny met Elder Peterson, Dr. Cheesman and Brewer, who was unaware of the two scholars' high academic credentials. They were not favorably impressed with Brewer and condemned his "find" as a hoax. Following their unsupportive reaction, an article entitled "John Brewer has a cave but he's not giving tours," appeared in the November 26, 1975 issue of Salt Lake City's *Deseret News,* in which Dr. Jesse Jennings of the University of Utah's Archaeology Department was quoted as saying that the sandstone tablet obtained from Brewer was a "ridiculous hoax."

Jennings referred to Dr. Ray Matheny, who said he "wasted his time exposing the man's works...a clumsy attempt to perpetrate a fraudulent claim of antiquity." Only Dr. Cheesman had mixed feelings: "They could be real." But Dr. Robert Heinerman, a Ph.D. in Anthropology from the University of Indonesia, recalled that he had formerly lived in Manti around 1975, when he learned of the alleged artifacts. He visited Brewer at his home, in Moroni, and heard the story of finding the cave with its bizarre contents. Unlike the BYU professors, Heinerman was more favorably impressed, and the two became close friends.

Late one night, two years later, Brewer unexpectedly appeared at Heinerman's home, and suggested they go off on a midnight hike. They drove to a quarry behind Temple Hill, in Manti, then walked south from the quarry, up the hill to its top, finally across to the mountain in the east. Suddenly Brewer stopped and told John to take off his shirt and pants, so he could squeeze into a tunnel and see the chamber they had so often discussed. Dr. Heinerman did as suggested and followed John into a tunnel that had been dug on a downward track, barely squeezing and squirming like a worm through the narrow passage. After what seemed an eternity, struggling through some thirty feet of utter darkness, they came to an opening. Reaching down with his hands, Heinerman felt the edge of stairs. These led into a chamber about twenty feet long and fourteen feet wide. The air was stifling and breathing difficult.

Several inches of fine dust covered the floor and puffed up with each step. Perhaps three dozen stone boxes were stacked against one wall and another twenty or so on the other. All of them were "wrapped with a cover of Juniper bark with pine pitch smeared all around, so as to make them literally water proof." In a smaller anti-chamber were two entombed mummies. They seemed an incredible eight or nine feet in length. Each had been placed in a cement sepulcher with removable lid. They were a male-female pair. The texture of their skin was almost moist, like tanned leather. Littering the cave was an abundance of weapons, swords, tools, copper and metal tablets of various sizes. Some of the plates lay shattered like glass into fibrous pieces, not unlike the broken windshield of a car.

Brewer said the steps led into the chamber when he first discovered them. But the overhanging rock had since collapsed over the entrance, so he had to spend some two years digging a tunnel parallel to the stairs, in order to regain entrance into the chamber. This work was accomplished at night to conceal his activity. Heinerman visited the cave several times thereafter with Brewer, always under cover of darkness, save only on one daylight occasion. The chamber, he says, was very warm during this daytime entry. Its interior is cool in winter, suggesting that the cave is not deep under ground, with temperatures regulated by outside weather conditions. Heinerman says that a wall inside the chamber features an illustration showing the location of several other caves in the Manti valley. It was from this map that Brewer discovered another cache on the west side of the valley.

Brewer eventually showed Heinerman his discoveries in another related site on the western side of the Manti Valley. After an extremely arduous journey west of Wales, Heinerman stood before the entrance to a natural cave. It lies under an overhanging ledge with a small crawl space underneath. The cave comprised several tunnels and chambers. Here too they found stone boxes containing plates covered with strange writing, together with metal weapons and tools, but no mummies. A wall mural depicted a hunting scene. Some of the boxes featured Mayan-type glyphs or illustrations, and weighed from sixty to ninety pounds each. In Heinerman's words, "the cemented stone boxes were highly decorated with ingenious art work." With great effort, a few of these containers were brought off the mountain. Heinerman still has several in his possession. He also owns a large number of the metal plates.

So far, Brewer and Heinerman are the only persons who claim to have visited the cave sites. No photographs of their interiors, with their giant, fair-haired mummies and metal weapons or tools, have been released. Nor are the precise whereabouts of these sites known to any but the two visitors. Until such time as professional investigators are allowed inside his alleged chambers, the authenticity of Brewer's finds cannot be established. But mitigating against allegations of his involvement in a hoax are the items he presents on behalf of the cave's legitimacy. Their sheer number and level of craftsmanship (beyond the abilities of Mr. Brewer to duplicate) should at least give critics pause for reconsideration. The really troubling aspect of his claims is less his personal account and description than the supposed artifacts themselves. They appear to be exceptionally well made and very old, but belonging to no known culture, ancient or modern. If authentic, they were the possessions of a thoroughly enigmatic people of which modern archaeologists are absolutely unaware.

Perhaps most unsettling, some of the "script" more resembles modern computer schematics than any form of writing. Other red-haired mummies were said to have been found in the West, most notably at Nevada's Lovelock Cave. Some may see in these questionable finds and unaccountable material evidence for Lemurians in ancient America. They were supposed to have been natives of a long-vanished civilization that dominated the Pacific with an advanced technology, until their islands were eventually engulfed by the sea, and a few of their wealth-laden leaders fled to the American West. Whatever the real identity of the Manti items, condemning them out of hand risks losing what may be our continent's most valuable cultural heritage. If ever validated and deciphered, they could release a prehistoric legacy far more valuable than the gold plates on which it was written.

Some of the plates were said to be so fragile they would shatter like precious china upon a drop. It sounds difficult to me for man to create and engrave something so fragile with ancient-like writings on them. Ancient Historical Research Foundation carbon dated the boxes 10 times to ensure their accurate measure of 5-390 B.C.. A ring-like artifact found near the female mummy was authenticated to around 1200 B.C.

The male mummy was said to have red hair, a copper armor-like breastplate and a crown or helmet of the same material. The female, who was blonde, also wore a copper/brass bust and had a magnificent head piece that bore similarity to a 'tablita' which is a native Hopi term meaning crown. The steps on the tablita symbolize a cloud altar or a stairway to the sky. The mummies were said to be in great condition and resembled a fine leather, bearing very few signs of wear.

VIRGINIA

A human jaw bone of great size was uncovered in a burial mound in Virginia in 1845. The teeth were set at an angle in the jawbone.

INDIANAPOLIS JOURNAL
Indianapolis, Indiana
March 15, 1888

HE FOUND A POT OF GOLD.

Treasure Trove Unearthed by a Virginia Farmer in Place of Skeletons.

[Baltimore American.]
Lorenzo Mears recently exhumed a large and valuable treasure on an old farm in the southern part of Accomack County. Virginia. Mears is a tenant on the farm situated on Nandua Creek, belonging to the heirs of the late John

Pitts, of Baltimore. A tradition in the neighborhood says a large amount of money was concealed on the farm during the American Revolution by its Tory proprietor, who, having gone to England during the war, died there without fixing the spot where he had buried the money.

Not many years ago, some of the descendants of the old Tory proprietor came over here and spent several hundred dollars in making excavations in a fruitless search for the money. All the ground around the old house was thrown up; and deep trenches were dug around the yard, signs of which still remain. It is said that these Englishmen brought over with them an old negro man, who had been a servant of the old Revolutionary proprietor, and who professed to know where his master had buried the money. The Englishmen finally gave up the search and went back to England. Nothing more was ever heard of the treasure till a few days ago, when it leaked out that Lorenzo Mears had accidentally struck upon it while planting some fence posts around the yard.

It seems that Mears tried to keep the matter a secret, but a little boy who lives with him went to the neighboring village of Pungo League and let the secret out. He informed some persons there that his "Uncle Renzi" now had piles of money, having recently dug up an iron pot full of gold and silver which two stout men could hardly carry. Mears is said to be reticent on the matter. And, while admitting that he has found a buried treasure, says that the quantity is not so large as has been reported. He has shown several of the gold coins to some of his neighbors. These coins are reported to be old English money, some of them being stamped with the image of Charles II, others with that of George III.

The affair created considerable talk here, and the story is generally believed by those who have had the amplest opportunities for investigation and are best acquainted with the locality and its old traditions. The place where the treasure is reported to have been found is one of the oldest on the eastern shore of Virginia. Two hundred and fifty years ago it was the seat of the Queen of Nandua. an Indian beauty who ruled over the savage tribes inhabiting that region. Nearby is the burial ground of the Nandua Indians. The creek has cut away the earth till many of the skeletons are exposed to view; and as the bank caves from time to time, the bones fall down into the water and drift with the ebbing tide out into the bay. Some of the skeletons are of giant size, and many of them are buried in coffins that were hewn out of solid logs.

These whitening skeletons, as they protrude from the side of the cliff, present a grim and ghastly spectacle, and rarely can the belated negro be seen in that haunted region after the sun is gone down and the shades of night have fallen on the earth.

WASHINGTON, D.C.

The skeleton of a giant found in Washington D.C. was the subject of an article entitled, *"The Army Medical Museum in Washington"* by Louis Bagger, *Appleton's Journal: A Magazine Of General Literature; Volume 9, Issue 206;* 1873: "The objects here collected which have not been given, or acquired by exchange, have been purchased for the use of the museum by order of the Surgeon General. There is a skeleton of a giant, who, in life, measured seven feet, prepared by Auzoux and mounted by Blanchêne's method, which, if I may use that term, is really a beauty. It is as white and clean as new fallen snow, and the brass joints and screws which keep it together are bright, and of the latest style and finish."

BREWERSVILLE, WEST VIRGINIA

1882 West Virginia, Brewersville: The remains of a giant human in a sitting position with artifacts of stone and flint were discovered near White Day Creek.

KANAWHA COUNTY, WEST VIRGINIA

A skeleton 7 ft. 6 in. long, was found in a massive stone structure that was likened to a temple chamber, within a Mound in Kanawha County, West Virginia. According to the publication, *Report on Mound Explorations of the Bureau of Ethnology, 12th Annual Report,* Smithsonian Bureau of Ethnology, 1890-91, the bones were black with "carbonization, which is indicative of great age; the specimen was composed of a leg bone broken off 4 inches above the knee, the knee cap and joint, the lower leg bones, and the complete foot. Doctors examined the bones, which size from knee to heel measured 38.9 inches. In life, the owner would have stood over 11 feet tall." Local newspapers ran stories of this marvelous find. Two museums sent investigators to look for more of the skeleton, but nothing else of this giant specimen was found.

HISTORY

OF THE

GREAT KANAWHA VALLEY

VOL. I.

BRANT, FULLER & CO.,
1891.

Within the village of Brownstown, ten miles above Charleston, and just below the mouth of Lens Creek, is another ancient burying ground. None of these have been systematically examined, but casual excavations are constantly disclosing the remains of these ancient people and their implements. At Brownstown, not long since, two skeletons were found together, one a huge frame about seven feet in length and the other about four feet, a dwarf and deformed. None of these graves at Loup, Paint, or Lens Creeks are marked by mounds, stone slabs, stone piles or any other surface indications. The probability naturally suggests itself that those who are buried there, and who built these stone enclosures, were a different race from the mound builders.

RIVESVILLE, WEST VIRGINIA

1875 West Virginia, Rivesville: Workmen constructing a bridge near the mouth of Paw Paw Creek uncovered three giant skeletons with strands of reddish hair clinging to the skulls. The skeletons had supported people approximately 8 feet tall.

WHEELING, WEST VIRGINIA

1856 West Virginia, Wheeling: A human skeleton was discovered by laborers while ploughing a vineyard measuring almost 11 feet tall.

LA CRESCENT, MINNESOTA

The 1911 publication, *Aborigines of Minnesota,* contains a report that, in 1888 at LaCrescent, Minnesota, burial mounds were found which held giant bones. Five miles north of Dresbach, the bones of humans over 8 feet tall were found. A story in the 2006 book *"Weird Minnesota"* by Eric Dregni, refers to a 1998 book by Jay Rath, entitled, *The M-Files,* in which the following statements are found:

> "We learn of many excavations from *Aborigines Of Minnesota.* In La Crescent, on the Mississippi River, 52 mounds were excavated. "When opened, they have been found to contain human remains of men of large stature; and it is said that, in grading for the railroad, a copper skillet and other trinkets were found at 18 feet below the surface." So reads the geological report on Houston County, part of a survey conducted in 1884."

> At Dresbach, also on the Mississippi, around 1885, Indian mounds yielded 8-foot skeletons; similar skeletons had earlier been unearthed nearby. "Large human bones" were also excavated from the Lanesboro group of mounds in Fillmore County. There were 600 sets of skeletons, all of full-grown men, no women or children.

> At Moose Island Lakes, an 1861 survey noted the recovery of 7-foot skeletons from mounds. At Pine City, a "gigantic"

skeleton was exhumed. At Rainy River in 1896, a 9-foot skeleton was found.

"In 1884, 52 men of 'exceptionally large stature' were uncovered in La Crescent, having been buried 18 feet underground. Even more impressive are the 600 huge skeletons that were found in Lanesboro." Rath continues, "George E. Powell, writing in 1907, said that, 27 years earlier, he had heard oral histories representing a battle said to have occurred 200 years before then. The dead were supposedly strangers slain by the Ojibwe; the story comes from a 100-year old Ojibwe man."

Aborigines of Minnesota, 1911, provides more details:

"Legends from Minnesota's Ojibwe (or Chippewa) Indians take the giant story back even further. They knew of a gigantic creature they called a Windigo. The Rev. Peter Jones was a missionary traveling in 1831 through what later became Minnesota, and he knew firsthand of the Windigo. An Ojibwe himself, he had been taken from his tribe and taught by missionaries. But he never forgot his childhood, when he had often listened with wonder and deep attention to the stories related of Waindegoos (Windigos), or giants. They are represented as beings 'tall as pine trees.' In their travels, they pull down and turn aside immense forests, as a man would the high grass as he passes through. They are said to live on human flesh; whenever they meet an Indian, they are sure to have a good meal; being also invulnerable to the shot of the arrow or bullet, they are the constant dread of the Indians. Persons who have been known to eat human flesh from starvation are also called "Windigos, after the giants."

Indeed, "the Windigo are powerful giants," wrote Charles Brown, director of the State Historical Society of Wisconsin, who collected Ojibwe Windigo stories in 1927.

The 1913 *Winona County History* book stated, "Indian mounds and relics are found in various parts of our area. While men were digging in Miners Bluff (hill on the south end of Dakota), 150 feet above the river, a skeleton of an unusual size was unearthed. On measuring, the giant skeleton, it was found to be 10 feet in length, with all parts in proper proportion. A copper hatchet and an arrowhead nine inches long, were found in the skull. Another skeleton, nine feet long, was found in the village of Dresbach, while some men were digging a road or trench."

"These skeletons were of an unusual size to those generally taken from Indian mounds. Their size, form and structure would lead those versed in paleontology to believe they belonged to a race prior to the Indian."

The 1882 *History of Houston County* said, "At La Crescent, there is a chain of mounds which indicate the existence of a race with characteristics quite distinct from, and unlike the Indians. The conformation of the skulls which have been found reveals them as having more of an animal nature than their exterminators; one striking peculiarity being in the size of the jaws, the lower one especially. It is true it was a human jaw and not an animal's, because it had a chin, which no mere animal has..."

An account by Jim Doville of Trempeleau, Wis., in an early 1900s era *La Crosse Tribune* and *Leader Press* also talked about "Indians who were of an average height of eight feet." The article said, "It was just after Doville returned from the Civil War that the Milwaukee [railroad] tracks were laid. Doville took an active part in the work, at the direction of the civil engineers. While building the right-of-way near Richmond, Minn., halfway between points of bluffs known as King's and Queen's mountains, the workmen were amazed to discover the skeletons of men, which then, even in the state they were found, were taller than the tallest pioneer workman in the big crew."

"A St. Louis scientist got wind of the find and he hastened north, and joined the railroad men. He declared, after assembling the bones of many of the skeletons, which now rest in glass cases in a municipal museum in St. Louis, that their stature averaged eight feet. No relics were found with the bodies. They were buried very deep in the ground and in large numbers, and are still to be found today, according to Doville, at the foot of King's and Queen's mountains, now better known as 'bluffs'...."

Doville, thought to be the first white child born on the Mississippi River above Fort Crawford at Prairie du Chien, Wis., whose mother was Winnebago, also spoke of "the great battle which the Red Men believed was fought at the base of King's bluff." He asked the tribe lots of questions. They Native Americans told Doville, "The mound builders were but dim memories to us, the recollections of them kept alive only in occasional story." The mound builders had been done away with entirely by the smaller, but more intelligent Natives which followed him, the descendants of whom ... still live in this section."

Perhaps the 1913 *Winona County History* summed it up the best, "Where they came from, when they lived, and whence they have gone, is only conjecture and speculation. That they were mighty races, skilled in the mode of warfare, understanding the mechanical arts, for all these we have conclusive evidence. But of their end we know nothing. Whether they were swept from the earth by some deadly epidemic, or annihilated themselves by intestine wars, or died of inherent weakness, we have nothing to inform us."

CODY, WYOMING

In his 1920 book, *Autobiography of Buffalo Bill (Colonel W.F. Cody)*, by Buffalo Bill (William Frederick Cody), Buffalo Bill Cody spoke of giants:

> "While we were in the sandhills, scouting the Niobrara country, the Pawnee Indians brought into camp some very large bones, one of which the surgeon of the expedition pronounced to be the thigh bone of a human being. The Indians said the bones were those of a race of people who long ago had lived in that country. They said these people were three times the size of a man of the present day, that they were so swift and strong that they could run by the side of a buffalo, and, taking the animal in one arm, could tear off a leg and eat it as they ran. These giants, said the

Indians, denied the existence of a Great Spirit. When they heard the thunder or saw the lightning, they laughed and declared that they were greater than either. This so displeased the Great Spirit that he caused a deluge. The water rose higher and higher till it drove these proud giants from the low grounds to the hills and thence to the mountains. At last, even the mountaintops were submerged and the mammoth men were drowned. After the flood subsided, the Great Spirit came to the conclusion that he had made men too large and powerful. He therefore corrected his mistake by creating a race of the size and strength of the men of the present day. This is the reason, the Indians told us, that the man of modern times is small and not like the giants of old. The story has been handed down among the Pawnees for generations, but what is its origin no man can say.

THE DAILY GATE CITY
Keokuk, Iowa
May 16, 1910:

GIANT'S SKELETON FOUND OUT WEST

Bones Discovered by Bursting Water Pipe, Which Dug Hole in the Ground.

ENCAMPMENT, Wyo., May 16.—That Carbon County, Wyoming, was inhabited by a race of men, or at least one man in the prehistoric age, has been proved by the discovery of a human skeleton which indicates that the man in life was nine feet, three inches in height. The bones were disclosed by the bursting of a large water pipe on the Tennan Ranch. The escaping water washed out a great hole in the hillside. The bones were in a good state of preservation, being in a fossiliferous condition.

In addition to giants, there is a lot of evidence that the countless stories of chance encounters with Little People are not just fairy tales, or hallucinations brought on by too much alcohol. Reports from the "New World" contain ample details of encounters with "wee folk." Every culture has their own version of fairies or "little people." The first thing that pops into our mind when we hear of fairies or elves, is often the leprechauns and fairies of Celtic countries. The Little People known to inhabit the mythology and archaeological discoveries of North America, have their own distinct appearance and habits. The most common source for reports of diminutive beings originate in Native American cultures. Most (if not all) of the aboriginal peoples of the United States and Canada, have their own beliefs in fairies. They called them "Little People." North American Natives have believed in mystical wee folk since the beginning of time.

In the book, *The Lost History of the Little People: Their Spiritually Advanced Civilizations around the World* (2013) by Susan Martinez, there is a reference to earlier author, Loren Eiseley, who also wrote about Little People. In *The Immense Journey,* 1957, there is an account of a two-foot-long cave mummy. Loren Eiseley, while at a bone hunters' camp on the western Plains of America, was approached by a rancher who attempted to sell him a two-foot-long cave mummy. "Two hundred bucks," declared the seller....

Eiseley may have passed up a rare hobbit, from the descriptions that appear elsewhere in his 1957 book, *The Immense Journey,* 1957:

> "A small people, like eight-year-olds," recall some of the Plains Indian Elders, once lived in the rocks near the Yellowstone. And as the Crow Indians recollect, Chief Red Plume, on a vision quest, won new mentors— three small men and women. These wee people, according to the Crow, created many of the paintings and rock carvings, and had a strong role in our tribal taboos and religion. It was at that mysterious monument, Crow Medicine Wheel, that Red Plume had his vision and where our forefathers claim the little people lived…it was a sacred place."

> Speaking of forefathers, when President Jefferson sent Lewis and Clark out West on their acclaimed Corps of Discovery, they camped one night at a hill near the Teton. The 'hill' was actually a mound, man-made. The intrepid explorers there learned that the Dakota Indians called the place *Mountain-of-the-Little-People* or *Spirit Mound.* Forty years later, when the Irish began migrating to America during the potato famines and beheld our 'Indian mounds' scattered across the land, they were certain these formations were the work of the little people, the Daoine Shia.

These poor Irish laborers had actually traced the origin of the American Mound builders more accurately than formidable intellects of the time like Prof. Schoolcraft who denied the "lost race" theory, insisting instead that the mounds had been built by the Red Indians. Yet the Indians themselves had no idea who the first mound builders were, although legend held that they were spirit people who lived in the Long Ago.

The region in which I live, here at the foothills of the Smoky Mountains – old Cherokee country – is rich in Little People lore and artifacts. When the Cherokee first migrated into Tennessee and North Carolina, they came upon some white people, similar perhaps to the "albinos" ensconced in the Kentucky hills or the "Jackson Whites" of old New Jersey. Moreover, there were mounds there, built–say the Cherokee–by a race of "moon-eyed" people (they had "bulging" eyes), much smaller than the Cherokee, with white skin and blue eyes....And the I'hins covered the earth over with mounds of wood and earth… hundreds and thousands of cities and mounds they built. In aftertime, the Cherokee held their most important and sacred councils upon the "Indian mound" in Nikwasi, today's Franklin, North Carolina.

The Little People who had built the Nikwasi mound were something like fairy folk and were called *Nunnehi* (The Immortals). There were also the *Yunwi Tsusdi* ("Little People") who were friendly to the Cherokee but avoided being followed; for these handsome, long-haired folk kept their houses and towns secret. But even the best-kept secrets of the Long Ago People were destined for the light of day, in this bright new Era of Rediscovery. And lo, Tennessee newspapers, in the 19th century, began reporting the discovery of burial grounds in Sparta, Smith, and White counties: "Very little people were deposited in tombs of stone; their bones were strong and well set, and the whole frames were well formed." Fine engravings of figures were also found in several of these sacramental burials. Bewildered by the Tennessee evidence, writers began to speculate about the origins of these unaccountable "little men," wondering if they were "beings from other worlds." Indeed, Dr. Newbrough found that "the North American Indians still have a legend of the mound builders, that they were people who came from another world to teach them of the Great Spirit, and of the Summer Land in the sky."

Historians, though, would not even consider that these strange burial specimens had anything to do with the "mysterious Mound builders." But then, more discoveries were made of "diminutive sarcophagi" in West Virginia, Ohio and Kentucky. The city of Lexington, Kentucky, averred historian George W. Ranck, is built on the "metropolis of a lost race [who] flourished centuries before the Indian." Was their remnant the "albinos" hiding in the Kentucky hills? And what about Mexico's Temple of Dwarves or Monte Alban (Mound of the Albinos) with its acclaimed "pygmy" tunnels and inscriptions left (as Edgar L. Larken, past director of Mt. Lowe Observatory, believed) by the "survivors of Pan?

Pan, an ancient name of the lost continent in the Pacific, is yet retained in Japan, where Shinto priests are familiar with the old name "I'hin," referring to the white-skinned Ainu people of northern Japan.

Another excerpt from Loren Eiseley's 1959 book, *The Immense Journey* is below:

LITTLE MEN AND FLYING SAUCERS
by Loren Eiseley

Today, as never before, the sky is menacing. Things seen indifferently last century by the wandering lamplighter now trouble a generation that has grown up to the wail of air raid sirens and the ominous expectation that the roof may fall at any moment. Even in daytime, reflected light on a floating dandelion seed, or a spider riding a wisp of gossamer in the sun's eye, can bring excited questions from the novice unused to estimating the distance or nature of aerial objects.

Since we now talk, write, and dream endlessly of space rockets, it is no surprise that this thinking yields the obverse of the coin: that the rocket or its equivalent may have come first to us from somewhere "outside." As a youth, I may as well confess, I waited expectantly for it to happen. So deep is the conviction that there must be life out there beyond the dark, one thinks that if they are more advanced than ourselves they may come across space at any moment, perhaps in our generation. Later, contemplating the infinity of time, one wonders if perchance their messages came long ago, hurtling into the swamp muck of the steaming coal forests, the bright projectile clambered over by hissing reptiles, and the delicate instruments running mindlessly down with no report.

Sometimes when young, and fossil hunting in the western Badlands, I had thought it might yet be found, corroding and long dead, in the tertiary sod that was once green under the rumbling feet of Titan heroes Surely, in the infinite wastes of time, in the lapse of suns and wane of systems, the passage, if it were possible, would have been achieved. But the bright projectile has not been found and now, in sobering middle age, I have long since ceased to look. Moreover, the present theory of the expanding universe has made time, as we know it, no longer infinite. If the entire universe was created in a single explosive instant a few billion years ago, there has not been a sufficient period for all things to occur even behind the star shoals of the outer galaxies. In the light of this fact it is now just conceivable that there may be nowhere in space a mind superior to our own.

If such a mind should exist, there are many reasons why it could not reside in the person of a little man. There is, however, a terrible human fascination about the miniature, and one little man in the hands of the spinner of folk tales can multiply with incredible rapidity. Our unexplainable passion for the small is not quenched at the borders of space, nor, as we shall see, in the spinning rings of the atom. The flying saucer and the much publicized little men from space equate neatly with our own projected dreams.

When I first heard of the little man there was no talk of flying saucers, nor did his owner ascribe to him anything more than an earthly origin. It has been almost a quarter of a century since I encountered him in a bone hunter's camp in the West. A rancher had brought him to us in a box. "I figured you'd maybe know about him," he said. "He'll cost you money, though. There's money in that little man."

"Man ?" we said.

"Man," he countered. "What you'd call a pygmy or a dwarf, but smaller than any show dwarf I ever did see. A mummy, too, a little dead mummy. I figure it was some kind of bein' like us, but little. They put him in the place I found him; maybe it was a thousand years ago. You'll likely know."

Our heads met over the box. The last paper was withdrawn. The creature emerged on the man's palm. I've seen a lot of odd things in the years since, and fakes by the score, but that little fellow gave me the creeps. He might have been two feet high in a standing posture, not more. He was mummified in a crouching position, arms folded. The face with closed eyes seemed vaguely evil. I could have sworn I was dreaming.

I touched it. There was a peculiar, fleshy consistency about it, still. It was not a dry mummy. It was more like what you would expect a natural cave mummy to be like. It had no tail. I know because I looked. And to this day the little man sits on there, in my brain, and as plain as yesterday I can see the faint half-smirk of his mouth and the tiny black hands at his knees.

"You can have it for two hundred bucks," said the man. We glanced at each other, sighed, and shook our heads. "We aren't in the market," we said. "We're collecting, not buying, and we're staying with our bones."

"Okay," said the man, and gave us a straight look, closing his box. "I'm going to the carnival down below tonight. There's money in him. There's money in that little man."

I think it may have been just as well for us that we made no purchase. I have never liked the little man, nor the description of the carnival to which he and his owner were going. It may be, I used to think, that I will yet encounter him before I die, in some little colored tent on a country midway. Once, in the years since, I have heard a description that sounded like him in another guise. It involved a fantastic tale of some Paleozoic beings who hunted among the tree ferns when the world was ruled by croaking amphibians. The story did not impress me; I knew him by then for what he was: an anomalous mummified stillbirth with an undeveloped brain.

I never expected to see him emerge again in books on flying saucers, or to see the "little men" multiply and become so common that columnists would take note of them. Nor, though I should have known better, did I expect to live to hear my little man ascribed an extraplanetary origin.

Lights come and go in the night sky. Men, troubled at last by the things they build, may toss in their sleep and dream bad dreams, or lie awake while the meteors whisper greenly overhead. But nowhere in all space or on a thousand worlds will there be men to share our loneliness. There may be wisdom; there may be power; somewhere across space great instruments, handled by strange, manipulative organs, may stare vainly at our floating cloud wrack, their owners yearning as we yearn. Nevertheless, in the nature of life and in the principles of evolution we have had our answer. Of men elsewhere, and beyond, there will be none forever.

The Elusive Little People

By PETER NETZEL

As I was working on the book *The Lost Treasures Of Montana: Custer Country,* I came across a very interesting story of Chief Plenty Coups, leader of the Crow Nation. In a detailed narrative, the old chief describes his personal experiences with the Little People of the Pryor Mountains and the profound effect they had on him and later, the lives of the Crow people.

To this day, the Crow believe in Little People whom they call the Nirumbee in their language. These dwarf size semi-human/semi-spirit beings inhabited the Pryor Mountains of Montana. It is said by some members of the Crow even to this day, that, if they pass through the Pryor Gap they leave offerings to the Little People in remembrance of their aid to the Crow nation.

As I read more and more about Native American culture, I realized that many tribes have stories of little people and giants as well. This led me to look further into the subject of Giants and Little People. Hence, this book was born.

The following is the section from my book that led me to write this book on Giants and Little People. The tale of the Little People of the Pryors which follows, is taken from my book, "The Lost Treasures Of Montana: Custer Country:"

The Native peoples of North America tell legends of a race of "little people" who lived in the woods, in the mountains, near sandy hills, and sometimes near rocks located along water, such as the Great Lakes. Often described as "hairy-faced dwarfs" in stories, petroglyph illustrations show some of the Little People with horns on their head and traveling in a group of 5 to 7 per canoe. Crow Chief, Plenty Coups, left behind an extensive chronicle of his interactions with the Little People of the

Pryors, in Montana and Wyoming. The Crow Chief's verbal account was written down by an interviewer in 1930. This fascinating account is quite believable. The excerpt from *The Lost Treasures of Montana: CUSTER COUNTRY,* by Peter Netzel, contains Chief Plenty Coups experiences with the Little People of the Pryors:

LITTLE PEOPLE OF THE PRYORS

There is an intriguing legend about the Little People of the Pryor Mountains which has been passed down in the folklore of the Crow Nation. The Little People were important to Chief Plenty Coups, giving him guidance through vision quests and dreams. Known as *Nirumbee* or *Awwakkulé* in the Crow language, the Little People are a race of warrior dwarves spoke of in the Crow Nation's traditions. The Little People were a group of tiny dwarf wise men who imparted spiritual wisdom.

Other Native American tribes in the West also have similar stories and beliefs about Little People. And, Lewis and Clark wrote of the Little People. While staying with the Wičhíyena Sioux on the Vermillion River in what is now South Dakota, Meriwether Lewis, William Clark, and 10 other men traveled to see the "Mountain of the Little People," about 9 miles north of the Vermilion River's junction with the Missouri River. Captains Lewis and Clark, and some of the men wrote of the Little People in their journal entries.

Excerpts from Captain Clark describe a two-day trip to Spirit Mound, where the Little People lived:

August 24, 1804

[Clark] 24th August Friday 1804....Capt. Lewis and myself concluded to visit a high hill situated in an immense plain three leagues N. 20° W. from the mouth of White Stone River; this hill appears to be of a conic form. And by all the different nations in this quarter is supposed to be a place of deavels [devils] or that they are in human form with remarkable large heads and about 18 inches high; that they remarkably are very watchful and are armed with sharp arrows with which they can kill at a great distance; they are said to kill all persons who are so hardy as to attempt to approach the hill; they have stated that tradition informs them that many Indians have suffered by these little people; and among others, that three Maha [Omaha] men fell a sacrifice to their merciless fury not many years since— so much do the Mahas, Sioux, Ottoes [Otoe], and other neighboring nations believe this fable, that no consideration is sufficient to induce them to approach this hill.

August 25, 1804

[Clark] Aug. 25th Saturday 1804....This morning Capt. Lewis & myself, Drouillard, Ordway, John Shields, Joseph Field, John Colter, Bratton, Cann, Labiche, Rich-ard Warfington, Robert Frazer, and York set out to visit this mountain of evil spirits....Capt. Lewis & myself concluded to go and see the mound which was viewed with such terror by all the different Nations in this quarter; we....dropped down to the mouth of White Stone River where we left the perogue with two men; and at 200 yards, we ascended a rising ground of about sixty feet, from the top of this highland; the country is level and open as far as can be seen, except some few rises at a great distance, and the mound which the Indians call Mountain of Little People or Spirits....this mound appears of a conic form and is N. 20° W. from the mouth of the Creek....This Mound is situated on an elevated plain in a level and extensive prairie, bearing N. 20° W. from the mouth of White Stone Creek nine miles; the base of the Mound is a regular parallelogram, the long side of which is about 300 yards in length, the shorter is 60 or 70 yards—from the longer side of the base, it rises from the North & South with a steep ascent to the height of 65 or 70 feet, leaving a level plain on the top it of 12 feet in width & 90 in length....the North & South part of this mound is joined by two regular rises, each in oval forms of half its height forming three regular rises from the plain....the ascent of each elevated part is as sudden as the principal mound at the narrower sides of its base—The regular form of this hill would in some measure justify a belief that it owed its origin to the hand of man; but as the earth and loose pebbles and other substances of which it was composed, bear an exact resemblance to the steep ground which borders on the creek in its neighborhood. We concluded it was most probably the production of nature. The only remarkable characteristic of this hill, admitting it to be a natural production, is that it is insulated or separated a considerable distance from any other, which is very unusual in the natural order or disposition of the hills....One evidence which the Indians give for believing this place to be the residence of some unusual Spirits is that they frequently discover a large assemblage of birds about this mound—is in my opinion a sufficient proof to produce in the savage mind a confident belief of all the properties which they ascribe it....from the top of this Mound we beheld a most beautiful land-scape....the plain to North N.W. & N.E. extends without interruption as far as can be seen....

The Sioux, who inhabited the region around the Spirit Mound of the Little People, described them as devils who are very alert to intrusions into their territory, that they carried sharp arrows which could strike at a great distance, and that they killed anyone who approached their mound. The Sioux have a traditional story which tells how a band of 350 warriors came near the mound late at night and were nearly wiped out by the ferocious Little People (the survivors were crippled for life).

Though most tribes feared the Little People, the Crow (or Absaroka) saw them as protectors and wise guides, powerful medicine. It is said that the Little People were protectors of the Crow people for untold years. Stories of these powerful dwarfs have been passed on from generation to generation.

1815 photo of Spirit Mound, eight miles north of Vermilion. This was reportedly home of the Little People. It is now within Spirit Mound Historic Prairie site in South Dakota.

The Crows were originally part of the Hidatsa Sioux people, who lived along the Missouri River in what is now western North Dakota and into the Yellowstone River Valley of south-central Montana. The Crow tribe lived on the plains and along the rivers and in the Big Horn, Pryor, and Wolf Mountains. Due to migrating eastern and midwestern Native American tribes moving Westward because of white encroachment, the Crows settled in the Yellowstone Valley.

Crow folklore says the "Little People" live in the Pryor Mountains, located in Carbon County, and Bighorn County, Montana. The mountains are sacred to the Crow. They say that petroglyphs on rocks in these mountains were made by the Little People, who are described as being about 18 inches tall (knee high). Crow folklore describes the Little People of the Pryor Mountains as having large, round bellies and little to no neck; and they are incredibly strong in spite of their very short arms and legs.

There is a Crow expression, "strong as a dwarf" which is a reference to the incredible strength of these Little People. The Crows tell of a Little Person who killed a full-grown bull elk, and tossing just the elk's head over his shoulder, he dragged it off effortlessly. Incredibly fierce warriors who fed primarily on meat, the Little People are said to have many sharp teeth in their mouths. Tribes tell stories of the Little People protecting the Crow against enemies. The dwarfs would lay in ambush for war parties, jumping out and tearing the hearts out of the enemies' horses.

The Little People (sometimes referred to as "spirit dwarves") were said to be able to bestow spiritual insight (maxpe) to certain individuals. Because of their fear and reverence of the Little People, the Crow would not enter the Pryor Mountains. The only exceptions were when, once in a while, a lone Crow would travel to the Medicine Rocks and fast and await a vision or dream conveying guidance or knowledge. Some of these seekers returned with reports of a Little Person appearing, sometimes as a being and sometimes as an animal, to give insights to the seeker.

The Crow tell of two ways to pass through the mountains without being harmed by the Little People. According to their folklore, the Little People had befriended a young Crow boy, who reported to the tribes that there was a pass through the mountains which the Crow could use.

This pass is now called Pryor Gap. The Crow name for Pryor Creek was "Arrow Creek," and the Pryor Mountains were known to them as the Baahpuuo or "Arrowhead Mountains." Arrow referring to the those of the Little People that were incredibly powerful and traveled long distances.

The famous chief of the Crows, Plenty Coups was greatly influenced by the Little People. Following are excerpts from the great chief telling of his experiences with these dwarflike creatures:

"PLENTY COUPS CHIEF OF THE CROWS"
as told to Frank B. Linderman
by Chief Plenty Coups, 1930

II

"I was nine years old, a happening made me feel that I was a grown-up man, almost in a day," he said. "I had a brother. I shall not speak his name, but if there were four brave, handsome young men in our tribe my brother was one of them. I loved him dearly, and he was always an inspiration to me." The names of the dead are seldom spoken by the Crows. "They have gone to their Father, Ah-badt-dadt-deah, and like him are sacred." This custom makes the gathering of tribal history extremely difficult. For a time Plenty-Coups would not violate this tribal custom which was threatening my success in getting his story. But finally, as his interest in his tale grew, he realized it was necessary, and graciously, and I believe a little fearfully, he named many men and women who had passed away.

One morning when our village was going to move, he went on the war-trail against our enemy, the Lakota [Sioux]. All that day he was in my thoughts. Even when we crossed Elk River, where usually there was satisfying excitement, I kept thinking of my brother. Rafts had to be made for the old people and children, and these, drawn by four men on good horses, had ever given me plenty to think about. But this day nothing interested me. That night I could not sleep, even when all but the wolves were sleeping.

When the village was set up on the Big River [Missouri], news reached us that my brother was gone, killed by Sioux on Powder River.

My heart fell to the ground and stayed there. I mourned with my father and mother, and alone. I cut my flesh and bled myself weak. I knew now that I must dream if I hoped to avenge my brother, and I at once began to fast in preparation, first taking a sweat-bath to cleanse my body.

Nobody saw me leave the village. I slipped away and climbed The-Buffalo's Heart, where I fasted two more days and nights, without success. I saw nothing at all and gave up to travel back to my father's lodge, where I rested.

The fourth night, while I was asleep, a voice said to me, *'You did not go to the right mountain, Plenty-Coups.'* I knew then that I should some-time succeed in dreaming.

The village was preparing to move to the Little Rockies, a good place for me; and before the women began to take down the lodges, I started out alone. Besides extra moccasins, I had a good buffalo robe; and as soon as I reached the mountains I covered a sweat-lodge with the robe and again cleansed my body. I was near the Two Buttes and chose the south one, which I climbed, and there I made a bed of sweet-sage and ground-cedar. I was determined that no smell of man should be on me and burned some e-say [a root that grows in the mountains] and sweet-sage, standing in their smoke and rubbing my body with the sage.

The day was hot; and naked I began walking about the top of the mountain crying for Helpers, but got no answer, no offer of assistance. I grew more tired as the sun began to go toward the west, and finally I went to my bed, lying down so my feet would face the rising sun when he came again. Weakened by my walking and the days of fasting, I slept, remembering only the last rays of the sun as he went to his lodge. When I wakened, looking into the sky, I saw that the Seven Stars [the Big Dipper] had turned round. The-Star-That-Does-Not-Move [North Star], this night was westward. Morning was not far away, and wolves were howling on the plains far below me. I wondered if the village would reach the Little Rockies before night came again. *'Plenty-Coups.'*

My name was spoken! The voice came from behind me, back of my head. My heart leaped like a deer struck by an arrow. 'Yes,' I answered, without moving. *'They want you, Plenty-Coups. I have been sent to fetch you,'* said the voice yet behind me, back of my head. 'I am ready,' I answered, and stood up, my head clear and light as air.

The night had grown darker, and I felt rather than saw some Person go by me on my right side. I could not tell what Person it was, but thought he beckoned me. 'I am coming,' I said, but the Person made no answer and slipped away in a queer light that told me where he was. I followed over the same places I had traveled in the afternoon, not once feeling my feet touch a stone. They touched nothing at all where the way was rough, and without moccasins I walked in the Person's tracks as though the mountain were as smooth as the plains. My body was naked, and the winds cool and very pleasant, but I looked to see which way I was traveling. The stars told me that I was going east, and I could see that I was following the Person downhill. I could not actually see him, but I knew I was on his trail by the queer light ahead. His feet stirred no stone, nothing on the way, made no sound of walking, nor did mine.

A coyote yelped on my right, and then another answered on my left. A little farther on I heard many coyotes yelping in a circle around us; and as we traveled they moved their circle along with us, as though they were all going to the same place as we. When the coyotes ahead stopped on a flat and sat down to yelp together, the ones behind closed in to make their circle smaller, all yelping loudly, as though they wished to tell the Person something. I knew now that our destination was not far off. The Person stopped, and I saw a lodge by his side. It seemed to rise up out of the ground. I saw that he came to it at its back, that it faced east, and that the Person reached its door by going around it to the right. But I did not know him, even when he coughed to let someone inside the lodge know he was there. He spoke no word to me but lifted the lodge door and stepped inside. *'Come, Plenty-Coups,'* he said gently. And I too stepped into the lodge.

There was no fire burning, and yet there was light in the lodge. I saw that it was filled with Persons I did not know. There were four rows of them in half-circles, two rows on each side of the center, and each Person was an old warrior. I could tell this by their faces and bearing. They had been counting coup. I knew this because before each, sticking in the ground, was a white coup-stick bearing the breath-feathers of a war-eagle. Some, however, used no stick at all, but only heavy first-feathers whose quills were strong enough to stick in the ground. These first-feathers were very fine, the handsomest I had ever seen, and I could not count them, they were so many. *'Why have you brought this young man into our lodge? We do not want him. He is not our kind and therefore has no place among us.'* The words came from the south side, and my heart began to fall down. I looked to see what Persons sat on the south side, and my eyes made me afraid. They were the Winds, the Bad Storms, the Thunders, the Moons and many

Stars, all powerful, and each of them braver and much stronger than men. (I believe the Persons on the south side of the lodge, the Winds, Bad Storms, the Moon, and many Stars, were recognized by Plenty-Coups as the great forces of nature, and that this is what he wished to convey to me.) *'Come, Plenty-Coups, and sit with us.'* This voice was kind. It came from the north side. *'Sit,'* said the Person who had brought me there, and then he was gone. I saw him no more.

They, on the north side of the lodge, made a place for me. It was third from the head on the left, and I sat down there. The two parties of Persons were separated at the door, which faced the east, and again in the west, which was the head of the lodge, so that the Spirit-trail from east to west was open, if any wished to travel that way. On neither side were the Persons the same as I. All were different, but I knew now that they had rights in the world, as I had, that Ah-badt-dadt-deah had created them, as he had me and other men. Nobody there told me this, but I felt it in the lodge as I felt the presence of the Persons. I knew that to live on the world I must concede that those Persons across the lodge who had not wished me to sit with them had work to do, and that I could not prevent them from doing it. I felt a little afraid but was glad I was there. *'Take these, Plenty-Coups,'* The Person at the head of the lodge on the north side handed me several beautiful first-feathers of a war-eagle. I looked into his eyes. He was a Dwarf-Person, Chief of the Little-People who live in the Medicine-Rock, which you can almost see from here, and who made the stone arrow points. I now saw that all on my side were the same as he, that all wore Dwarfs not tall as my knee. (The Dwarfs or Little-People are legendary beings, supposed to possess great physical strength. In the story of "Lost Boy" a Crow saw one of the Dwarfs shoulder a full-grown bull elk and walk with it on his shoulder. They dwell in Medicine-Rock, near Pryor, Montana. The Little-People made the stone arrow heads, the Crows believe. All the Indian tribes of the Northwestern plains, with whom I am acquainted, possess legends that deal with the makers of the stone arrow points which are scattered so plentifully over North America. These legends, together with the knowledge that identical stone arrow points are found in Europe, led me, long ago, to the belief that our plains Indians neither made nor used them that some other people made them. Careful inquiry among very old Indians, beginning in 1886, has not discovered a single tribesman who had ever heard of his own people making stone arrow points. These old men have told me that before the white man came their arrow points were of bone.) *'Stick one of your feathers in the ground before you and count coup," said the Dwarf-Chief.'*

I hesitated. I had never yet counted coup, and here in this lodge with old warriors was no place to lie. *'Count coup!'* commanded the Dwarf-Chief. I stuck a first-feather into the ground before me, fearing a dispute. *'That,'* said the Dwarf-Chief, *'is the rider of the white horse! I first struck him with my coup-stick, and then, while he was*

unharmed and fighting, I took his bow from him.'
The Thunders, who sat at the head of the lodge on
the south side, said, *'Nothing can be better than
that.' 'Stick another feather before you, Plenty-
Coups.'* said the Dwarf-Chief. I stuck another
first-feather in the ground, wondering what the
Dwarf-Chief would say for it. But this time I was
not afraid. *'That,'* he said, *'is the rider of the
black horse. I first struck him with my bow. Then,
while he was armed with a knife and fighting me,
I took his bow from him, also his shield.'*
'Enough!' said the Persons on the south side. *'No
Person can do better than that. Let us leave off
counting coups.' 'We are glad you have admitted
this young man to our lodge,'* said the Bad Storms,
'and we think you should give him something to
take back with him, some strong medicine that
will help him.' Plenty-Coups had been speaking
rapidly, his hands following his spoken words
with signs, acting parts, while his facial
expressions gave tremendous emphasis to his
story. He was perspiring and stopped to brush his
face with his hand.

"I had not spoken," he went on, "and could not
understand why the Dwarf-Chief had ordered me
to stick the feathers, nor why he had counted coups
in my name before such powerful Persons." *'He
will be a Chief.'* said the Dwarf-Chief. *'I can give
him nothing. He already possesses the power to
become great if he will use it. Let him cultivate his
senses, let him use the powers which Ah-badt-
dadt-deah has given him, and he will go far. The
difference between men grows out of the use, or*

non-use, of what was given them by Ah-badt-dadt-deah in the first place.' Then he said to me, *'Plenty Coups, we, the Dwarfs, the Little-People, have adopted you and will be your Helpers throughout your life on this world. We have no medicine-bundle to give you. They are cumbersome things at best and are often in a warrior's way. Instead, we will offer you advice. Listen! In you, as in all men, are natural powers. You have a will. Learn to use it. Make it work for you. Sharpen your senses as you sharpen your knife. Remember the wolf smells better than you do because he has learned to depend on his nose. It tells him every secret the winds carry because he uses it all the time, makes it work for him. We can give you nothing. You already possess everything necessary to become great. Use your powers. Make them work for you, and you will become a Chief.'*

A medicine-bundle contains the medicine or talisman of its possessor. Often the skin and stuffed head of an animal as large as a wolf is used. Sometimes, however, the bundles are small, containing the skin, claws, teeth, or heads of lesser creatures, depending wholly upon what animal or bird offered "help" to the dreamer. The medicine-bundle is of first importance, the possessor believing implicitly that the superlative power of the animal or bird that offered aid in his dream is always at hand and at his service when he is in need. The contents of these bundles are secret and sacred to the Indian.

When I wakened, I was perspiring. Looking into the early morning sky that was growing light in the north, I went over it all in my mind. I saw and understood that whatever I accomplished must be by my own efforts, that I must myself do the things I wished to do. And I knew I could accomplish them if I used the powers that Ah-badt-dadt-deah had given me. I had a will and I would use it, make it work for me, as the Dwarf-Chief had advised. I became very happy, lying there looking up into the sky. My heart began to sing like a bird, and I went back to the village, needing no man to tell me the meaning of my dream. I took a sweat-bath and rested in my father's lodge. I knew myself now. Here, the old Chief, as though struck with remorse, turned his head aside and whispered, "O Little-People, you who have been my good Helpers through a long life, forgive me if I have done wrong in telling this to Sign-Talker. I believed I was doing right. Be kind. I shall see you very soon and explain all."

He appeared shaken, and I wondered if he would go on. Coyote-Runs and Plain-Bull felt as much relieved as I did when the old man said, "I was nine years old and undeveloped, but I realized the constant danger my people were in from enemies on every side. Our country is the most beautiful of all. Its rivers and plains, its mountains and timber lands, where there was always plenty of meat and berries, attracted other tribes, and they wished to possess it for their own. To keep peace, our chiefs sent out clans to the north, east, south, and west. They were to tell any who wished to come into our country that they were welcome. They were told to say, 'You may hunt and may gather berries and plums in our country, but when you have all you can carry you must go back to your own lands. If you do this all will be well. But if you remain overlong, we will warn you to depart. If you are foolish and do not listen, your horses will be stolen; and if even this does not start you homeward, we will attack you and drive you out.'" The country belonging to the Crows was not only beautiful, but it was the very heart of the buffalo range of the Northwest. It embraced endless plains, high mountains, and great rivers, fed by streams clear as crystal. No other section could compare with the Crow country, especially when it was untouched by white men. Its wealth in all kinds of game, grass, roots, and berries made enemies for the Crows, who, often outnumbered, were obliged continually to defend it against surrounding tribes.

I decided to go afoot to the Crazy Mountains, two long day's journey from the village. The traveling without food or drink was good for me, and as soon as I reached the Crazies I took a sweat-bath and climbed the highest peak. There is a lake at its base, and the winds are always stirring about it. But even though I fasted two more days and nights, walking over the mountain top, no Person came to me, nothing was offered. I saw several grizzly bears that were nearly white in the moonlight, and one of them came very near to me, but he did not speak. Even when I slept on that peak in the Crazies, no bird or animal or Person spoke a word to me, and I grew discouraged. I could not dream. Back in the village I told my closest friends about the high peaks I had seen, about the white grizzly bears, and the lake. They were interested and said they would go back with me and that we would all try to dream. There were three besides myself who set out, with extra moccasins and a robe to cover our sweat-lodge. We camped on good water just below the peak where I had tried to dream, quickly took our sweat-baths, and started up the mountains. It was already dark when we separated, but I found no difficulty in reaching my old bed on the tall peak that looked down on the little lake, or in making a new bed with ground-cedar and sweet-sage. Owls were hooting under the stars while I rubbed my body with the sweet-smelling herbs before starting out to walk myself weak. When I could scarcely stand, I made my way back to my bed and slept with my feet toward the east. But no Person came to me, nothing was offered; and when the day came I got up to walk again over the mountain top, calling for Helpers as I had done the night before. All day the sun was hot, and my tongue was swollen for want of water; but I saw nothing, heard nothing, even when night came again to cool the mountain. No sound had reached my ears, except my own voice and the howling of wolves down on the plains. I knew that our great Crow warriors of other days sacrificed their flesh and blood to dream, and just when the night was leaving to let the morning come I stopped at a fallen tree, and, laying the first finger of my left hand upon the log, I cut part of it off with my knife. [The end of the left index finger on the Chief's hand is missing] But no blood came. The stump of my finger was white as the finger of a dead man, and to make it bleed I struck it against the log until blood flowed freely.

Then I began to walk and call for Helpers, hoping that some Person would smell my blood and come to aid me. Near the middle of that day my head grew dizzy, and I sat down. I had eaten nothing, taken no water, for nearly four days and nights, and my mind must have left me while I sat there under the hot sun on the mountain top. It must have traveled far away, because the sun was nearly down when it returned and found me lying on my face. As soon as it came back to me I sat up and looked about, at first not knowing where I was. Four war-eagles were sitting in a row along a trail of my blood just above me. But they did not speak to me, offered nothing at all. I thought I would try to reach my bed, and when I stood up I saw my three friends. They had seen the eagles flying over my peak and had become frightened, believing me dead. They carried me to my bed and stayed long enough to smoke with me before going back to their own places. While we smoked, the four war-eagles did not fly away. They sat there by my blood on the rocks, even after the night came on and chilled everything living on the mountain.

Again the Chief whispered aside to the Little-People, asking them if he might go on. When he finally resumed, I felt that somehow he had been reassured. His voice was very low, yet strained, as though he were tiring.

I dreamed. I heard a voice at midnight and saw a Person standing at my feet, in the east. He said, *'Plenty-Coups, the Person down there wants you now.'* He pointed, and from the peak in the Crazy Mountains I saw Buffalo-Bull standing where we are sitting now. I got up and started to go to the Bull, because I knew he was the Person who wanted me. The other Person was gone. Where he had stood when he spoke to me there was nothing at all. The way is very long from the Crazies to this place where we are sitting today, but I came here quickly in my dream. On that hill over yonder was where I stopped to look at Buffalo-Bull. He had changed into a Man-Person wearing a buffalo robe with the hair outside. Later I picked up the buffalo skull that you see over there, on the very spot where the Person had stood. I have kept that skull for more than seventy years. The Man-Person beckoned me from the hill over yonder where I had stopped, and I walked to where he stood. When I reached his side he began to sink slowly into the ground, right over there [pointing]. Just as the Man-Person was disappearing, he spoke. *'Follow me.'* he said. But I was afraid. *'Come.'* he said from the darkness. And I got down into the hole in the ground to follow him, walking bent-over for ten steps. Then I stood straight and saw a small light far off. It was like a window in a white man's house of today, and I knew the hole was leading us toward the Arrow

Creek Mountains [the Pryors]. In the way of the light, between it and me, I could see countless buffalo, see their sharp horns thick as the grass grows. I could smell their bodies and hear them snorting, ahead and on both sides of me. Their eyes, without number, were like little fires in the darkness of the hole in the ground, and I felt afraid among so many big bulls. The Man-Person must have known this, because he said, *'Be not afraid, Plenty-Coups. It was these Persons who sent for you. They will not do you harm.'* My body was naked. I feared walking among them in such a narrow place. The burrs that are always in their hair would scratch my skin, even if their hoofs and horns did not wound me more deeply. I did not like the way the Man-Person went among them. *'Fear nothing! Follow me, Plenty-Coups.'* he said.

I felt their warm bodies against my own, but went on after the Man-Person, edging around them or going between them all that night and all the next day, with my eyes always looking ahead at the hole of light. But none harmed me, none even spoke to me, and at last we came out of the hole in the ground and saw the Square White Butte at the mouth of Arrow Creek Canyon. It was on our right. White men call it Castle Rock, but our name for it is The-Fasting-Place. Now, out in the light of the sun, I saw that the Man-Person who had led me had a rattle in his hand. It was large and painted red. [The rattle is used in ceremonials. It is sometimes made of the bladder of an animal, dried, with small pebbles inside, so that when shaken it gives a rattling sound.] When he reached the top of a knoll he turned and said to me, *'Sit here!'* Then he shook his red rattle and sang a queer song four times. *'Look!'* he pointed. Out of the hole in the ground came the buffalo, bulls and cows and calves without number. They spread wide and blackened the plains. Everywhere I looked great herds of buffalo were going in every direction, and still others without number were pouring out of the hole in the ground to travel on the wide plains. When at last they ceased coming out of the hole in the ground, all were gone, all! There was not one in sight anywhere, even out on the plains. I saw a few antelope on a hillside, but no buffalo not a bull, not a cow, not one calf, was anywhere on the plains. I turned to look at the Man-Person beside me. He shook his red rattle again. *'Look.'* he pointed. Out of the hole in the ground came bulls and cows and calves past counting. These, like the others, scattered and spread on the plains. But they stopped in small bands and began to eat the grass. Many lay down, not as a buffalo does but differently, and many were spotted. Hardly any two were alike in color or size. And the bulls bellowed differently too, not deep and far-sounding like the bulls of the buffalo but sharper and yet weaker in my ears. Their tails were different, longer, and nearly brushed the ground. They were not buffalo. These were strange animals from another world. I was frightened and turned to the Man-Person, who only shook his red rattle but did not sing. He did not even tell me to look, but I did look and saw all the Spotted-Buffalo go back into the hole in the ground, until there was nothing except a few antelope anywhere in sight. *'Do you understand this which I have shown you, Plenty-Coups?'* he asked me. "No." I answered. How could he expect me to understand such a thing when I was not yet ten years old?

During all the time the Spotted-Buffalo were going back into the hole in the ground the Man-Person had not once looked at me. He stood facing the south as though the Spotted-Buffalo belonged there. *'Come, Plenty-Coups,'* he said finally, when the last had disappeared. I followed him back through the hole in the ground without seeing anything until we came out right over there [pointing] where we had first entered the hole in the ground. Then I saw the spring down by those trees, this very house just as it is, these trees which comfort us today, and a very old man sitting in the shade, alone. I felt pity for him because he was so old and feeble.

'Look well upon this old man,' said the Man-Person. *'Do you know him, Plenty-Coups?'* he asked me. "No," I said, looking closely at the old man's face in the shade of this tree. *'This old man is yourself, Plenty-Coups,'* he told me. And then I could see the Man-Person no more. He was gone, and so too was the old man. Instead I saw only a dark forest. A fierce storm was coming fast. The sky was black with streaks of mad color through it. I saw the Four Winds gathering to strike the forest, and held my breath. Pity was hot in my heart for the beautiful trees, I felt pity for all things that lived in that forest, but was powerless to stand

with them against the Four Winds that together were making war. I shielded my own face with my arm when they charged! I heard the Thunders calling out in the storm, saw beautiful trees twist like blades of grass and fall in tangled piles where the forest had been. Bending low, I heard the Four Winds rush past me as though they were not yet satisfied, and then I looked at the destruction they had left behind them. Only one tree, tall and straight, was left standing where the great forest had stood. The Four Winds that always make war alone had this time struck together, riding down every tree in the forest but one. Standing there alone among its dead tribesmen, I thought it looked sad. "What does this mean?" I whispered in my dream. *'Listen, Plenty-Coups,'* said a voice. *'In that tree is the lodge of the Chickadee. He is least in strength but strongest of mind among his kind. He is willing to work for wisdom. The Chickadee-Person is a good listener. Nothing escapes his ears, which he has sharpened by constant use. Whenever others are talking together of their successes or failures, there you will find the Chickadee-Person listening to their words. But in all his listening he tends to his own business. He never intrudes, never speaks in strange company, and yet never misses a chance to learn from others. He gains success and avoids failure by learning how others succeeded or failed, and without great trouble to himself. There is scarcely a lodge he does not visit, hardly a Person he does not know, and yet everybody likes him, because he minds his own business, or pretends to. The lodges of countless Bird-People were in that forest when the Four Winds charged it. Only one is left unharmed, the lodge of the Chickadee-Person. Develop your body, but do not neglect your mind, Plenty-Coups. It is the mind that leads a man to power, not strength of body.'* I wakened then.

My three friends were standing at my feet in the sunshine. They helped me stand. I was very weak, but my heart was singing, even as my friends half carried me to the foot of the mountain and kindled a fire. One killed a deer, and I ate a little of the meat. It is not well to eat heartily after so long a time of fasting. But the meat helped me to recover my strength a little. Of course we had all taken sweat-baths before touching the meat, or even killing the deer, and I was happy there beside the clear water with my friends. Toward night two of them went back to the village to bring horses for me and the man who stayed with me at the foot of the mountains. I was yet too weak to travel so far afoot. Lying by the side of the clear water, looking up into the blue sky, I kept thinking of my dream, but could understand little of it except that my medicine was the Chickadee. I should have a small medicine-bundle, indeed. And I would call upon the Wise Ones [medicine-men] of the tribe to interpret the rest. Perhaps they could tell the meaning of my dream from beginning to end.

In the middle of the third day my ears told me that horses were coming. My friend and I walked a little way to meet them, and very soon I heard the voices of my uncles, White-Horse and Cuts-The-Turnip.

They were singing the Crow Praise Song with several others who were leading extra horses for my friend and me.

I was stronger now and could ride alone, but the way seemed very far indeed. Of course I had spoken to nobody of my dream, but when I came in sight of the village my uncles began again to sing the Praise Song, and many people came out to meet us. They were all very happy, because they knew I now had Helpers and would use my power to aid my people. None spoke to me, not because he did not wish to be kind but because the people knew I must first cleanse myself in a sweat-lodge before going about the village with my friends. I saw my young sweetheart by her father's lodge, and although she did not speak to me I thought she looked happier than ever before.

While I was in the sweat-lodge my uncles rode through the village telling the Wise Ones that I had come, that I had dreamed and wished interpretation of my vision in council. I heard them calling this message to those who had distinguished themselves by feats of daring or acts of wisdom, and I wondered what my dream could mean, what the Wise Ones would say to me after I had told them all I had seen and heard on the peak in the Crazy Mountains. I respected them so highly that rather than have them speak lightly of my dream I would willingly have died. Plenty-Coups hesitated, his dimmed eyes staring over my head into the past. His last words, spoken in a whisper, had lifted him away. He had forgotten me and even the two old men who, like himself, appeared to be under a spell and scarcely breathed.

My father was gone, the Chief went on, brushing his forehead with his hand, so that I had only my uncles to speak for me before the Wise Ones. But my uncles were both good men. Both loved me and both belonged to the tribal council, whose members had all counted coup and were leaders. No man can love children more than my people do, and while I missed my father this day more than ever, I knew my uncles looked on me as a son and that they would help me now. Both of them were waiting, and when I was ready they led me to the lodge of Yellow-Bear, where our Chiefs sat with the Wise Ones. When I entered and sat down, Yellow-Bear passed the pipe round the lodge, as the sun goes, from east to west. Each man took it as it came, and smoked, first offering the stem to the Sun, the father, and then to the Earth, the mother of all things on this world. But no one spoke. All in that lodge had been over the hard trail and each knew well what was in my heart by my eyes. The eyes of living men speak words which the tongue cannot pronounce. The dead do not see out of their bodies' eyes, because there is no spirit there. It has gone away forever. In the lodge of Yellow-Bear that day seventy years ago I saw the spirits [souls] of my leaders in their eyes, and my heart sang loudly because I had dreamed. When the pipe was finished, my uncle, White-Horse, laid his hand on my shoulder. "Speak, Plenty-Coups," he said. "Tell us your dream. Forget nothing that happened. You are too young to understand, but here are men who can help you."

At this point a rolling hoop bumped violently against the Chief's chair and fell flat beside it. The old man did not start or show the least displeasure, even when a little bright-eyed girl ran among us to recover it. He did not reprove her with so much as a look. Instead, he smiled. "I have adopted many children," he said softly.

I told my dream, all of it. Even a part I forgot to tell you, about trying to enter a lodge on my way back from this place to the Crazies. A Voice had spoken. *'Do not go inside,'* it said. *'This lodge contains the clothes of small babies, and if you touch them or they touch you, you will not be successful.'* Of course I did not enter that lodge, but went on to my bed in the mountains. This I told in the order it came in my dream. When I had finished, Yellow-Bear, who sat at the head of the lodge which faced the east, lighted the pipe and passed it to his left, as the sun goes. Four times he lit the pipe, and four times it went round the lodge, without a word being spoken by anybody who took it. I grew uneasy. Was there no meaning in my dream? "White-Horse," the voice of Yellow-Bear said softly, "your nephew has dreamed a great dream."

My heart began to sing again. Yellow-Bear was the wisest man in the lodge. My ears were listening. "He has been told that in his lifetime the buffalo will go away forever," said Yellow-Bear, "and that in their place on the plains will come the bulls and the cows and the calves of the white men. I have myself seen these Spotted-Buffalo drawing loads of the white man's goods. And once at the big fort above the mouth of the Elk River [Fort Union, above the mouth of the Yellowstone] on the Big River [Missouri] I saw cows and calves of the same tribe as the bulls that drew the loads. The dream of Plenty-Coups means that the white men will take and hold this country and that their Spotted-Buffalo will cover the plains. He was told to think for himself, to listen, to learn to avoid disaster by the experiences of others. He was advised to develop his body but not to forget his mind. The meaning of his dream is plain to me. I see its warning. The tribes who have fought the white man have all been beaten, wiped out. By listening as the Chickadee listens, we may escape this and keep our lands. The Four Winds represent the white man and those who will help him in his wars. The forest of trees is the tribes of these wide plains. And the one tree that the Four Winds left standing after the fearful battle, represents our own people, the Absarokees, the one tribe of the plains that has never made war against the white man."

"The Chickadee's lodge in that standing tree is the lodges of this tribe pitched in the safety of peaceful relations with white men, whom we could not stop even though we would. The Chickadee is small, so are we against our many enemies, white and red. But he was wise in his selection of a place to pitch his lodge. After the battle of the Four Winds he still held his home, his country, because he had gained wisdom by listening to the mistakes of others and knew there was safety for himself and his family."

"The Chickadee is the medicine of Plenty-Coups from this day. He will not be obliged to carry a heavy medicine-bundle, but his medicine will be powerful both in peace time and in war. He will live to be old and he will be a Chief.

He will someday live differently from the way we do now and will sit in the shade of great trees on Arrow Creek, where the Man-Person took him in his dream. The old man he saw there was himself, as he was told. He will live to be old and be known for his brave deeds, but I can see that he will have no children of his own blood. This was told him when he tried to enter that lodge on his way from Arrow Creek to the peak in the Crazy Mountains where he dreamed. When the Voice told him not to enter, that the lodge was filled with the clothes of babes, that if he touched them he would not succeed, it meant he would have no children. I have finished."

"Your dream was a great dream. Its meaning is plain," said the others, and the pipe was passed so that I might smoke with them in the lodge of Yellow-Bear. "Ho I" said Plenty-Coups, making the sign for "finished."

Chief Plenty Coup & his wife, Kills Together; 1908.

"And here I am, an old man, sitting under this tree just where that old man sat seventy years ago when this was a different world."

CHIEF PLENTY COUPS
1848-1932

Chief Plenty Coups is a famous Crow Chief who led the Crow Nation through its transition from the nomadic days of the buffalo, to reservation life. He encouraged Crows to settle down and begin farming, and not to fight the further settlement of the white men between 1880 and 1920. He often negotiated for his people with U.S. Representatives in Washington and on the reservation. He famously said to his people: "Education is your most powerful weapon. With education you are the white man's equal; without education you are his victim." He died in 1932, still fighting for the rights of his people.

The existence of "little people" has been insisted upon as the truth by rational human beings for eons. Native American tribal culture is replete with credible stories of the Little People. These myths are ancient and reside deep within the folklore of tribal cultures. Even today, there are people who relate face-to-face encounters with these tiny, magical beings.

Encounters with Little People are still being reported. The internet is full of tales like the ones that follow:

One story that runs through many websites and books is the late Harry Anderson's childhood memory of a long ago summer night in Barron County, Wisconsin. It was the summer of 1919:

One night, as he walked down an isolated country road near Barron, Wisconsin, 13-year-old Harry Anderson saw something distinctly odd. Twenty little men, trooped in single file and heading in his direction, were visible in the bright moonlight. Even as they passed him, they paid him no attention. Anderson noticed they were dressed in leather knee pants held up by suspenders. They wore no shirts; they were bald; and their skin was pale white. All were making "mumbling" sounds, but they did not appear to be communicating with each other. The biggest of the little folk was about three feet high. "I could see them as plain as I do you. I ran home and called three women to come back with me and see them. But when we got to the place, they were all gone." The bizarre encounter remained vivid in his memory for the rest of his life.

Native American tribes around Wisconsin report sightings of fairy folk. The Winnebago (Hochunk people) speak of a little being called Wakdjunkaga. This trickster (his name literally means "tricky one") was sent to help and protect the Hochunk people; but his clownish and sometimes inappropriate antics cause more trouble than they are worth. Wakdjunkaga stories range from light-hearted fables, to cautionary tales about the consequences of bad behavior, to ribald jokes.

WISCONSIN TRIBAL LITTLE PEOPLE

The *Wisconsin Archeologist, Vol. 18, No. 4*, published by the Wisconsin Archaeological Society in 1937, contains references to fairies and spirits found in the myths and legends of Wisconsin's waterfalls:

> In the mythology of the Winnebago, the waterfalls—like the springs, lakes, streams and rapids—were associated with the water-spirits. The knowledge of and the care of such places was within the province of their Water-spirit clan.

> Water was one of the immaterial possessions of the Water-spirit people. Water was sacred to them as it also was to the Wolf clan of this tribe. Tobacco and other offerings were made to these spirits at their dens or retreats. Ulysses S. White, a Winnebago, gives the Indian name for a waterfall as *nee-ho-har-nee-la* and says that falls were the homes of Water-spirits. Falls were sometimes spoken of as "talking waters;" they were hallowed shrines. From the spirit "voices" in the falling water, the Indian received inspiration and encouragement. Indian fairy-folk, commonly spoken of as "Little People," frequented the vicinity of waterfalls. The Chippewa name them as Munidogewazas, or "little manitou men." Sister M. Macaria, St. Mary's School, Odanah, in a recent letter to Charles E. Brown (May 24, 1938) mentions these fairy-folk: "These little men roam about near bodies of water. Bad River Falls in the Bad River is one of their favorite haunts, Marble Point is another, and the Apostle Islands (Lake Superior) are one of their main stomping grounds. They may be seen from a distance, but to approach them is an impossibility. These little men give great power if dreamed about."

An old Chippewa, traveling years ago over the trail from the Lac Court Oreille country to Lake Superior, saw a gathering of these *puckwidjinees* near the base of a waterfall. They were dressed like Indians, apparently holding a council. He very wisely did not attempt to approach them.

WISCONSIN WATERFALLS

Such myths, legends and stories as it has been possible to obtain from Indians and other sources about the many beautiful waterfalls in Wisconsin are interesting and deserve to be recorded for the use of students of Wisconsin Indian folklore and folk ways. Big and Little Manitou Falls. These waterfalls are located in Pattison State Park 12 miles south of the City of Superior in Douglas County.

The Black River at this point, flowing northward to Lake Superior, breaks over the trap rock ledge in a series of two falls, the first or Little Manitou Falls, about 30 feet in height, the second, Big Manitou Falls, plunging into a mountain gorge with a sheer drop of 165 feet.

This largest and most beautiful waterfall in Wisconsin is dedicated to the Great Spirit, Gitchee Manido, and was, according to the Chippewa Indians, one of his greatest creations. "Out of its thundering waters," writes Fred L. Holmes, "came the voices which held Indians in superstitious awe."

Waters of the Black River, approaching the falls, seem to sense the compelling mystery of the fearful plunge and hurry faster as each step of the precipice is neared. On the crest of the brink the waters roll and toss, but momentarily are transformed into a white spray that turns more vaporous down the glide. The receiving basin seethes and foams like a boiling cauldron. The gorge below is very narrow for a short distance and the walls are twisted forms indicating volcanic origin. In this foaming cataract, several spirits lived. Sometimes, say the Indians, one could hear their voices or their war songs above the roar of the Falls of the Great Spirit.

Woe to those who in years past paid no heed to the warnings or commands of these spirit voices. The "Little People," puckwidjinees, have also been seen near these waterfalls.

HARDSCRABBLE FALLS.

This attractive waterfall tumbles down a rocky incline in the wild and rugged hardscrabble area of Barron and Rusk Counties in northwestern Wisconsin. It is the least known of our falls. This region has been proposed for preservation as a state park. Besides swift running streams and unusual rock formations, there are many acres of virgin maple forest, with unspoiled floor covered with wild flowers and ferns. In past years, Indian fairy folk or "Little Indians" have been seen by Chippewa near this waterfall. It has been said that these dwarf aborigines were the first to discover and make use of the red pipestone found at various places in the Barron quartzite range; and that from them, the Chippewa people learned of the quarry locations. In some of these places, Indian hunters have heard the noise made by their stone hammers when parties of these little folks were engaged in quarrying the stone for pipe and ornament making.

YUNDI TSUNDI

The Little People of the Cherokee are dwarf Spirits who stand about 2 feet tall. They live in rock caves on the mountain sides. These Little People are believed to be here to teach lessons about living in harmony with nature and with others. Their appearance is described as well-shaped and handsome, with hair that almost touches the ground. The Yundi Tsundi of the Cherokee are said to be helpful, kind-hearted, and work great magic. In spite of their gentle nature, these little folk do not like to be disturbed. The Yundi Tsundi love music and spend most of their time drumming, singing, and dancing. It is not safe to follow the sounds of their drumming and singing, because they do not like to be disturbed; and they will throw a spell over the stranger to cause him to become confused, losing his way. Even if the intruder manages to get back to his settlement, remains in a dazed state forever. There are Cherokee stories that tell of hearing the voices of these little people nearby at night. Even though the people inside hear talking, they must not go out. If anyone should go out, he would die.

In the morning, they find the corn gathered or the field cleared as if a whole force of men had been at work.

In the old days, the Cherokee Medicine Man would travel to the rock caves to meet with the Little People and share in their secrets. The medicine men would stay in the mountains for seven days and nights telling stories around the campfire. On the first night, they would tell the story of the bear and sing the songs the bear had taught the Cherokee. The songs were for good hunting. On the second night, they would dance the Green Corn Dance for good crops, singing and dancing all night long. On the third night, a song was sung to invoke the deer spirit to be kind to the Cherokee hunters. The fourth, fifth and sixth nights were spent on more storytelling, dancing and singing. Each medicine man told about the sacred formula that the Little People had entrusted to him. On the seventh night, at the darkest hour, the Little People, or Yundi Tsundi, danced into the circle. They danced and chanted sacred songs. Then the Little People told the medicine men to return the secrets that had been shared with them that year. One by one the medicine men gave the secrets to the Little People. The medicine men left the cave and returned to their homes. They would repeat the rituals with the Yundi Tsundi every year.

When a hunter finds anything in the woods, such as a knife or a trinket, he must say, 'Little People, I would like to take this' because it may belong to them. If he does not ask their permission, the little people will throw stones at him as he goes home. The little people of the Cherokee are known to retrieve lost children and return them to their village. One Cherokee tale tells of a hunter, who, one winter, found tracks in the snow like the tracks of little children. He wondered how they could have come to be there and followed them until they led him to a cave. Inside were a large group of Little People, young and old men, women, and children. They brought him in and were kind to him. The hunter stayed with them for some time. When he decided to leave, they warned him that he must not tell of them or he would die. The hunter went back to the settlement. His friends were anxious to know where he had been. For a long time, he refused to say; until at last, he could not stay quiet any longer. He told the story, and within a few days, he died. Only a few years ago two hunters from Raventown, going behind the high fall near the head of Oconaluftee on the East Cherokee reservation, found there a cave with fresh footprints of the Little People all over the floor.

Another story tells that, during the smallpox epidemic among the East Cherokee just after the war, one sick man wandered off. His friends searched, but could not find him. After several weeks, he came back and said that the Little People had found him and taken him in to one of their caves and tended to him until he was cured.

About twenty five years ago a man named Tsantawu was lost in the mountains on the head of Oconaluftee. It was winter time and very cold and his friends thought he must be dead, but after sixteen days he came back and said that the Little People had found him and taken him to their cave, where he had been well treated, and given plenty of everything to eat except bread. This was in large loaves, but when he took them in his hand to eat, they seemed to shrink into small cakes so light and crumbly that though he might eat all day he would not be satisfied. After he was well rested they had brought him a part of the way home until they came to a small creek, about knee deep, when they told him to wade across to reach the main trail on the other side. He waded across and turned to look back, but the Little People were gone and the creek was a deep river. When he reached home, his legs were frozen to the knees and he lived only a few days.

There are three kinds of Little People. The Laurel People, the Rock People, and the Dogwood People.

The Rock People are the mean ones who practice getting even; who steal children; and the like. But they are like this because their space has been invaded.

The Laurel People play tricks and are generally mischievous. When you find children laughing in their sleep, they are said to be playing with the Laurel People, who are humorous and enjoy sharing joy with others.

Then there are the Dogwood People who are good and take care of humans.

The lessons taught by the Little People are clear. The Rock People teach us that if you do things to other people out of meanness or intentionally, it will come back on you. We must always respect other people's limits and boundaries. The Laurel People teach us that we shouldn't take the world too seriously, and we must always have joy and share that joy with others. The lessons of the Dogwood People are simple–if you do something for someone, do it out of the goodness of your heart. Don't do it to have people obligated to you or for personal gain.

In Cherokee beliefs, many stories contain references to beings called the Little People. These people are supposed to be small mythical characters, and in different beliefs they serve different purposes.

There are a lot of stories and legends about the Little People. You can see the people out in the forest. They can talk and they look a lot like Indian people except they're only about two feet high, sometimes they're smaller. Now the Little People can be very helpful, and they can also play tricks on us, too. And at one time there was a boy. This boy never wanted to grow up. In fact, he told everyone that so much that they called him "Forever Boy" because he never wanted to be grown. When his friends would sit around and talk about: "Oh when I get to be a man, and when I get to be grown, I'm gonna be this and I'm gonna go here and be this," he'd just go off and play by himself.

He didn't even want to hear it, because he never wanted to grow up. Finally his father got real tired of this, and he said, 'Forever Boy, I will never call you that again. From now on you're going to learn to be a man, you're going to take responsibility for yourself, and you're going to stop playing all day long. You have to learn these things. Starting tomorrow you're going to go to your uncle's, and he's going to teach you everything that you are going to need to know.' Forever Boy was broken hearted at what his father told him, but he could not stand the thought of growing up. He went out to the river and he cried. He cried so hard that he didn't see his animal friends gather around him. And they were trying to tell him something, and they were trying to make him feel better, and finally he thought he understood them say, 'Come here tomorrow, come here early.' Well, he thought they just wanted to say goodbye to him. And he drug his feet going home.

He couldn't even sleep he was so upset. The next morning he went out early, as he had promised, to meet his friends. And he was so sad, he could not bear the thought of telling them goodbye forever. Finally he began to get the sense that they were trying to tell him something else, and that is to look behind him.

As he looked behind him, there they were, all the Little People. And they were smiling at him and laughing and running to hug him. And they said, 'Forever Boy you do not have to grow up. You can stay with us forever. You can come and be one of us and you will never have to grow up...we will ask the Creator to send a vision to your parents and let them know that you are safe and you are doing what you need to do.' Forever Boy thought about it for a long time. But that is what he decided he needed to do, and he went with the Little People.

And even today when you are out in the woods and you see something, and you look and it is not what you really thought it was, or if you are fishing and you feel something on the end of your line, and you think it is the biggest trout ever, and you pull it in, and all it is, is a stick that got tangled on your hook, that is what the Little People are doing. They are playing tricks on you so you will laugh and keep young in your heart. Because that is the spirit of Little People, and Forever Boy, to keep us young in our hearts.

SIOUX HOLY MAN, BLACK ELK

Oglala Sioux holy man, Black Elk, who lived from 1863 to 1950, and toured with Buffalo Bill's Wild West Show as a young man, wrote of spiritual things. In the following passage from Black Elk, *The Sacred Ways of a Lakota* by Wallace Black Elk and William Lyon, 1990, the Sioux shaman spoke of Little People:

> So when I went to vision quest, that disk came from above. The scientists call that a…Unidentified Flying Object, but that's a joke, see? Because they are not trained, they lost contact with the wisdom, power and gift. So that disk landed on top of me. It was concave, and there was another one on top of that. It was silent, but it lit and luminesced like neon lights. Even the sacred robes there were luminesced, and those tobacco ties lying there lit up like little light bulbs. Then these little people came, but each little group spoke a different language. They could read minds, and I could read their minds. I could read them. So there was silent communication. You could read it, like when you read silent symbols in a book. So we were able to communicate…They are human, so I welcomed them. I said, "Welcome, Welcome…"

LEGEND OF SPIRIT MOUND

The Yankton Sioux people believe that Spirit Mound, in South Dakota, is home to Little People. When the Lewis

313

and Clark Expedition passed through the region in 1804, the Yanktons pointed it out to the explorers, warning them to stay away from it. Spirit Mound, or *Paha Wakan*, was well-known to tribes for miles around. The Yankton, the Omaha, and Oto tribes believed that the mound was occupied by little people, spirits in dwarf form, who killed any human that ventured too close. They were said to be eighteen inches tall, with oversized heads. Although there are other hills nearby, Spirit Mound stands out from them. Lewis called it "The Hill of Little Devils" in his journal. In addition to the mound, these Little People also live in the woods of the Yankton Reservation. Thomas Constantine Maroukis, wrote in his 2005 book, *Peyote and the Yankton Sioux: The Life and Times of Sam Necklace*:

> These "little people" are described by such respected elders as Henry Hare, Sr.; Joe Rockboy; and Asa Primeaux. Rockboy said that "they were the enemies of the Sioux from the time that the Sioux entered this region." Asa Primeaux said that the "little people" inhabit some of the woods between Choteau Creek and Greenwood, just north of the Missouri River.

> While we were touring the area, Asa explained that people avoided the woods even though they contained plenty of dead trees for firewood. He added that the "little people" are dangerous, but that they are here for a reason: "This is God's land and you have to respect God's ways. If you follow God's ways, you can get through the woods okay; but if not, if you are a doubter, you may see one of the little people and they will get you."

> Lewis and Clark may have doubted the existence of the "little people," but they are part of the Yankton belief system. Their presence in Yankton tradition has been documented for almost two hundred years.

YEHASURI

The Catawba, also known as Kowi Anukasha (forest dwellers) or Iswä (people of the river), are a tribe of Native Americans, known officially as the Catawba Indian Nation. They live in the Southeast United States, along the border of North Carolina near the city of Rock Hill, South Carolina. Living along the Catawba River, they were named one of the most powerful tribes in the South. Decimated by smallpox epidemics, tribal warfare, and social disruption, the Catawba declined drastically in number in the late 18th and 19th centuries. As of 2006, the population of the Catawba Nation was about 2600, mostly in South Carolina; with smaller groups in Oklahoma, Colorado, and Ohio.

The Little People of the Catawba are called *Yehasuri*. They are two-foot-tall creatures who appear in ancient Catawba legends. They are said to live on the Catawba Indian Reservation in South Carolina. Their name translates to "wild little people." These characters possess high intelligence and powerful secret knowledge. The Yehasuri use their high intellect to play tricks, to disobey normal rules, or to exhibit unacceptable behavior. The Catawba Yehasuri are generally depicted as small, but otherwise ordinary looking people who are said to live in tree stumps. They reportedly eat a wide variety of forest food, like frogs and bugs.

Said to be vicious on occasion, the Catawba believe the only way to stop these little terrorists is to rub tobacco on one's hand and recite an ancient Catawba prayer. Other precautions against Yehasuri were to be sure that no possessions were left out where they could get at them; bringing in clothing at night; sweeping away the tracks and footprints of children before night; and avoiding places in the forest where the Yehasuri tricksters might be encountered. However, although the Yehasuri have strong magic and can be very dangerous, they sometimes also bestow special powers upon people who treat them respectfully.

In the sample page above, cartoonist Andrew Cohen incorporates the naughty-but-playful Yehasuri into the layout.

(Taken from an article in *Indian Country Today, June 26, 2008*)

THE LITTLE PEOPLE: A CHOCTAW LEGEND

A long time ago, in ancient time, while the Choctaw Indians were living in Mississippi, the Choctaw legends say that certain supernatural beings or spirits lived near them. These spirits, or "Little People," were known as Kowi Anukasha or "Forest Dwellers." They were about two or three feet tall. These pygmy beings lived deep in thick forest, their homes were in caves hidden under large rocks.

When a boy child is two, three, or even four years old, he will often wander off into the woods, playing or chasing a small animal. When the little one is well out of sight from his home, "Kwanokasha," who is always on watch, seizes the boy and takes him away to his cave, his dwelling place. Many times his cave is far away and Kwanokasha and the little boy must travel a very long way, climbing many hills and crossing many streams. When they finally reach the cave, Kwanokasha takes him inside where he is met by three other spirits, all very old, with long white hair.

The first one offers the boy a knife; the second one offers him a bunch of poisonous herbs; the third offers a bunch of herbs yielding good medicine. If the child accepts the knife, he is certain to become a bad man and may even kill his friends. If he accepts the poisonous herbs, he will never be able to cure or help his people. But, if he accepts the good herbs, he is destined to become a great doctor and an important and influential man of his tribe and win the confidence of all his people. When he accepts the good herbs, the three old spirits will tell him the secrets of making medicines from herbs, roots, and barks of certain trees, and of treating and curing various fevers, pains, and other sickness.

That is the reason the "Little People" take the boy child to their home in the wilderness, in order to train Indian doctors, transmitting to them their special curative powers and to train them in the manufacture of medicines. The child will remain with the spirits for three days after which he is returned. He does not tell where he has been or what he has seen or heard. Not until he becomes a man will he make use of the knowledge gained from the spirits, and never will he reveal to others how it was acquired. It is said among the Choctaws that few children wait to accept the offering of the good herbs from the third spirit, and that is why there are so few great doctors and other men of influence among the Choctaws.

It is also said that the "Little People" are never seen by the common Choctaws. The Choctaw prophets and herb doctors, however, claim the power of seeing them and of holding communication with them. During the darkest nights in all kinds of weather, you can see a strange light wandering around in the woods. This light is the Indian doctor and his little helper looking for that special herb to treat and cure a very sick tribesman.

NUNUPI

The Nunupi have been a myth of the Comanche people since the earliest times. Some oral legends and myths of the Comanche Nunupi can be traced back to their Shoshone relatives, hundreds of years prior. The Nunupi are small bi-pedal humanoids, ranging from twelve to eighteen inches in height, some with larger heads, large dark eyes, long arms, different skin tones, long hair of varying colors or no hair. Sightings or close encounters of more than one individual Nunupi are rare. The Nunupi can be mischievous, contrary, or humorous according to various legends. Some believe they are spirits or ghosts and that they can come into a person's dreams. In some myths, they have powers to heal or can cause sickness or death.

Nunupi are said to appear and disappear at will and live near creeks, caverns and in mountain valleys. It is claimed they have super strength to carry large animals or move heavy rocks. Many Nunupi stories include descriptions of them appearing as very small "Indian men" dressed in buckskin clothing and moccasins, carrying tiny war shields, and using bows and arrows tipped with alligator bone. When the Nunupi shot their arrows, they looked like lightning strikes and would never miss. Their arrows could even go around corners and through solid rock.

Some oral myths suggest they originated from the heavens as "Star People," and have the ability to circumvent Earth's physics, gravity, and human logic.

In Comanche legends, there are stories of eagles, with their superior vision, tormenting the Nunupi from the sky—swooping to steal Nunupi babies and drop them from high above. To defend against this, the Nunupi were said to pluck the eagle's tail feathers to keep them from flying. They would also steal the eagles' eggs, in return.

Like most native tribes, Comanche children learned of the Nunupi by the light of the campfire. Stories were told of the Nunupi and Mupitsi (Moo-Peets), a hairy man-like giant, to frighten the children from wandering from the camp alone. In other Nunupi stories, they are protectors, helpers and healers—sometimes musical, amusing, and comical.

In Comanche oral history, there were certain men and women who allegedly communicated with the Nunupi. The Comanche language term used is Nunupi Puha (Pooh-Ah) or Nunupuhi (power or medicine from the little people), referring to those who were allegedly contacted and "given or taught" certain magical powers and knowledge.

A person who encountered the Nunupi felt disoriented; and some were said to have forever-altered minds afterward. Reported Nunupi encounters in dreams and on vision quests suggest the medical phenomenon known as sleep paralysis, or sleep telepathic communication had occurred. According to the nunupi.com website, people who had encountered a Nunupi described something like the "Oz Effect" (being taken out of our reality and put into a new dimension where magical things happened, like the Land of Oz). The nunupi.com website reports modern day Nunupi sightings:

> Historical and modern day sightings of Nunupi foot-prints and encounters of various kinds have occurred in and around the Wichita Mountains north of Lawton, Oklahoma. More reported Nunupi gathering sites are

along the creeks in Faxon, Cache, and Cyril, Oklahoma; and around Stephenville, Killeen, and Quanah, Texas.

Strange occurrences of singing and drumming attributed to the Nunupi at the Comanche Nations' governmental headquarters located north of Lawton, Oklahoma, have occurred. The Nunupi were heard singing by night workers in one of the offices on more than one occasion.

STICK INDIANS

In the traditions of many Salish and other Northwest Indian tribes, Stick Indians are evil-minded and extremely dangerous forest spirits. These Little People of myth and legend are described as being everything from bringers of good luck and health and raising human orphans, to pushing humans off of cliffs. Physical details about Stick Indians vary from tribe to tribe. In the Salish culture, they are described as large, hairy bigfoot-like creatures. The Cayuse and Yakami describe them as forest dwarves. In some traditions, Stick Indians have powers to paralyze, hypnotize, or cause insanity in hapless humans, while in others, they merely lead people astray by making eerie sounds of whistling or laughter in the woods at night. In some stories Stick Indians may eat people who fall prey to them, kidnap children, or molest women. They also take aggressive revenge against people who injure or disrespect them, no matter how unintentionally. There are not a lot of legends regarding Stick Indians recorded, likely due to taboos related to these deadly creatures. Saying the actual Salish name of these beings in public is considered to be provoking their attacks, a belief many Native people still adhere to today, choosing to refer to them only in English, or not at all.

According to Yakama folklore, the true nature and physical attributes of Stick Indians are unknown. No one has ever encountered a Stick Indian and survived to tell about it. Stick Indians are small, vicious and cunning, half-humans about three to four feet tall. They are skinny, with elongated arms and legs, and sharp teeth. They have claws on their hands and feet. Stick Indians live in deep forests, and are occasionally heard, but never seen. They lure their victims by emitting sounds like small children laughing out in the forest. Any person who tries to find where the laughter is coming from, becomes disoriented and lost as they attempt to find the "children" playing in the woods. If the victim is an adult, they are attacked and eaten; the body's remains are never found. If the victim is a small child, the Stick Indians turn them into one of them through some demonic Stick Indian Magic.

MEMEGWESI

Memegwesi are alternately described as a species of Little People that live in high remote ledges; and small riverbank-dwelling water spirits, depending on the tribe. They are part of the folklore of the Ojibway, Algonquin, Ottawa, Cree, Metis, Innu, and Menominee tribes. They are generally harmless creatures, but are sometimes known to blow canoes astray or steal things when they are not shown proper respect. In some Ojibwe traditions, Memegwesi can only be seen by children and medicine people. In others, they can appear to anyone, and may help humans who give them tobacco and other gifts. Most often Memegwesi are described as being child-sized and have hair growing all over their bodies. A Memegwesi has a large head and a strange voice that sounds like the whine of a dragonfly. The Cree and Innu describe these dwarf-like creatures as having narrow, ugly faces that they seek to hide when they meet with humans. Some Menominee storytellers have said that they have no noses. Some legends say that the Memegwesi were originally created from the bark of trees. These little people are said to carve symbols on rocks; they sometimes carve small canoes for themselves out of stone. Some people believe that their name comes from the Ojibwa word for "hairy," *memii,* since Memegwesi are usually described as having hairy faces and bodies. Other people believe that the name is related to the word for butterfly, *memengwaa.* There is a tale told of a meeting with these creatures at Lake Timiscaming. The Indians where passing the high ledge of rock a few miles below Haileybury, where the water was very deep and where they had set their nets. They found that somebody had been stealing fish. They proceeded to watch the nets and soon saw three *Memegwesi* come out astride of an old log for a canoe, using sticks for paddles. The Indians pursued them, the fairies meanwhile hiding their faces. Finally the Indians caught one.

Then one Indian said, "Look behind!" When the fairy turned quickly they got a glimpse of how ugly he was. The Indians then took a knife from this fairy and the rest disappeared, riding their log through the rock wall to the inside, where they could be heard crying, as this was where they lived. The Indians then threw the knife at the rock and it went right through to the inside to its owner.

THE LEGEND OF BURNT FACE

Thomas Yellowtail was born near Lodge Grass on the Crow Reservation of Montana in 1903. His Indian name was Medicine Rock Chief, given to him from Medicine Crow, the famous warrior and chief born around 1848. Tom had also received the name *Dashbiilaa,* Fire Heart. It was this name that you would hear, spoken in *Apsaalooke,* calling him to the center pole of the Sun Dance lodge to "doctor" someone.

Tom Yellowtail tells the oral story of the Little People in "Burnt Face," which is included in *Stories That Make the World: Oral Literature of the Indian Peoples of the Inland Northwest,* a publication of the University of Oklahoma Press, in 1999:

BURNT FACE.

As told by TOM YELLOWTAIL; June 1993.

The edited segments of Tom Yellowtail's telling of Burnt Face included here highlight the journey of a young boy.

In the days when they were still moving about the country–in the territory where the Crow Indians roamed about, moving from one place to another—is this area comprised of the Little Bighorn River, the Bighorn River, the Yellowstone River, and the Missouri River. The Indians would follow some of these rivers; they moved about every few days, from way down there next to the North Dakota border line, on up this way toward these Bighorn Mountains.

In the evening, in the camp, the children would play, build a bonfire or something like that, and play. This one night, they did build a bonfire and they were chasing each other around playing games, when a young lad of about the age of this boy here now....I'd say the lad was probably about ten years old. They were all playing around this bonfire chasing each other; and while they were playing like that, chasing each other, some were standing back. Somebody gave a push to this one boy as he was going by the fire. When he got pushed the boy fell into that bonfire, which burned him pretty bad, before they rescued him. They pulled him out, but he was burned already pretty bad from the big bonfire he fell into. When that accident happened, the other children all quit playing.

The burned child was taken to his parent's camp, and they took care of him. In the next few days, the sores started from the burns on his face. He was burned so much that his whole face was covered with sores. When they finally began to heal as scabs, he would still try to play with his other friends. But, because his face was disfigured after the sores had healed and tightened up, the other kids would make fun of him. "Ahh, look at him....look at Burnt Face. He has a funny, ugly face!"

All that made the boy ashamed. He felt ashamed the way the other kids would make fun of him and his ugly face. He didn't like that and he wanted to leave camp, get away from staying in camp. So, he got bedding and things to stay away from the camp. When the camp moved about, he would travel along the side of them, I'd say probably a half a mile away from them or so. He doesn't come into camp for he is ashamed of what the other kids would say to make fun of him when they looked at him. And so, he stayed that way. His parents would try to bring him back and he would not do it. He has his bedding; he stays there and they bring food for him; and he's sad and he doesn't come back into the camp to play with the other children.

As the camp moves about, moving toward the Bighorn Mountains, he had an idea. As they were approaching the Bighorn Mountains, he thought to himself : "Now, when we get to these Bighorn Mountains, I will quit staying alone alongside my parents. I'll leave them when we get to these mountains. I will go up somewhere and fast."

So, he told his parents to make him several pairs of moccasins and extra clothing, and to save up plenty of jerky to take with him when he leaves the camp, when they get to the mountains.

The camp could go on and he'd take to the mountains and fast somewhere. "If I am lucky in my fasting, I will return to my people after. If not, if something happens to me, that will be alright."

So the parents prepared all those extra pairs of moccasins for him, the things he would need for him to get along with, and the jerky for food, so he could spend quite a few days before he would return to his people. When they got to the mountains, he bid his folks goodbye for awhile, saying: "Now you folks go on and I'll take these mountains and I'll find a place where I'll fast for quite awhile. He left the camp and he took to the mountains and went south along the range. He kept on traveling into Wyoming; kept traveling south and finally he came to a place where he said, "I believe this is a good place." It is where the present Medicine Wheel is now. He comes to that place that overlooks the country for miles. "Right here is where I will fast!"

So he did; he started fasting there, right where the Medicine Wheel is now, he fasted. Where he fasted, a lot of the place is just rocky formations all around him. During the day, he would gather rocks; and he started forming a circle representing the Lodge...the Lodge you see nowadays that comprises...the Sundance Lodge. He built that large circle. Every day he'd pile up rocks on top to form a circle, with the doorway toward the rising Sun to the east. He made it big; it had spokes that lead to the center.

The boy must of stayed there a mouth or so and he fasted there, every day saying his prayers. He has tobacco with him, a good supply of tobacco. He would fill up his pipe and offer smokes to the Great Spirit.

Right by where he fasted and made offerings, are the cliffs, and caves where you hear about the Little People. They were there then; and they're there yet today. Finally, the Little People come out. They had been watching him. They said: "Young man, you have been here for awhile. We have been watching you fasting; you have said your prayers; and you have spent enough time here building this Sundance Lodge. Now we want to adopt you. We want to give you medicine. We want you to quit your fasting and you go back to your people. Your parents and the rest of them, get back to them; do not stay away from them. We will take those scars away from you so you will look fine, so you won't be ashamed to get back into your people's comfort. The medicine things we will give you, you will have them; you will pray for people and doctor them when you are back home. You will show the power we are giving you. We give you all these powers so that, using your medicines, you will be a medicine man among your people, a healer. You will eventually become a chief of your tribe."

"Alright. I will leave. I'll go back." And so, he started back the way he came and went to the place where the Little People had told him he would find the people.

When he came into the camp, the chief looked at him. He has grown up; he's a young man now. The chief didn't recognize him as the young lad who had left the camp. The young man explained to the chief: "I am the boy that got my face burned and I stayed away from the camp. I'm the boy, but I've grown up now. I fasted like I wanted to; I received my medicine. I was asked to return to my people and here I am. I've come back. My parents are here somewhere."

So the chief called the herald to come and told him the story. "Go around camp and tell the different chiefs to come together and come to my camp. We have this young man who has returned to us; we will hear his story. They gathered in a big tipi, and had a ceremony, filling and smoking their pipes. The chief says: "Young man, we are now ready to hear your story."

So the young man says "I am the boy, that quite awhile back, when we were moving up from way down the Missouri headed this way up the Bighorn River, when we got to the Bighorn mountains where I left you. I went quite aways down and came to a place where I fasted and stayed. I spent all my time there. The Little People there around close by came to me and talked with me. They advised me to leave that place and come back to my parents and all of you. I'm a member of your group. They called me Burnt Face. I was disfigured, but those Little People took the disfigurations off my face and made me look different. So here I am. I'm the boy who left your camp."

"That is great," the chief said. "We welcome you back to our camp. From now on we will depend on you when we are sick; you have been given the power to doctor you and make us well."

Poor little Burnt Face became the man that the group called on to doctor them. He was given great respect.

Those who had made fun of him, now said: "Oh! This man has the power. We must respect him. We cannot make fun of him any more." As time went on, he finally become the great chief as the Little People had predicted. The great chief, Burnt Face.

For Tom Yellowtail and so many other elders, the way of the world is as a "great circle." It has no beginning, nor an end, for time is as a circle, always repeating itself. The life of any four-legged or two-legged is as a circle, from birth, to maturity, to old age, and back to where one came.
The sun, the moon, the stars and the earth are as circles and move in circles as well. The great winds move in circles, move around the stones, trees and flowers that are all rounded as the circle.

The birds make their nests as circles and their young
are born out of the circles of eggs.

This we all see with the circles of our eyes and come
to know in our hearts. This we live by. Our lodges
were once round as the nests of birds; now we are
reminded of this when we set up our tepees each
August at Crow Fair. Throughout our land our
ancestors built great circles of rock, which we now
call medicine wheels. At our pow wows at New
Year's and during Crow Fair we dance the round
dance. We give prayer and clean ourselves from the
inside out each time we enter the circle of our sweat
lodges. When the medicine bundles are opened, we
sit in a prayer circle and watch the smoke circle from
our cigarettes, carrying our prayers with it. Each
summer, when we build and give of ourselves within
the circle of our Sun Dance lodge, we are reminded
of the great circle of life and of the world.

Our lives and the lives of all the peoples make up a
"great wagon wheel." Though the non-Indian came
to this land traveling on them, we've always had the
"wheel." Ours can be seen in the rock "Medicine
Wheel" of the Bighorn Mountains and in the
Sundance Lodges. Each spoke of the great wheel is
as a particular religion, a particular people – the Sun
Dance, the Christian, the Muslim, the Hindu, the
Buddhist, the Indian, the non-Indian, the two-
leggeds, the four-leggeds, the wingeds. Each is
unique, with its own language and traditions. But all
are of equal worth; all are of the same length. To
shorten or even remove one of the spokes

would only cause the wheel to wobble and fall. All
are needed. Nevertheless, all the spokes are linked to
the same hub, the same God.

Though each of us may address it differently, each with our own way of praying, it is the same God, uniting all the peoples. To live is to live in the circle, as a part of the great wheel.

In the Crow story *"The Little People,"* a hunter goes hunting in the Pryor Mountains and has little luck. He asks the Little People for guidance. A Little Person's voice tells him that he has to provide them with an offering. The man shoots a deer, and then drops it over a cliff in Black Canyon as an offering to these little spirits. He then goes on to have great luck at hunting. After returning home with his meat, the man goes back to the mountains the next day; he is curious to see if the dead deer is still where he left it. When he looks at the place where he dropped it, the deer's body is gone.

According to *Wikipedia,* as of the late 20th century, some Crow remained convinced that the Little People exist. Members of the Crow Nation passing through Pryor Gap sometimes still leave offerings for the Little People. Members of the modern Crow Nation say they have even encountered them while hunting in the Pryor Mountains. Others, taking a wrong road or footpath, say they have seen them blocking the road, and Little People are claimed to have even healed some sick people. Several white people in the area also claim to have seen the Little People, including a local bar owner, ranch hands, and hunters.

MANNEGISHI

The Cree are one of the largest groups of the First Nations (the predominant indigenous peoples in Canada south of the Arctic Circle). The major proportion of Cree in Canada live north and west of Lake Superior, in Ontario, Manitoba, Saskatchewan, Alberta, the Northwest Territories and Nunavut. In the United States, this Algonquian-speaking people historically lived from Lake Superior westward. Today, they live mostly in Montana, where they share a reservation with the Ojibwe (Chippewa). The *Mannegishi* are a race of trickster people in Cree folklore, who are described as being somewhat humanoid, with thin, lanky arms, six fingers on each hand, and big heads with no nose. According to Cree mythology, there are two humanoid races: the first one is our human species; and the other is the "Little People," like the Mannegishi. These Little People of the Cree are said to live between rocks in the rapids of streams and rivers. They delight in crawling out of the rocks and capsizing the canoes of people coming through the rapids, often sending them to their death.

The Mannegishi has resurfaced in recent years. In 1977, there was a purported modern sighting of the Mannegishi in the Dover Demon stories in New England:

BANGOR DAILY NEWS
Bangor, Maine
May 16, 1977

Teen'ers Report "Creature"

DOVER, Mass. (AP)

Police say recent reports of strange orange-eyed creatures were probably nothing more than a school vacation hoax. But a few nagging doubts linger.

Three teenagers have reported seeing a creature resembling comic book conceptions of a spaceman at night last month along dark, lonely roads in this community of 5,000 about 15 miles southwest of Boston.

"The only thing that worries me is the story of Bill Bartlett," 17, one of the witnesses, said Police Chief Carl Sheridan.

He described the youth as an "outstanding artist and a reliable witness."

A police spokesman said reports of the sightings were not made public by police until last week. He said officers searched the areas of the reported sightings without finding anything.

The teenagers say the creature has no ears, no mouth and no nose. It is described as three and a half feet tall with a white, melon-like head, rough skin and glowing eyes.

Two of the teenagers made sketches. One was by Bartlett, who is a member of Boston's Copley Art Society, a wellknown amateur arts guild.

"It scared me to death. I couldn't go back and see it," said Bartlett, the first person to report seeing the creature.

He told The Associated Press he was driving along Farm Street at 10:30 p.m. April 21 when he spotted something on top of a broken stone wall.

THE BOSTON GLOBE
Boston, Massachusetts
October 29, 2006

By MARK SULLIVAN

DECADES LATER, THE DOVER DEMON STILL HAUNTS.

DOVER—Twenty-nine years later, William Bartlett stands by his story of what he saw on Farm Street that night. It was an eerie human-like creature, he said, about 4 feet tall with glowing orange eyes and no nose or mouth in a watermelon-shaped head.

"I have no idea what it was," Bartlett, now a 46-year-old artist living in Needham, said in a recent interview. "I definitely know I saw something."

The "Dover Demon" that Bartlett and two other teenagers reported seeing over a two-day span in April 1977 has since gained worldwide attention, not unlike Bigfoot, the Loch Ness monster, and the Latin American goat-sucker, the Chupacabra. Internet pages are devoted to the Dover Demon. You can play a video game featuring the creature, or buy a figurine of it as far away as Japan.

"In a lot of ways it's kind of embarrassing to me," said Bartlett. "I definitely saw something. It was definitely weird. I didn't make it up. Sometimes I wish I had."

He has made a career as a painter, his work displayed in galleries on both coasts, but a Google search on "Bill Bartlett," he noted, invariably turns up his teenage encounter with the unknown.

Once, his wife, Gwen, browsing the horror section of a bookstore, flipped open an encyclopedia of monsters — and there was an entry about her husband and the Dover Demon.

331

"It's a thing that's been following me for years," Bartlett said. "Not the creature — the story. Sometimes I dread every Halloween getting calls about it."

On April 21, 1977, Bartlett, then 17, was driving along Farm Street at around 10 p.m. when, he said, he saw the creature atop a broken stone wall. Two hours later, according to news accounts from that time, John Baxter, 15, was walking home from his girlfriend's house when he got within 15 feet of the creature along a creek in a heavily wooded area along Miller Hill Road.

At midnight the next night, Abby Brabham, 15, was driving home with her boyfriend when she spotted the creature sitting upright on Springdale Avenue.

A drawing made by Baxter showed a humanoid figure with large eyes standing by a tree. Bartlett's large-eyed creature crawled with tendril-like fingers across a stone wall. "I, Bill Bartlett, swear on a stack of Bible's that I saw this creature," he wrote on the sketch. The locations of the sightings, plotted on a map, lay in a straight line over 2 miles. All the sightings were made in the vicinity of water.

No sightings have been reported since, though Bartlett says a weird experience a year later left him wondering if he had had a return visit from the creature.

The following year, he said, he was in a parked car with his girlfriend when he heard a thump on the car. He made out a small figure leaving the scene. He remains unsure who — or what — banged the car, he said, though it could have been a youngster playing a prank. Farm Street on a recent evening could have been a modern-day Sleepy Hollow, with woods lining the fieldstone walls, and what little light there was coming from the moon. Since at least the 17th century, the vicinity of the second-oldest road in Dover has been associated with strange occurrences.

In his 1914 town history, *"Dover Farms,"* Frank Smith writes of Farm Street:

In early times this road went around by the picturesque Polka Rock [on the farm of George Battelle] which was called for a man by that name, of whom it is remembered, that amid the superstitions of the age he thought he saw his Satanic Majesty as he was riding on horseback by this secluded spot.

The location has long been looked upon as one in which treasures are hid, but why anyone should go so far inland to hide treasures has never been told; however, there has been at times unmistakable evidence of considerable digging in the immediate vicinity of this rock.

Loren Coleman of Portland, Maine, a well-known crypto-zoologist, or researcher of "hidden animals," from Sasquatch to sea serpents, led the original investigations into the Dover Demon, whose name he coined. Studying Dover's history, Coleman said in a telephone interview, he was struck by the fact that the area in which the Demon was sighted had a tradition of unexplained activity.

"In the same area you had three major legends going on," he said, citing the apparition of the devil on horseback, the tales of buried treasure, and then the Dover Demon. "I think it certainly says something. It's almost as if there are certain areas that 'collect' sightings, almost in a magnetic way."

Coleman theorized that the large geologic outcropping in the woods off Farm Street that historian Smith called the "Polka Stone" might actually have been called the Pooka stone, after the fairy folk of Celtic folklore.

When the Dover Demon was sighted in 1977, it might not have been the first time a strange creature was spotted in the woods by local teenagers.

Mark Sennott of Sherborn, who was buying a bagel and coffee at Isabella's Groceries in Dover Center on a recent Saturday morning, said there was talk at Dover-Sherborn High School in the early 1970s of strange things seen in the woods.

In fact, Sennott said, he and his friends might have seen a "demon" themselves at Channing Pond on Springdale Avenue in 1972.

"I don't know if we really saw something," he said. "We thought we did. We saw a small figure, deep in the woods, moving at the edge of the pond. We could see it moving in the headlights. We didn't know—it could have been an animal," Sennott said the group told police, who investigated. But, "nothing came of it."

When Bartlett saw this creature five years later, he said, he was driving with two friends on Farm Street near Bridge Street on the way to Sherborn about 10 p.m. They had not had any beer: "We were probably looking for it," he said, "but we didn't see any that night."

Bartlett said the car was traveling maybe 35 to 40 miles per hour when he saw the thing "standing on a wall, its eyes glowing" in the headlights. "It was not a dog or a cat," he said. "It had no tail. It had an egg-shaped head." He said he saw it from about 10 feet away, over the duration it took the car to travel from one utility pole to the next. His two friends did not report seeing the creature.

He grew up around animals, and had seen the odd mangy fox, Bartlett said. "This definitely wasn't," he said. "It was some kind of creature," with "long thin fingers" and "more human-like in its form than animal."

Its shape reminded him of "kids with distended bellies," he said. "I' have always tried to guess what it was. I never had any idea."

This was no prank, Bartlett said. "I wasn't trying to be funny. People who know me know I didn't make this up."

Coleman, who began an investigation within days of the sightings in 1977 and spotlights the Dover Demon case in the 2001 edition of his book "Mysterious America," believes Bartlett.

"We have a credible case, over 25 hours, by individuals who saw something," said Coleman, who interviewed all three teens within a week of the reported sightings and said he was convinced they had not concocted a hoax.

Nothing quite like the Demon has been reported seen before or since, he said. The Dover creature does not match the descriptions of the Chupacabra, or of Roswell aliens, or of the bat-eared goblins said to have attacked a family in Hopkinsville, Ky., in 1955.

"It doesn't really fit any place,"

Coleman said. "It's extremely unique. It has no real connections to any other inexplicable phenomena."

Is it possible the teens actually saw a foal, or perhaps a moose calf, as some have suggested? Coleman said he canvassed local horse owners after the incident and none reported missing a horse. Moreover, it was not foaling season, he said.

As for the moose theory, only two moose were reported in Massachusetts in 1977 and 1978, both of them in Central Massachusetts, he said. A yearling moose by that time in April would weigh more than 600 pounds and be "bigger than the Volkswagen Bartlett was in," said Coleman.

"To have a bipedal moose with long fingers and orange skin and no hair and no nose would be more of a phenomenon than the Dover Demon," he said.

So what did those teens see?

"It's OK to say we don't know," said Coleman.

"I think the Dover Demon's mystery lives on. It's an unknown phenomenon whose fame has stretched worldwide, and I think Dover should be very proud."

In Dover, a quiet community dotted with horse farms and one of the richest towns in the state, people are still not quite sure what to make of the story.

"That thing has haunted me for 29 years," said Carl Sheridan, a former police chief. "I knew the kids involved. They were good kids . . . pretty reliable kids. God only knows what they saw," Sheridan said. "I still don't know. Strange things have happened. The whole thing was unusual."

He got calls from all over the world when the case made the news, the former chief said, and he still does, from time to time.

"The thing will not die," Sheridan said. "I'm telling you, the thing will not go away."

In Town Clerk Barrie Clough's office at Town Hall, municipal reports share shelf space with a file of materials related to the Dover Demon case, including a book titled "Weird New England" and a newspaper clipping headlined "Bizarre four-foot creature with orange skin and glowing eyes stalking a town."

"Every once in a while people will come in and ask about it," said Clough. "I have no idea if it's true or untrue."

Downtown Dover was decorated recently with pumpkins as children arrived for a Halloween fair, and a steady stream of regulars bought coffee and newspapers at Isabella's. Located in the old Dover Pharmacy, now with an Italian deli counter added to the old soda fountain, the grocery remains a town hub. Behind the counter at Isabella's, Scott Bielski, 17, of Dover, a senior at Dover-Sherborn High, said the demon gives his small town a unique claim to fame.

"Home of the Dover Demon has a nice ring to it," he said with a smile. As far as he knows, the creature had never stopped in to the soda fountain. "Let us know if he wants anything," he said.

A customer who gave his name as Jimmy said he has lived in town for four years but has yet to see the demon. "Maybe I will some day," he said. "I'm one of those realists — if I don't see it, I don't believe it."

Customer Ed Tourtellotte of Dover said: "I think it's probably as real as the Easter Bunny, but it's fun."

Nearly three decades after seeing something very strange on Farm Street, Bartlett has decidedly mixed feelings about the experience. "It was my 15 minutes of fame, without wanting it," he said.

"It was a little embarrassing. It still is." He said he hasn't talked much to his two children, 8 and 5 years old, about the creature: "I don't want to scare them." And the professional artist has never drawn another picture of the thing he saw. "I don't have enough memory of it," he said. "I haven't wanted to. I'm a serious fine-arts painter. I don't want people to think I'm some freak. I don't usually tell anybody."

"I shouldn't be embarrassed, but you see these people on TV and they're made to look like idiots," he said.

"I really do wish that I had made it up. I might have profited from it. It's a great story."

"I wish it was seen again so everyone would know it was true."

CHOCTAW NATION:
EPIC BATTLE OF GIANTS & DWARFS

Newspapers from early 1898, carried such headlines as "Thousands of Skulls Dug Up With Arrow Points In Them;" "Major Archaeological Discovery Occurs in Kansas:" "The Greatest Prehistoric Battle and Burying Ground Yet Discovered in the United States Found Near Redlands, Kansas On Northern Border of the Choctaw Indian Reservation Near the Arkansas River." Professor Edwin Walters, the archaeologist who discovered the massive battle site, stated that nearly 100,000 warriors met death at that point; the battle occurred 20,000 years ago. Walters hypothesized that the battle was fought between the mound builders and the Maya Toltec race who came from Yucatan to take the Mississippi Valley from the mound builder tribes. The skeletons varied greatly in length, some being those of dwarfs and others of a giant race:

FARMERS' REVIEW
Chicago, Illinois
January 5, 1898

The greatest prehistoric battle and burying ground yet discovered in the United States has just been found near the little town of Redlands, I.T. It lies on the northern border of the Choctaw Indian reservation and near the Arkansas River. Professor Edwin Walters, the archaeologist who discovered it, states that from extensive excavations he has made, he believes that nearly 100,000 warriors met death at that point, and that the battle occurred 20,000 years ago. He goes a step further and declares that the battle was fought between the mound builders and the Maya Toltec race, the latter coming from Yucatan and striving to wrest the Mississippi Valley from the mound builders. The battle ground is thirty acres in area. The bones are buried near the top of a deep strata of sand and covered first with a sort of adobe, a formation of the quaternary period; then with an alluvial top soil. Almost every skull has from one to five arrow points sticking into it. Sharp arrow points and javelins are also found embedded in other bones of the body. The skulls have narrow, retreating foreheads and projecting chins and the skeletons vary greatly in length, some seeming to be those of dwarfs and others of a giant race. The bodies are buried in a circle, feet toward the center; and most of them, in a sitting posture. At the side of each is found a clay vessel that was evidently filled with food to stay the soul of the departed warrior on his way to the spirit land.

~ ~ ~ ~ ~

CLARENCE AND RICHMOND EXAMINER
Grafton, NSW
February 15, 1898

An Awful Battle of Prehistoric Times.

Evidences of a mighty battle between barbaric races contending for the possession of the great valley of the Mississippi twenty thousand years ago, in which sixty thousand and perhaps a hundred thousand tawny-skinned warriors gave up their lives, have been discovered in the Indian Territory—that wild and almost unknown portion of the public domain set apart for the use and benefit of the nation's wards.

The initial discovery was made by laborers employed in grading a road bed for the Kansas City, Pittsburg, and Gulf Railway, a few months ago, near Redlands, I.T., in the northern parts of Choctaw Indian Reservation. They were surprised to find, at a depth of six to eight feet, a deposit of human bones, ancient pottery and stone weapons of warfare.

The road, at this point, went through one of the terraces of the Arkansas River bottom for a considerable distance; and as the grading progressed, cartloads of human bones, most of which crumbled when exposed to the air, and great quantities of rude battle axes, arrow points, long daggerlike javelin points, and pieces of pottery were unearthed.

THIRTY ACRES OF SKELETONS.

The workmen made no effort to preserve the relics, and the real value and extent of the prehistoric remains might never have been known had not Professor Edwin Walters, an archaeologist and geologist in the employ of the road, happened along about that time. He recognized the importance of the find, and has recently made extensive excavations. By digging and sounding, he has ascertained that thirty acres, most of which is heavily timbered, are underlaid with human bones ranging in height from dwarf to giant.

His first theory was that he had found an ancient burying-ground, in which, for many successive generations, the tribesmen had been laid to rest. But, when he picked up a skull in which thirteen moss agate arrow points were embedded, the conclusion was forced upon him that he had come upon a prehistoric battleground. Further excavations revealed other skulls pierced with arrow points, and many skeletons in portions of which arrow points or stone javelin heads were buried. One of them was dug up with a stone javelin head thrust through the spine, and projecting for several inches through the breastbone. Scarcely a skull has been found that does not bear the marks of violence. The great number of stone war implements that are being found confirms Professor Walters' theory that one of the bloodiest struggles of prehistoric times occurred there.

FOUGHT HAND TO HAND.

Less than fifty thousand men were killed in the bloodiest battle of the Civil War. What fearful carnage must there have been when between sixty thousand and one hundred thousand men, armed only with bows and arrows, javelins and rude battle axes, went down? Little wonder that almost every skull is crushed in with a blow from a battle axe or pierced with arrows whose tips had previously been dipped in poison. The work of mapping the earthworks, battle grounds, and burial places along the great battle line is one of the most stupendous undertakings yet attempted by students of America.

ALASKA'S INUKIN OR IRCINRRAQS

Alaska, 49th of the United States, has persistent tales of strange little people roaming about. The native tribes of the region, such as the Inuit and Yup'ik have had tales of little people living in the forests and frigid tundra dating back to prehistory. Depending on the tribe or tradition, these mystical little creatures go by many names: *Ircinrraqs*, E*nukin*, *Ircenrraat*, *Ingnakalaurak*, *Egassuayaq*, *Ircinrraqs* and *Paalraayak*. Most commonly and collectively these dwarfs are referred to as the Inukin. They are most often described as being between 1 to 3 feet in height; they dress in animal skins; they have pointed heads and pointy ears. These little people prefer to stay underground or hidden away in the tundra during the day, only venturing out at night, when everyone is supposed to be asleep. They rummage through the trash, steal fish off drying racks, and snatch up items left loose.

The Inukin are mischievous, bad-tempered, and they seem to enjoy tormenting people. It is said that the Inukin will intentionally try to get travelers lost or throw rocks at them. They have a bad habit of stealing the kills of hunters, even though they are hunters themselves, using bows and arrows. At their worst, the Inukin are thought to abduct women or children and drag them off, never to be seen again. The Inukin are said to have superhuman strength and supernatural powers such as shapeshifting, invisibility, and the power to create confusion in the minds of those who actually see them. A persistent story, appearing on the Internet since around 2009 is credited to "an old Inupiaq man named *Majik Imaje*." Of these little people and their great strength, he says:

> They live in the old ways to this very day they dress in caribou skins. They still hunt with bow & arrow. They live underground, and in caves all throughout this vast area. They possess super human qualities that you will never believe. They are incredibly strong and they can run, very fast; they sneak around the villages stealing food. When any hunter shoots and kills a caribou, it requires two adult Inupiaq men to lift that caribou to place on a sled. It only takes one Ingnakalaurak or Enukin to pick one up and run with it, over his head. Hunters, experienced hunters, often talk about caribou that they have shot & killed dead, and the caribou will disappear before they reach it to dress it out. Make no mistake, these people are very good in what they do, they are perhaps the best hunters in the world. Some bush pilots have reported seeing the strange sight of caribou running on their sides, only to fly lower and see that they are actually being carried along by an Inukin.

> This is no legend or folklore; new sightings are prevalent and constant each and every year. Although they are avoided by humans because of their malevolent tendencies, these creatures are also said to have a benevolent side as well. For instance, it is supposedly good luck to receive a gift from them when they are feeling generous. On occasion, instead of playing pranks, they will take pity on a lost soul out in the woods and guide the way. When a hunter is lost or stuck or in trouble these little people seemingly appear out of nowhere to assist and then are gone in a flash.

Another report appearing on the Internet seems to bear this out. According to the account, an Inupiaq man, Luke Koonuk, was out hunting one day. He had traveled many miles from Point Hope, Alaska, into a desolate region. His 4-wheel-drive Honda became stuck in the mud. After prolonged attempts at trying to free the vehicle from the ruts, Koonuk had to stop. Exhausted and bent over trying to catch his breath Koonuk suddenly, out of the corner of his eye, saw his Honda rise in the air and come bouncing down on firmer ground. A small creature was running away, moving so rapidly that it was sort of a blur.

The old Inupiaq man, Majik Imaje, goes on with his report of the Enukins:

> This is a vast area we are talking about in square miles, roughly the size of all the New England states put together, empty, with no inhabitants. A long time before the whaling companies arrived, the Ignaugalurauk's lived among the people of Point Hope, AK. One of their young was eaten by a dog, and they moved out of the village. These Enukin people are small, 3-4 feet in height! They live in the old ways to this very day. They dress in caribou skins. They still hunt with bow & arrow. They live underground, and in caves all throughout this vast area. They possess superhuman qualities that you will never believe. They are incredibly strong and they can run, very fast. When any hunter shoots and kills a caribou, it requires two adult men to lift that caribou to place it on a sled. It only takes one Ingnakalaurak or Enukin to pick up a caribou and run with it over his head. Running with a dead caribou? How do you make sense out of that? Bush Pilots have reported seeing caribou moving, quickly, in a horizontal position.

> Let's stop right here and let me extend an invitation to you. Anyone can come on up here and talk to the bush pilots. They will tell you what they have seen with their own eyes. I have lived almost 3 decades among the Inupiaq peoples. Hunters, experienced hunters, often talk about caribou that they have shot & killed, and the caribou will disappear

before they reach it to dress it out. Make no mistake, these people are very good in what they do.

Jump on a 4 wheel Honda or a snowmobile, and go 200 miles out into this empty region at 50 below zero and stay out there for weeks. You see a caribou and shoot it, it falls down, motionless. They wait and watch; have a smoke… wait and watch. "That caribou is dead," said Inupiaq man Joe Oktillik. "I got on my machine and drove over those hills, and — Where is it? I know this is the spot. There are tracks to the left or the right and no tracks going straight ahead. The last place I looked Joe said, "was up!?" Caribou is gone, no tracks? This happens a lot up here.

DETROIT MICHIGAN'S LITTLE PEOPLE

The tale has its origins with the Ottawa tribe of Native American, who inhabited the region of what is now Detroit, Michigan. Curious spirit folk known as the Nain Rouge, or "Red Dwarfs," once inhabited this untamed wilderness. These creatures were said to be indeed mischievous, like many little folk in other traditions. But, the Nain Rouge were powerful nature spirits and caretakers of the earth. These mostly benevolent forest dwellers, can also be harbingers of doom and destruction; a human who sees one of them takes it as an omen of bad things to come. The Nain Rouge were described as small, child-sized humanoids with ruddy faces of old men. These gnomes had glowing eyes and jagged and yellowed, rotten teeth. They are sometimes described as wearing no clothes, but being covered in matted, reddish-brown hair. Other descriptions say that Nain Rouge dress in shabby garments, pointy hats, and fur boots.

One of the earliest such reports occurred on March 10, 1701, when the founder of Detroit, Antoine de la Mothe Cadillac, was having a party. A mysterious fortune teller appeared at the gathering. She read Antoine de la Mothe Cadillac's palm, telling him that he was destined to start a great city; but this new colony would be the place of great strife and bloodshed. She also warned him to pay heed to the Nain Rouge; he was warned not to upset any of the little people, because this would certainly mean his downfall.

The skeptical Cadillac scoffed at her warnings. After the founding of his city, while walking one evening, Cadillac reported that a deformed, dwarf-like creature, crooked, horrendous teeth, covered in blackish-red fur, and with fierce, beady red eyes, shuffled up to him. Cadillac recognized the Nain Rouge, but in spite of warnings, he bashed the creature over the head with his cane and told it to go away. The gnome just laughed and ran off. From that point in time, Cadillac was plagued with a constant misfortunes, eventually dying alone and penniless.

The Nain Rouge was spotted at other times in the Detroit area. One of the more well-known of these sightings occurred on July 30, 1763, when the Battle of Bloody Run was fought between the British and Ottawa Chief Pontiac's band of insurgents. Eyewitnesses, including many of the soldiers, claimed that they had seen one of the Nain Rouge sitting on the banks of the creek watching the carnage. When the fighting stopped, the fearsome little dwarf began to frolic and dance among the corpses that littered the ground and to splash about in the blood stained waters of the creek.

The reputation of the Nain Rouge portending death and disaster continued. In the days before the great Detroit fire of 1805, which would burn most of the city to the ground, the dreaded Nain Rouge was reportedly seen numerous times. Some even claimed that they saw the evil little man dancing in the flames.

The creature was seen again at the end of the War of 1812. The defeated General William Hull reported seeing a Nain Rouge peering out of the fog, with an evil grin on its face during his surrender of Detroit in 1813.

The malevolent little beasts were still up to their tricks in the 20th century. The creature was sighted a few times before the 1967 Detroit riot, one of an epidemic of race riots sweeping the U.S. at the time. The Detroit riot was one of the most destructive and violent riots the nation has ever seen. One witness at the time described the creature as "doing back flips and cartwheels" down 12th Street during the police raid of a bar that ignited the whole fiasco.

Then, in March of 1976, two workers reported seeing a Nain Rouge climbing up a utility pole. The utility workers thought it was a child climbing the pole until it leapt down to the ground and they could see that it was actually the legendary Nain Rouge. Immediately after this, one of the worst snowstorms in the Detroit's history hit.

There are more recent alleged sightings of the Nain Rouge as well. In 1996, the *Michigan Believer* ran a story about a pair of witnesses who claimed that they had just exited a nightclub when they saw a tiny, hunched over man wearing what looked like a filthy tattered old fur coat flee from a car that it was attempting to burglarize, while making a "cawing sound, similar to a crow."

In 2017 there were reports of the Nain Rouge around Detroit. One commenter on *Reddit,* called "theinfamous99," gave two accounts of what appears to be this creature:

> These 2 stories came from 2 people who knew nothing of the other. My great Aunt says when she was little, she saw a gnome on several occasions. It would stare at her and even followed her. The last time she saw it was at a funeral home, where it attempted to get her to go into a cellar. When she told me and my sister this story many years later, she looked disturbed. She said that she has carried a cross ever since.

> The next person to tell me a related account was my close friend's older sister. She said she was chased by an "evil little creature" at her bus stop. She described it as a gnome. My friends would tease her about it at the time. But, now that I'm older and more mature, I regret not listening to her. She had a hard time even talking about it. She said the gnome was very small, smaller than she was as an 8 year old girl. It had white fur and a pointy red hat.

Why would the Nain Rouge go from the beneficial spirit and protector of nature, that it was traditionally seen as in Native American lore; to evil creature depicted by people of European descent. Could it be that the Nain Rouge simply did not take kindly to outsiders coming into their land? Or, could it be that we have misunderstood them, and that they are not causing the disasters in any way, but rather trying to warn us in their own way, and in this sense they could still be considered protectors or guardians of a sort?

Regardless of whether the Nain rouge is actually real or not, the city of Detroit has adopted it as sort of a mascot. There has historically been a yearly parade called the Marche du Nain Rouge, in which costumed revelers ceremoniously chase the red dwarf out of the city and conclude with burning an effigy of the creature, which will banish the imp from the city for another year.

FROM BROOKLYN TO COLOMBIA & BACK

A internet blog website, "From the Shadows: True Tales of the Paranormal" by Jason Offutt, from December 9, 2010, featured a story of an encounter with little people in Brooklyn, New York. Fabian Hernandez, 30, a veteran of the U.S. Army 82nd Airborne Division, and his brother, an aircraft engineer, were born in Brooklyn, N.Y., in the 1980s. "We lived in a small apartment in Brooklyn with our parents," he said. "I have Native Indian blood from the natives of Colombia, South America, from my mother's side." Due to financial struggles, the family soon moved back to their mother's home country, Colombia. There, Hernandez saw little people in his room. Hernandez and his brother were sleeping when a vibration woke Fabian. He wasn't prepared for what he saw. "I can recall seeing a group of small men working around my bed, silently," Hernandez said. "It was like as if I was looking at characters (from another) dimension."

Hernandez laid in his bed, just staring at the little men. "These creatures got the most of me and I started to be more curious," Hernandez said. "I observed them walking around like they were working in a mine of some kind, like digging or something." The little men were three inches tall and bright white. "They were minding their own business," Hernandez said. "The following day I told my parents and I just simply got brushed off. At that time, I got a little scared and did not know what to do, so I simply forgot it as time passed."

Four years later, the Hernandez family moved back to Brooklyn. "I was around the age of nine and my brother was just a few years older than me," Hernandez said. "We lived in a small apartment where we shared the same bed in our parent's room." One night, Hernandez went to sleep early because of the flu. When he woke in the early morning, he saw something he'd seen years before, a continent away. "I slept against the wall and my brother towards the edge," he said. "I think it was around two or three in the morning when I noticed a white, long bright light, like when window blinds close and the light comes in." Something moved in the light. "I had awakened my brother laying next to me, to see what I was seeing," he said. "This long, bright light transformed, and my brother said 'look, it's moving.' I said, 'what is that?'" Both Hernandez and his brother saw little white figures, about three inches tall, moving in that light. "They were talking amongst each other, moving around rapidly in a (different) dimension sort of way," Hernandez said. The light drew across the ceiling and onto the wall next to Hernandez before it disappeared.

Since this incident, Hernandez hasn't seen the little people, but the thought of them still frightens him. "I get the chills talking about it, as (does) my brother," Hernandez said. "This has been something that has been bothering my brother and I for many years, thinking that it was just my mind or eyes playing tricks on me, but I know it wasn't a child problem, since my older brother had confirmed it."

FIRST-HAND ENCOUNTERS

There are quite a few postings on internet forums by readers who have either heard stories of encounters with Little People, or have actually experienced them first-hand. Here are some examples:

- I learned that a bored young boy playing along a creek near Bend, Oregon, saw two little people who crossed the creek and stood looking at him. He said they were no more than 15 to 18 inches high and very dark complexion. They wore skins as garments, and after a period of 10 to 15 seconds, walked back across the creek and into the forest. The boy showed their footprints to his parents, who had contracted to a logging company to clean up slash piles. The prints were obvious and his parents were flabbergasted, but chose not to follow the little beings into the woods. He believes now that the little men weren't happy about the logging and destruction in the forest.

- The last time I saw little people was around 1957 in Fort Worth, Texas. I had been sleeping and something made me open my eyes. I saw two small people looking back at me. I was too tired and sleepy at the time to pursue further investigation of these two little guys who had very little hair and wore shabby strange clothes. They sort of smiled at me and I fell back to sleep. I know what I saw and they were real.

- I don't know if what I saw was a "little person," but when I was younger, around seven or eight, these little shadows or elves, maybe the size of a pinky, would come out in my room. I can't remember the feelings I had. I wouldn't go to bed with the lights out and I insisted that my parents stay with me in my room until I fell asleep. I think they thought I was crazy or something! But I know what I saw. Most of the time, they walked on my window, but then when I turned the other direction, they would jump in front of me as if they wanted me to see them. I don't think I was all that scared, but I can still remember clearly what they looked like. Over a period of time, they disappeared. I think it lasted a year. Also, I remember that when I wanted them to go away, I would ask them to leave. If they didn't, then I would try to smack them with my hand, but they would disappear before I could. I don't recall them talking. It was strange, but I know it happened.

- Last year when my daughter and friends were four-wheeling in the woods in Washington state, they were stuck and having problems getting out. When working at getting out, an elf-like person came out and looked at them. The elf had a bow and arrow, pointed hat and pointed ears. Six people saw it." The experience lasted only about 10 seconds for the friends, but seemed to play out as if in slow motion. "We turned and ran as fast as we could toward our vehicle," Paul says. "On arriving, we tried to make sense of what we witnessed. We returned to the spot and saw nothing but bush. No lights, no little people, no rock formation, just bush.

- One bizarre report comes from a witness who had just moved to Puerto Rico with his mother when he was 17 years old. He claimed that one day he had gone to take a shower and suddenly heard the family dog frantically barking at something outside. It seemed that the dog was quite worked up and upset over something, so the witness got out of the shower to go take a look out the window, where he saw something far weirder than what he had perhaps been expecting. There in the yard lurking behind a tree was what the witness described as a "diminutive man dressed completely in white, and complete with a white cone-shaped hat and white, pointed shoes." The odd little man apparently stared at the witness for a moment and proceeded to vanish into thin air. A few days later, the strange creature appeared again, this time outside of the witness's window. The strange tiny man then smiled and disappeared again until a few days later, when he appeared yet again. This time the witness claims to have tried to communicate with it, asking it what its name was, to which it surprisingly replied that its name was "Sebastian Polizar." Things had gotten so incredibly odd that the witness, who had to this point not mentioned it to anyone else, told his mother, who perhaps not surprisingly didn't believe him. The witness then called out to the gnome by name and it apparently appeared out of nowhere right there in front of them to cause the mother to scream out in shock. This gnome reportedly would continue to make regular appearances around the house and in the yard until the family had had enough and moved out.

- Another early account of an apparent gnome comes from the rural town of Farmersville, Texas, in the United States, in 1913. The witness, a man by the name of Silbie Latham, claimed that while he and his two brothers were out toiling away on their cotton farm one day their dogs began to bark and snarl off in the distance. The brothers thought nothing of it at first, but the barking and growling became steadily more intense and chaotic until they decided that it was probably best to see what was disturbing the animals so much. When the oldest of the brothers, Clyde, went to have a look he shouted to the others that he could see that the dogs were upset by a "little man." When the others ran to go see what he meant they were purportedly met with the sight of a diminutive humanoid around 18 inches tall and a dark green in color and wearing a large, pointed hat, and the thing was just standing there with its arms at its sides. Silbie would describe the scene thus: He didn't seem to have any shoes, but I don't really remember his feet. His arms were hanging down just beside him, like they was grew down the side of him. He had on a kind of hat that reminded me of a Mexican hat. It was a little round hat that looked like it was built onto him. He didn't have on any clothes. Everything looked like a rubber suit including the hat. He just stood still. I guess he was just scared to death… Right after we got there, the dogs jumped him. ravaged the little creature, tearing it apart, although of course the body has become lost to the mists of time, as is often the case in these accounts. Another early report from 1919 was told by a witness named Harry Anderson, who claimed that one night when he was 13 years old he had seen a procession of around 20 tiny men marching along in the moonlight. The strange little people were described as having pale white skin and wearing leather knees pants and suspenders. The odd little humanoids were walking along in a single file line and allegedly chattering with each other in some unintelligible language. Although Harry was terrified, the creatures marched right on by him and didn't even seem to notice that he was there at all.

- Starting from 1952, when he was just a child, the household of Dan Bortko, of Wyandotte County, Kansas, would be haunted by a gnome for years. The family had moved to a two-story home on a rural farm property in Liberty, Mo. complete with a barn, and from a very young age Bortko claims he frequently saw a small humanoid about 3 feet tall and fully decked out in German lederhosen and with a smoking pipe, lurking about their house, often appearing in his room at night. The creature would often stand there looking at him before smiling or winking and disappearing through the closet. Bortko also said that he would often look outside his window at night to see "little people" congregating out around the barn. He once drew a picture of the one he had seen up close, and it was so frightening to his little brother that he would cry whenever he saw it. Bortko would say of his first encounter with the creature: I had just awakened from a nap and was rubbing my eyes and saw what you would call a troll. I'll call him a troll because that's what he reminded me of. It was an old man with a long beard, large nose, about three feet tall, standing at the foot of my bed. I was astounded.

- There was another case in the early 1960s from a witness known as Jerry, who claimed that he saw a "gnome" or "troll" at his home in Orange, N.J. Jerry claimed that one day he had gone outside into the backyard and seen a "a small gnome-like man with a long beard" standing by the steps leading up to the porch. According to the witness the little man "had funny clothes on and a pointed hat and all." Years later this strange creature would make another appearance at the home, when Jerry's 5-year-old nephew woke from a nap crying to run downstairs and claim that he had been woken by a small man with a flowing white beard who had been staring at him as he slept.

- As if gnomes and elves aren't already quite strange enough, there have even been reports of actual leprechauns. One of the weirdest of these occurred in the last place one might expect for a leprechaun sighting. In 2006 a large crowd amassed on Le Cren Street in Mobile, Alabama; they were creating considerable commotion.

When an NBC affiliated news station arrived to see what was going on, they were told that a leprechaun had been spotted up in a tree, which had slowly materialized there out of nowhere, and was hiding within the branches. One witness produced a sketch of the creature. Although the video of the scene, complete with commentaries by people who had seen the creature, went viral on YouTube at the time, many thought it was all a St. Patrick's Day hoax. However, numerous witnesses were adamant that they had actually seen what has become known as the "Alabama Leprechaun," with some swearing that they continued to sight the strange creature in the area afterwards. Considering the parodies made of the incident and all of the fun poked at the story it is nearly impossible to tell if there is anything more to this than a big joke; but it is a truly weird tale all the same.

Giants & Little People

of

SCANDINAVIA

"Scandinavia" is the region of the world that encompasses the countries of Norway and Sweden, Denmark, Finland, Iceland, and the Faroe Islands. The term, "Norse mythology" is the body of myths and folklore of the North Germanic people of Scandinavia. The giants and giantesses, also called Jotuns or Jötunns in Norse mythology, are said to be the first living beings, a race of Giants. A Jotun is a giant with superhuman strength who lives in the land of Jotunheim, which is one of the nine worlds in Norse mythology. Jotunheim is mostly made of rocks, mountains, wilderness and dense forests. The Giants mostly eat the fish in the water, and the animals from the dense forests, because there is no fertile land.

The first of these giants was a giant called Ymir, and it is from the corpse of Ymir the world created. According to the medieval Icelandic scholar, Snorri Sturluson, Ymir was born when fire and ice met. Ymir was suckled by the cow Audhumla for his nourishment, and several other giants spontaneously sprang from his sweat. Audhumla, in turn, was nourished by a salt lick; and as she licked it, a being named Buri, the first of the Aesir gods, was freed from the salt. He produced a son, Borr, who mated with Bestla, one of Ymir's descendants. From their union came Odin, the chief of the Aesir, and his two brothers, Vili and Ve. The brothers then slew Ymir and fashioned the cosmos from his corpse.

As one of the poems in the *Poetic Edda*, *Grímnismál* or "Song of the Hooded One," words it this way:

> *From Ymir's flesh the earth was created,*
> *And from his sweat the sea,*
> *Mountains from bone,*
> *Trees from hair,*
> *And from his skull the sky.*

> *And from his eyebrows the blithe gods made*
> *Midgard, home of the sons of men*
> *And from his brains*
> *They sculpted the grim clouds.*

Of the countless giants in Norse legends, Hrungnir was reported to be one of the biggest and baddest. One day Odin, the leader of the Norse gods of Asgard, challenged Hrungnir to a horse race. Odin rode his fast eight-legged steed Sleipnir; and Hrungnir rode his four-legged horse, Gullfaxi. Not surprisingly, Sleipnir outran Gullfaxi and led him into the realm of Asgard. There, feeling sorry for the loser, Odin invited Hrungnir for a drink. Unfortunately, Hrungnir was not a pleasant drunk. He soon become belligerent and argumentative, claiming that he could kill all the gods of Asgard, except for the goddesses Freya and Sif, whom he would carry off with him to Jotunheim, the realm of the Giants. Becoming tired of Hrungnir's arrogance, the other gods called upon Thor, who challenged Hrungnir to a duel.

Hrungnir agreed. On the day of the fight, he turned up clad in stone armor and carrying a giant whetstone as a weapon. Thor threw his trusty hammer, Mjolnir, and it smashed through both the whetstone and Hrungnir's head. The latter fell to his death. It is said that the fragments of the whetstone fell to the earth and became the flint we see around us today.

In addition to Giants in Norse folklore and mythology, there were real live men of gigantic stature throughout the region, throughout history. A brief listing of some of these notable Scandinavian Giants follows:

ROLV THE WALKER
Norway, England: Ganger-Rolv, Rolv the Walker, later known as Rollo, was a Norwegian Viking. One of the most famous of the Viking chieftains was

"Rollo the Walker," so called because he was "a giant so tall that no horse could carry him." Therefore, he always had to walk. But, because of his immense size and strength, he did on foot what few could do on horseback.

In his 1904 history, *Famous Men of the Middle Ages,* John Henry Haaren describes Rollo:

CHAPTER XII: ROLLO THE VIKING
(Died 931 A.D.)

I.

For more than two hundred years during the Middle Ages the Christian countries of Europe were attacked on the southwest by the Saracens of Spain, and on the northwest by the Norsemen, or Northmen. The Northmen were so called because they came into Middle Europe from the north. Sometimes they were called Vikings, or pirates, because they were adventurous sea-robbers who plundered all countries which they could reach by sea. Their ships were long and swift. In the center was placed a single mast, which carried one large sail. For the most part, however, the Norsemen depended on rowing, not on the wind, and sometimes there were twenty rowers in one vessel. The Vikings were a terror to all their neighbors; but the two regions that suffered most from their attacks were the Island of Britain and that part of Charlemagne's empire in which the Franks were settled. Nearly fifty times in two hundred years the lands of the Franks were invaded. The Vikings sailed up the large rivers into the heart of the region which we now call France and captured and pillaged cities and towns.

Some years after Charlemagne's death they went as far as his capital, Aix, took the place, and stabled their horses in the cathedral which the great emperor had built. In the year 860 they discovered Iceland and made a settlement upon its shores. A few years later they sailed as far as Greenland, and there established settlements which existed for about a century. These Vikings were the first discoverers of the continent on which we live. Ancient books found in Iceland tell the story of the discovery. It is related that a Viking ship was driven during a storm to a strange coast, which is thought to have been that part of America now known as Labrador. When the captain of the ship returned home he told what he had seen. His tale so excited the curiosity of a young Viking prince, called Leif the Lucky, that he sailed to the newly discovered coast. Going ashore, he found that the country abounded in wild grapes; and so he called it Vinland, or the land of Vines. Vinland is thought to have been a part of what is now the Rhode Island coast. The Vikings were not aware that they had found a great unknown continent. No one in the more civilized parts of Europe knew anything about their discovery; and after a while the story of the Vinland voyages seems to have been forgotten, even among the Vikings themselves. So it is not to them that we owe the discovery of America, but to Columbus; because his discovery, though nearly five hundred years later than that of the Norsemen, actually made known to all Europe, for all time, the existence of the New World.

II.

The Vikings had many able chieftains. One of the most famous was Rollo the Walker, so called because he was such a giant that no horse strong enough to carry him could be found, and therefore he always had to walk. However, he did on foot what few could do on horseback. In 885 seven hundred ships, commanded by Rollo and other Viking chiefs, left the harbors of Norway, sailed to the mouth of the Seine, and started up the river to capture the city of Paris. Rollo and his men stopped on the way at Rouen, which also was on the Seine, but nearer its mouth. The citizens had heard of the giant, and when they saw the river covered by his fleet they were dismayed. However, the bishop of Rouen told them that Rollo could be as noble and generous as he was fierce; and he advised them to open their gates and trust to the mercy of the Viking chief. This was done, and Rollo marched into Rouen and took possession of it. The bishop had given good advice, for Rollo treated the people very kindly. Soon after capturing Rouen he left the place, sailed up the river to Paris, and joined the other Viking chiefs. And now for six long miles the beautiful Seine was covered with Viking vessels, which carried an army of thirty thousand men. A noted warrior named Eudes was Count of Paris, and he had advised the Parisians to fortify the city. So not long before the arrival of Rollo and his companions, two walls with strong gates had been built round Paris. It was no easy task for even Vikings to capture a strongly walled city. We are told that Rollo and his men built a high tower and rolled it on wheels up to the walls. At its top was a floor well manned with soldiers. But the people within the city shot hundreds of arrows at the besiegers, and threw down rocks, or poured boiling oil and pitch upon them. The Vikings thought to starve the Parisians, and for thirteen months they encamped round the city. At length food became very scarce, and Count Eudes determined to go for help. He went out through one of the gates on a dark, stormy night, and rode post-haste to the king. He told him that something must be done to save the people of Paris. So the king gathered an army and marched to the city. No battle was fought-- the Vikings seemed to have been afraid to risk one. They gave up the siege, and Paris was relieved. Rollo and his men went to the Duchy of Burgundy, where, as now, the finest crops were raised and the best of wines were made.

III.

Perhaps after a time Rollo and his Vikings went home; but we do not know what he did for about twenty-five years. We do know that he abandoned his old home in Norway in 911. Then he and his people sailed from the icy shore of Norway and again went up the Seine in hundreds of Viking vessels. Of course, on arriving in the land of the Franks, Rollo at once began to plunder towns and farms. Charles, then king of the Franks, although his people called him the Simple, or Senseless, had sense enough to see that this must be stopped. So he sent a message to Rollo and proposed that they should have a talk about peace. Rollo agreed and accordingly they met. The king and his troops stood on one side of a little river, and Rollo with his Vikings stood on the other. Messages passed between them. The king asked Rollo what he wanted. "Let me and my people live in the land of the Franks; let us make ourselves home here, and I and my Vikings will become your vassals," answered Rollo. He asked for Rouen and the neighboring land. So the king gave him that part of Francia; and ever since it has been called Normandy, the land of the Northmen. When it was decided that the Vikings should settle in Francia and be subjects of the Frankish king, Rollo was told that he must kiss the foot of Charles in token that he would be the king's vassal. The haughty Viking refused. "Never," said he, "will I bend my knee before any man, and no man's foot will I kiss." After some persuasion, however, he ordered one of his men to perform the act of homage for him. The king was on horseback and the Norseman, standing by the side of the horse, suddenly seized the king's foot and drew it up to his lips. This almost made the king fall from his horse, to the great amusement of the Norsemen. Becoming a vassal to the king meant that if the king went to war Rollo would be obliged to join his army and bring a certain number of armed men--one thousand or more. Rollo now granted parts of

Normandy to his leading men on condition that they would bring soldiers to his army and fight under him. They became his vassals, as he was the king's vassal. The lands granted to vassals in this way were called feuds, and this plan of holding lands was called the Feudal System. It was established in every country of Europe during the Middle Ages. The poorest people were called serfs. They were almost slaves and were never permitted to leave the estate to which they belonged. They did all the work. They worked chiefly for the landlords, but partly for themselves. Having been a robber himself, Rollo knew what a shocking thing it was to ravage and plunder, and he determined to change his people's habits. He made strict laws and hanged robbers. His duchy thus became one of the safest parts of Europe. The Northmen learned the language of the Franks and adopted their religion. The story of Rollo is especially interesting to us, because Rollo was the forefather of that famous Duke of Normandy who, less than a hundred and fifty years later, conquered England and brought into that country the Norman nobles with their French language and customs.

DANIEL CAJANUS

Standing above eight feet high, the Swedish giant Daniel Cajanus was born in Paldamo, Finland in 1704. At that time, Finland was still a province of Sweden. Even though Daniel grew up during a famine, he attained the great height of seven feet, eight inches. Cajanus left his home in 1723. He made his living by acting in plays and exhibiting himself in theaters for a fee. One day, in Prussia, a well-known strong man challenged Daniel Cajanus to a bizarre duel: they would slap each other's faces until one of them was out cold. Although he was a peaceful man, Cajanus accepted the challenge. The strong man won a coin toss and delivered the first blow, which almost toppled the giant. Infuriated, Cajanus dealt the Prussian such a powerful box on the ear, that the man fell dead. Since the bizarre duel was illegal, Daniel Cajhanus had to flee Prussia.

On February 27, 1749, the 46-year-old giant died in his house in Haarlem Proveniershuis, Amsterdam. The funeral of Daniel Cajanus was said to be grand, just the way he would have like it. The coffin was twice the size of an average human's. His enormous silver-hilted sword and his gloves were displayed on the hearse's sides. The hearse and coffin, with its many pairs of pallbearers, were viewed by several thousand spectators.

In addition to mythological Giants and real human Giants, Scandinavian fairy tales include them. One such fairy story follows:

POPULAR TALES FROM THE NORSE
Edinburgh, Scotland; 1888

THE GIANT WHO HAD NO HEART
IN HIS BODY

By DAVID DOUGLASS

Once on a time there was a King who had seven sons, and he loved them so much that he could never bear to be without them all at once, but one must always be with him. Now, when they were grown up, six were to set off to woo, but as for the youngest, his father kept him at home, and the others were to bring back a princess for him to the palace. So the King gave the six the finest clothes you ever set eyes on, so fine that the light gleamed from them a long way off, and each had his horse, which cost many, many hundred dollars, and so they set off. Now, when they had been to many palaces, and seen many princesses, at last they came to a King who had six daughters; such lovely king's daughters they had never seen, and so they fell to wooing them, each one, and when they had got them for sweethearts, they set off home again, but they quite forgot that they were to bring back with them a sweetheart for Boots, their brother, who stayed at home, for they were head and ears in love with their own sweethearts.

But when they had gone a good bit on their way, they passed close by a steep hillside, like a wall, where the giant's house was, and there the giant came out, and set his eyes upon them, and turned them all into stone, princes and princesses and all. Now the King waited and waited for his six sons, but the more he waited the longer they stayed away; so he fell into great trouble, and said he should never know what it was to be glad again.

"And if I had not you left," he said to Boots, "I would live no longer, so full of sorrow am I for the loss of your brothers."

"Well, but now I've been thinking to ask your leave to set out and find them again; that's what I'm thinking of," said Boots.

"Nay, nay!" said his father; "that leave you shall never get, for then you would stay away too."

But Boots had set his heart upon it; go he would; and he begged and prayed so long that the King was forced to let him go. Now, you must know the King had no other horse to give Boots but an old broken-down jade, for his six other sons and their train had carried off all his horses; but Boots did not care a pin for that, he sprang up on his sorry old steed.

"Farewell, father," said he; "I'll come back, never fear, and like enough I shall bring my six brothers back with me." And with that he rode off.

So, when he had ridden a while, he came to a Raven, which lay in the road and flapped its wings, and was not able to get out of the way, it was so starved.

"Oh, dear friend," said the Raven, "give me a little food, and I'll help you again at your utmost need."

"I haven't much food," said the Prince, "and I don't see how you'll ever be able to help me much; but still I can spare you a little. I see you want it."

So he gave the Raven some of the food he had brought with him.

Now, when he had gone a bit further, he came to a brook, and in the brook lay a great Salmon, which had got upon a dry place, and dashed itself about, and could not get into the water again.

"Oh, dear friend," said the Salmon to the Prince; "shove me out into the water again, and I'll help you again at your utmost need."

"Well!" said the Prince, "the help you'll give me will not be great, I daresay, but it's a pity you should lie there and choke." And with that, he shot the fish out into the stream again.

After that he went a long, long way, and there met him a Wolf, which was so famished that it lay and crawled along the road on its belly.

"Dear friend, do let me have your horse," said the Wolf; "I'm so hungry the wind whistles through my ribs; I've had nothing to eat these two years."

"No," said Boots, "this will never do; first I came to a raven, and I was forced to give him my food; next I came to a salmon, and him I had to help into the water again; and now you will have my horse. It can't be done, that it can't, for then I should have nothing to ride on."

"Nay, dear friend, but you can help me," said Graylegs the wolf. "You can ride upon my back, and I'll help you again in your utmost need."

"Well! The help I shall get from you will not be great, I'll be bound," said the Prince; "but you may take my horse, since you are in such need." So when the wolf had eaten the horse, Boots took the bit and put it into the wolf's jaw, and laid the saddle on his back. Now, the wolf was so strong, after what he had got inside him, that he set off with the Prince like nothing. So fast he had never ridden before.

"When we have gone a bit farther," said Graylegs, "I'll show you the Giant's house."

So after a while they came to it.

"See, here is the Giant's house," said the Wolf; "and see, here are your six brothers, whom the Giant has turned into stone; and see here are their six brides, and away yonder is the door, and in at that door you must go."

"Nay, but I daren't go in," said the Prince; "he'll take my life."

"No! no!" said the Wolf; "when you get in you'll find a Princess, and she'll tell you what to do to make an end of the Giant. Only mind and do as she bids you."

Well! Boots went in, but, truth to say, he was very much afraid. When he came in the Giant was away, but in one of the rooms sat the Princess, just as the wolf had said, and so lovely a Princess Boots had never yet set eyes on.

"Oh! heaven help you! whence have you come?" said the Princess, as she saw him; "it will surely be your death. No one can make an end of the Giant who lives here, for he has no heart in his body."

"Well! Well!" said Boots; "but now that I am here, I may as well try what I can do with him; and I will see if I can't free my brothers, who are standing turned to stone out of doors; and you, too, I will try to save, that I will."

"Well, if you must, you must," said the Princess; "and so let us see if we can't hit on a plan. Just creep under the bed yonder, and mind and listen to what he and I talk about. But, pray, do lie as still as a mouse."

So he crept under the bed, and he had scarce got well underneath it, before the Giant came.

"Ha!" roared the Giant, "what a smell of Christian blood there is in the house!"

"Yes, I know there is," said the Princess, "for there came a magpie flying with a man's bone, and let it fall down the chimney. I made all the haste I could to get it out, but all one can do, the smell doesn't go off so soon." So the Giant said no more about it, and when night came, they went to bed. After they had lain a while, the Princess said—

"There is one thing I'd be so glad to ask you about, if I only dared."

"What thing is that?" asked the Giant.

"Only where it is you keep your heart, since you don't carry it about you," said the Princess.

"Ah! that's a thing you've no business to ask about; but if you must know, it lies under the door-sill," said the Giant.

"Ho! Ho!" said Boots to himself under the bed, "then we'll soon see if we can't find it."

Next morning the Giant got up cruelly early, and strode off to the wood; but he was hardly out of the house before Boots and the Princess set to work to look under the door-sill for his heart; but the more they dug, and the more they hunted, the more they couldn't find it.

"He has baulked us this time," said the Princess, "but we'll try him once more."

So she picked all the prettiest flowers she could find, and strewed them over the door-sill, which they had laid in its right place again; and when the time came for the Giant to come home again, Boots crept under the bed. Just as he was well under, back came the Giant.

Snuff-snuff, went the Giant's nose. "My eyes and limbs, what a smell of Christian blood there is in here," said he.

"I know there is," said the Princess, "for there came a magpie flying with a man's bone in his bill, and let it fall down the chimney. I made as much haste as I could to get it out, but I daresay it's that you smell."

So the Giant held his peace, and said no more about it. A little while after, he asked who it was that had strewed flowers about the door-sill.

"Oh, I, of course," said the Princess.

"And, pray, what's the meaning of all this?" said the Giant.

"Ah!" said the Princess, "I'm so fond of you that I couldn't help strewing them, when I knew that your heart lay under there."

"You don't say so," said the Giant; "but after all it doesn't lie there at all."

So when they went to bed again in the evening, the Princess asked the Giant again where his heart was, for she said she would so like to know.

"Well," said the Giant, "if you must know, it lies away yonder in the cupboard against the wall."

"So, so!" thought Boots and the Princess; "then we'll soon try to find it."

Next morning the Giant was away early, and strode off to the wood, and so soon as he was gone Boots and the Princess were in the cupboard hunting for his heart, but the more they sought for it, the less they found it.

"Well," said the Princess, "we'll just try him once more."

So she decked out the cupboard with flowers and garlands, and when the time came for the Giant to come home, Boots crept under the bed again.

Then back came the Giant.

Snuff-snuff! "My eyes and limbs, what a smell of Christian blood there is in here!"

"I know there is," said the Princess; "for a little while since there came a magpie flying with a man's bone in his bill, and let it fall down the chimney. I made all the haste I could to get it out of the house again; but after all my pains, I daresay it's that you smell."

When the Giant heard that, he said no more about it; but a little while after, he saw how the cupboard was all decked about with flowers and garlands; so he asked who it was that had done that? Who could it be but the Princess?

"And, pray, what's the meaning of all this tomfoolery?" asked the Giant.

"Oh, I'm so fond of you, I couldn't help doing it when I knew that your heart lay there," said the Princess.

"How can you be so silly as to believe any such thing?" said the Giant.

"Oh yes; how can I help believing it, when you say it?" said the Princess.

"You're a goose," said the Giant; "where my heart is, you will never come."

"Well," said the Princess; "but for all that, 'twould be such a pleasure to know where it really lies."

Then the poor Giant could hold out no longer, but was forced to say—

"Far, far away in a lake lies an island; on that island stands a church; in that church is a well; in that well swims a duck; in that duck there is an egg, and in that egg there lies my heart,—you darling!"

In the morning early, while it was still gray dawn, the Giant strode off to the wood.

"Yes! now I must set off too," said Boots; "if I only knew how to find the way." He took a long, long farewell of the Princess, and when he got out of the Giant's door, there stood the Wolf waiting for him. So Boots told him all that had happened inside the house, and said now he wished to ride to the well in the church, if he only knew the way. So the Wolf bade him jump on his back, he'd soon find the way; and away they went, till the wind whistled after them, over hedge and field, over hill and dale. After they had travelled many, many days, they came at last to the lake. Then the Prince did not know how to get over it, but the Wolf bade him only not be afraid, but stick on, and so he jumped into the lake with the Prince on his back, and swam over to the island. So they came to the church; but the church keys hung high, high up on the top of the tower, and at first the Prince did not know how to get them down.

"You must call on the raven," said the Wolf.

So the Prince called on the raven, and in a trice the raven came, and flew up and fetched the keys, and so the Prince got into the church. But when he came to the well, there lay the duck, and swam about backwards and forwards, just as the Giant had said. So the Prince stood and coaxed it and coaxed it, till it came to him, and he grasped it in his hand; but just as he lifted it up from the water the duck dropped the egg into the well, and then Boots was beside himself to know how to get it out again.

"Well, now you must call on the salmon to be sure," said the Wolf; and the king's son called on the salmon, and the salmon came and fetched up the egg from the bottom of the well.

Then the Wolf told him to squeeze the egg, and as soon as ever he squeezed it the Giant screamed out.

"Squeeze it again," said the Wolf; and when the Prince did so, the Giant screamed still more piteously, and begged and prayed so prettily to be spared, saying he would do all that the Prince wished if he would only not squeeze his heart in two.

"Tell him, if he will restore to life again your six brothers and their brides, whom he has turned to stone, you will spare his life," said the Wolf. Yes, the Giant was ready to do that, and he turned the six brothers into king's sons again, and their brides into king's daughters.

"Now, squeeze the egg in two," said the Wolf. So Boots squeezed the egg to pieces, and the Giant burst at once.

Now, when he had made an end of the Giant, Boots rode back again on the Wolf to the Giant's house, and there stood all his six brothers alive and merry, with their brides. Then Boots went into the hill-side after his bride, and so they all set off home again to their father's house. And you may fancy how glad the old king was when he saw all his seven sons come back, each with his bride. "But the loveliest bride of all is the bride of Boots, after all," said the king, "and he shall sit uppermost at the table, with her by his side."

So he sent out, and called a great wedding-feast, and the mirth was both loud and long; and if they have not done feasting, why, they are still at it.

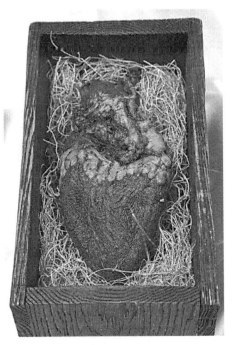

PRESERVED HEART OF A 5TH CENTURY NORSE GIANT IN AN OAK BOX.

While going through his famous grandfather's belongings after his passing in 1937, violinist Lars Sigerson discovered this casket and its gruesome contents. It has been passed from generation to generation within his family for hundreds of years. The explanation and story that goes with it, has been lost to the ages. Inscribed on the little casket in old Norse runes is the following: *"Behold! Within this casket lies the heart of the fierce and terrible giant known as Hrungnir, slain this day by Fafrd the Red, whose bravery and cunning shall live forever!"* The human heart housed in the box came from a larger than average man. Research indicates it was roughly cut out and preserved with salts, the same process the ancient Norse would use to preserve fish and meat for their Viking voyages and to survive the long winters. Little is known about Fafrd the Red, who is only mentioned briefly in *Eymundar Pattr Hrings,* the Tale of Eymundu. In this tale, he is described only as a tall, red-haired youth with a strong arm and a clever wit.

Little People

Hafnarfjördur, Iceland, is famous for having one of the largest settlements of elves, dwarves and other mystical beings on the planet. They are collectively called "Hidden Folk." Centuries-old folklore says that whole clans of such beings reside in the rocks that make up part of the town's center, as well as many other places in Iceland. Though elves are visible only to those with "second sight," a great many Icelanders believe in their existence. Stories abound of instances where new roads or housing developments were under construction and strange happenings, caused by Hidden Folk, took place.

According to visitreykjavik.is, there is even a "Hidden Worlds Tour" that takes you to the home sites of these Little People, stopping at places like Hellisgerdi Park and the base of the cliff Hamarinn, which is said to be "home to the Royal Family of the Hidden Folk." Along the way, the guide relates ancient folk tales of the magical hidden worlds and describes how the town grew and developed in harmony with the Hidden Folk.

Iceland is not the only Scandinavian country that is home to Little People. The dwarves of Scandinavia are so prevalent, that they formed the basis for J.R.R. Tolkien's depiction of dwarves in his writings. The dwarves in *The Hobbit* all have names drawn from Norse mythology. In Norse mythology, *Dökkálfar* (Old Norse for "Dark Elves") and Ljósálfar (Old Norse for "Light Elves"), are two contrasting types of Little People. The Dokkalfar dwell within the earth and are swarthy and dark-skinned. The Ljósálfar live in Álfheimr, and are "fairer than the sun to look at."

The Dökkálfar and the Ljósálfar appear in the *Prose Edda*, written in the 13th century by Snorri Sturluson:

XVII.

Then said Gangleri: "Thou knowest many tidings to tell of the heaven. What chief abodes are there more than at Urdr's Well?" Harr said: "Many places are there, and glorious. That which is called Alfheimr is one, where dwell the peoples called Light-Elves; but the Dark-Elves dwell down in the earth, and they are unlike in appearance, but by far more unlike in nature. The Light-Elves are fairer to look upon than the sun, but the Dark-Elves are blacker than pitch. Then there is also in that place the abode called Breidablik, and there is not in heaven a fairer dwelling. There, too, is the one called Glitnir, whose walls, and all its posts and pillars, are of red gold, but its roof of silver. There is also the abode called Himinbjorg; it stands at heaven's end by the bridge-head, in the place where Bifrost joins heaven."

Another great abode is there, which is named Valaskjalf; Odin possesses that dwelling; the gods made it and thatched it with sheer silver, and in this hall is the Hlidskjalf, the high-seat so called. Whenever Allfather sits in that seat, he surveys all lands. At the southern end of heaven is that hall which is fairest of all, and brighter than the sun; it is called Gimle. It shall stand when both heaven and earth have departed; and good men and of righteous conversation shall dwell therein: so it is said in Voluspa:

A hall I know standing than the sun fairer.
Thatched with gold in Gimle bright;
There shall dwell the doers of righteousness
And ever and ever enjoy delight.

Then said Gangleri: "What shall guard this place, when the flame of Surtr shall consume heaven and earth?"

"It is said that another heaven is to the southward and upward of this one, and it is called Andlangr; but the third heaven is yet above that, and it is called Vidblainn; and in that heaven we think this abode is. But we believe that none but Light-Elves inhabit these mansions now."

Following is a brief list of some of the notable Little People of Scandinavia:

ALBERICH

Alberich was a powerful magician that lived between the 5th and 8th centuries A.D., during the era of the French Merovingian rulers. He lived underground in a castle carved out of rock and decorated with precious gems and stones. German folktales—particularly the *Nibelungenlied*, an epic poem written in Old German—tell that he was a dwarf and responsible for guarding the treasures of Nibelung, ruler of a Scandinavian race of dwarfs who owned a hoard of gold and magic treasures.

They lived in Nibelheim, "land of mist." He fought Seigfried. When he was defeated, he had to part with the sword *Balmung* and a cloak which made its wearer invisible. The name Alberich is derived from the terms *Elbe* (elves) and *Reix* (king) thereby indicating that he was King of Elves.

German composer, Richard Wagner immortalized Alberich in his opera *Der Ring des Nibelungen*, where Alberich is portrayed as the dwarf chieftain of the Nibelungen, and protector of the "Rhinegold treasure," which is a fabled fortune in gold lying at the bottom of the Rhine River.

DVERGAR

Dvergar are dwarves in Norse mythology that are associated with rocks, the earth, craft and metal work, wisdom, and greed. Dvergar are ill-tempered, greedy, miserly, and grudging. Skilled craftsmen, they are known to curse objects they are forced to make, or that are stolen from them. They almost never willingly teach their magical knowledge. At the same time, they can be surprisingly friendly and loyal to those who treat them kindly. Known for their strength and overall hardiness, the Dvergar were said to be able to hold their own in a fight. Like trolls, Norse dwarves are sometimes depicted as turning to stone if exposed to direct sunlight.

These dwarves were formed from maggots that formed on the body of the dead Ymir. He was the first being, a giant who was created from the drops of water that formed when the ice of Niflheim, one of the Nine Worlds in Norse mythology, met the heat of Muspelheim, the Fire World. Ymir was killed by the Norse gods, Odin, Ve, and Vili, ending the rule of the primordial giants.

The Norse epic poem, *Voluspa-The Song of the Sybil* tells what happened after Ymir was killed:

> The sons of Borr, after they had made the earth from
> the body of the proto-giant Ymir, took the giant's

skull and made of it the heaven, and set it up over the earth with four corners.

Under each corner they set a dwarf: their names are Norðri, Suðri, Austri, and Vestri.

The Dvergar were blacksmiths who built weapons for war between the gods. They also created many precious and magical objects for the gods. Dvergar have been traditionally known to the Norse as the craftsmen of gold and silver. The ones called Ívaldi's sons made various precious objects, among which Odin's spear (called Gungnir: the unfailing one); and Thor's hammer (called Mjöllnir: the bright and shining one).

Álfrigg, Dvalinn, Berlingr, and Grérr as the dwarfs who gave a gold necklace to Freyja in exchange for her spending the night with each one of them. Dwarfs also made Gleipnir, the unbreakable fetter used to bind the giant wolf Fenrir. Two other dwarfs, Dáinn and Nabbi, made Freyja's golden-bristled hog Hildisvíni (who was really her lover Ottar). The sons of Sólblindi made the gate Þrymgjöll, which shuts so fast that it traps those who attempt to use it. Nine other dwarfs helped Loki build her hall Hyrr, a hall which is surrounded by a flickering flame.

The dwarfs Fjalarr and Galarr made mead out of the blood of Kvasir, whom they had murdered. They blended honey with the blood, and the outcome was mead that caused the one who drinks it to becomes a skald (a court poet), or a scholar. The dwarf Andvari provided Loki with the gold needed to pay the blood-debt for the death of Ótr, which was two kennings of gold. Another dwarf, called Thiodreyrir, sang strength to the Aesir, wealth to all elves, and wisdom to Odin. In the saga, *Ynglinga*, king Svegðir saw a stone with a dwarf sitting under it. The dwarf stood in the door and invited Svegðir to come in. Svegðir ran into the stone, which instantly closed behind him, and he was never seen again.

The Dvergar are mentioned in many Norse epic poems, like
Voluspa-The Song of the Sybil:

Silence I ask of the sacred folk,
Silence of the kith and kin of Heimdal:
At your will Valfather, I shall well relate
The old songs of men I remember best.

I tell of giants from times forgotten.
Those who fed me in former days:
Nine worlds I can reckon, nine roots of the tree.
The wonderful ash, way under the ground

When Ymir lived long ago
Was no sand or sea, no surging waves.
Nowhere was there earth nor heaven above.
But a grinning gap and grass nowhere.

At Ida's Field the Aesir met:
Temple and altar they timbered and raised,
Set up a forge to smithy treasures,
Tongs they fashioned and tools wrought;

Played chess in the court and cheerful were;
Gold they lacked not, the gleaming metal
Then came three, the Thurs maidens,
Rejoicing in their strength, from Giant-home.

The high Gods gathered in council.
In their hall of judgement: Who of the dwarves
Should mould man by master craft
From Brimir's blood and Blain's limbs?

Motsognir was their mighty ruler,
Greatest of dwarves, and Durin after him :
The dwarves did as Durin directed,
Many man forms made from the earth.

Nyi and Nidi, Nordri, Sudri, Austri and Vestri, Althjof,
Dvalin, Bivor, Bavor Bombur, Nori, An and Anar, Ai,

Mjodvitnir, Veignr and Gandalf, Vindalf, Thorin, Thror
and Thrain, Thekkur, Litur, Vitur, Nar and Nyradur, Fili,
Kili, Fundin, Nali Hefti, Vili, Hanar, Sviur, Billing, Bruni,
Bildur, and Buri, Frar, Hornbori Fraegur, Loni, Aurvangur,
Jari, Eikinskjaldi:
(All Durin's folk I have duly named,)

I must tell of the dwarves in Dvalin's host;
Like lions they were in Lofar's time:
In Juravale's marsh they made their dwelling,
From their Stone hall set out on journeys,

There was Draupnir and Dolgthrasir, Har, Haugspori,
Hlevangur, Gloi, Dori, Ori, Dufur, Andvari, Skirvir, Virvir
Skafidur, Ai, Alf and Yngvi, Eikinskjaldi, Fjalar and Frosti,
Finn and Ginnar:
Men will remember while men live
The long line of Lofar's forbears.

Interestingly, the Dvergar are
said to dwell in dark places;
they appear to be vulnerable
to the rays of the sun. In
Alvísmál, the dwarf Alvíss
shows up at Thor's home to
claim his daughter as his
bride, but Thor makes their
contest last until sunrise;
whereupon the dwarf is
turned into stone. In the same
poem the sun is called
"Deceiver of Dvalinn," since
Dvalinn, like other dwarfs
living underground, cannot
live in its light.

Giants & Little People

of

SOUTH

AMERICA

As far back as the 1500s, when Spanish navigators were exploring the coast of the Americas, sightings of live giants were recorded. Several captains of the Spanish ships reported taller-than-average native people on their expeditions to the Americas. Eyewitnesses included Sir Francis Drake, Captain John Smith, a Smithsonian professor, as well as a few other notable persons.

In 1523, Spanish fleets monopolized the Caribbean Islands. Historian Peter Martyr, who assisted at the Council of the Indies, issued an unusual report. The details of this report was originally shared by a native who was Christianized and taken to Spain. He said:

> The report ran that the natives were white and their king and queen giants, whose bones, while babies, had been softened with an ointment of strange herbs, then kneaded and stretched like wax by masters of the art, leaving the poor objects of their magic half dead, until after repeated manipulations they finally attained their great size.

Francisco Gordillo was a Captain in the Spanish Navy of the early 1520s; he reported to Lucas Vasquez de Allyon. Lucas Vasquez de Allyon, a judge of the court on Hispaniola. In 1521, De Allyon sent Captain Francisco Gordillo on an expedition to search the Bahamas for Indians to be sold as slaves. If that failed, the slavers were supposed to go back to the coastal area that Salazar had called the "land of giants." Captain Francisco Gordillo, departed Hispaniola in early 1521. He sailed to the Bahamas but found no natives. (Previous slave-hunters had visited these islands on numerous occasions and had captured so many people that only a handful remained.)

Somewhere along the way, Captain Gordillo had met up with Pedro de Quejo, a Spanish "slaver." They are the first known Spaniards to sail along the Georgia, South Carolina, North Carolina, and Virginia coasts. The Chicora natives who lived in a portion of what is now South Carolina, were famed for their height; the Spaniard slavers managed to capture about 70 of them to take back to Spain.

Although Gordillo and Quejo treated the Chicora natives badly, their relationships with the Duhare peoples were much more gentlemanly. This may have been because the inhabitants of Duhare were described as looking European, with red or brown hair, tanned skin and gray eyes. These strange people did not appear to be Native American; they had full beards and towered over the Spanish. The report on the Duhare from the voyage, stated:

> Ayllon says the natives are white men, and his testimony is confirmed by Francisco Chicorana. Their hair is brown and hangs to their heels. They are governed by a king of gigantic size, called Datha, whose wife is as large as himself. They have five children. In place of horses, the king is carried on the shoulders of strong young men, who run with him to the different places he wishes to visit.

> The Spanish describe Datha as being the largest man they had ever seen. He had a wife as tall as him. He wore brightly colored paint or tattoos on his skin that distinguished him from the commoners.

PATAGONIAN GIANTS

In a 1908 publication called *The Independent*, Dr. Frederick A. Cook writes of giant humans found on the southern tip of South America, in the Patagonia region. The first mention of this mythical race of Giants surfaced in the 1520s in the account of Antonio Pigafetta, chronicler of Ferdinand Magellan's expedition. His piece in the 1908 edition of *The Independent,* states the following:

> Since the days of Magellan, Patagonia has been a name with which to conjure up scenes of strange animals and giant people. On the mainland, there are two distinct tribes of Indians: the Auracanians in the North; and the Tehuelches in the South. The latter are the far-famed giants. Although not as large as they have at times been represented, are people of magnificent physical development....The name *Patagones*, meaning "clumsy foot" was a misnomer, for these people really have small

feet and small hands for their size. They do, however, wear a very clumsy boot made out of guanaco skin.

Dr. Frederick Cook with two Patagonian Giants, 1898.

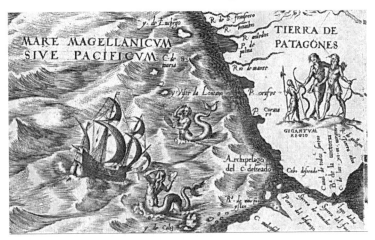

In *The World Encompassed by Sir Francis Drake: Being His Next Voyage To Nombre de Dios* (London, 1628), we are given this account of Patagonia's giants:

> But one day (without anyone expecting it) we saw a giant who was on the shore [near today's Puerto San Julián, Argentina], quite naked, and who danced, leaped, and sang, and while he sang he threw sand and dust on his head. Our captain sent one of his men toward him, charging him to leap and sing like the other in order to reassure him and to show him friendship. Which he did. Immediately the man of the ship, dancing, led this giant to a small island where the captain awaited him. And when he was before us, he began to marvel and to be afraid, and he raised one finger upward, believing that we came from heaven. And he was so tall that the tallest of us only came up to his waist. Withal he was well proportioned. . . . The captain named the people of this sort Patagoni. The etymology of the word is unclear, but Patagonia came to mean "Land of the Bigfeet."

John Byron's book, *A Voyage Round the World in His Majesty's Ship the Dolphin* (London, 1767), has this to say about the Patagonian giants:

> Magellan was not altogether deceived, in naming them Giants; for they generally differ from the common sort of men, both in stature, bigness, and strength of body, as also in the hideousness of their voice: but yet they are nothing so monstrous, or giantlike as they were reported; there being some English men, as tall, as the highest of any that we could see, but peradventure, the Spaniards did not think, that ever any English man would come thither, to reprove them; and thereupon might presume the more boldly to lie: the name Patagones, Five cubits viz. 7 foote and a halfe, describing the full height (if not somewhat more) of the

highest of them. But this is certain, that the Spanish cruelties there used [referring to Magellan's hostage taking], have made them more monstrous, in mind and manners, then they are in body; and more inhospitable, to deal with any strangers, that shall come thereafter.

He reduced the height of the Patagonians from ten feet to seven and a half feet but was obviously more intent on discrediting the Spanish and blaming them for the "monstrosity" of the giants. Ironically, though, he was really confirming the basic facts behind the myth.

Found on a princeton.edu website is this excerpt:

In the 1700s, the myth was still alive and entertaining Europeans. Horace Walpole, the English historian and gothic novelist, published *An Account of the Giants Lately Discovered: In a Letter to a Friend in the Country* following the return in 1766 of Captain John Byron, who had circumnavigated the world in the HMS *Dolphin*. Word leaked that the crew had seen nine-foot giants in South America. Byron's May docking and Walpole's July publication suggests the rapidity with which rumors passed along the London grapevine. In his thirty-one-page pamphlet, Walpole satirizes the whole idea and facetiously suggests that a limited number of the giant women could be imported "for the Sake of mending our Breed." The official account of Byron's voyage, appearing in 1773, finally debunks the myth, but not without respecting the Patagonians' vertical features:

When we came within a little distance from the shore, we saw, as near as I can guess, about five hundred people, some on foot, but the greater part on horseback....one of them, who afterwards appeared to be a Chief, came towards me: he was of a gigantic stature, and seemed to realize the tales of monsters in a human shape....if I may judge of his height by the proportion of his stature to my own, it could not be much less than seven feet....Mr. Cumming [one of Byron's officers] came up with the tobacco [a gift], and I could not but smile at his astonishment which I saw expressed in his countenance, upon perceiving himself, though six feet two inches high, become a pigmy among giants; for these people may indeed more properly be called giants than tall men....the shortest of whom were at least four inches taller. In all probability, these accounts were describing the Tehuelche Indians, native to the Patagonian area of Argentina, who are typically tall—but not monstrous giants.

TIERRA DEL FUEGO, ARGENTINA

A Voyage Round the World, in His Majesty's Ship the Dolphin, Commanded by the Honourable Commodore Byron, Newbery and Carnan; 1768, mentions Argentinian giants:

During the Renaissance, the notion of terra australis became more than just hypothetical as European explorers such as Marco Polo and Amerigo Vespucci discovered new coastlines in the south, and cartographers creatively, if not accurately, incorporated them into their new maps. It is also at this point that ideas of *terra australis* intersect with giant lore, for on the same voyage, Magellan's crewman, Antonio Pigafetta, recorded that they saw a giant standing on the beach north of Tierra del Fuego. He claimed that the tallest was "so tall that our heads did not reach his belt" and that he was "a size like a giant, who had a voice like a bull."

This encounter was forever engraved on the history of this land, for it was subsequently named Patagonia (from Patagón, or "big-foot") after the colossal people seen there, and seventeenth-century maps of this

"Here, have some bread—so that you don't eat me."

territory, for example those of Jocodus Hondius and Willem Janszoon Blaeu, were adorned by illustrations of giants. Magellan's sighting inaugurated the giants' entry into the menagerie of fantastic beings, amongst skiapods and antipodes, depicted as inhabiting the still not completely charted southern extremes of the world.

QUONIAMBEC

Andreas Thevet was a famous 16th century cosmographer (the science that deals with the whole order of nature; a cosmographer maps the general features of the cosmos and the universe, describing both heaven and Earth). He traveled in South America to study the natives for the King of France. A likeness of Quoniambec, a "giant-like man," appears in his *Portraitures & Lives*. In the text accompanying the copperplate engraving of the Indian's portrait, Thevet wrote: I have seen him and sufficiently observed him upon the River of Janaira. He had a great body, proportionably gross, exceeding strong. His portraiture, I brought from that country, with two green stones in his cheeks and one on his chin."

BRAZILIAN GIANTS

William Turner, a botanist who wrote the first original work of scientific botany in the English language, wrote that, on the coast of Brazil, near the river Polata, he saw a tribe of very gigantic naked savages, one of whom he estimated to be twelve feet tall. He also told of an Indian that he had seen who, still a youth, towered to a height of thirteen spans.

Anthony Knivet was an English sailor who fell into Portuguese hands in Brazil in 1591, while on a voyage around the world with English privateer, Thomas Cavendish. Suffering from frostbite while passing through the Strait of Magellan, Knivet and 19 other sick or mutinous men were left on the remote island of Ilhabela. He was captured by the Portuguese and put to work as a slave on a sugar plantation. He managed to escape and made it to an indigenous Brazilian tribe of Tupi people. Knivet lived for a while with the tribe, and wrote about his adventures after his return to Britain, in 1601. Knivet said that, several times, he saw an Indian who, though still a youth, who towered to a height of thirteen spans.

ECUADOR

According to a press clipping, dated May 14, 1926, from Nayarit, Mexico, Capts. D. W. Page and F. W. Devalda discovered the bones of a race of giants who averaged over ten feet in height. Local legends state that they came from Ecuador. Nothing more has been heard of this, but that is not surprising; the word "giant" will flutter the feathers of any scientist into rapid flight, metaphorically speaking, in the opposite direction.

So also, with a report from the *Washington Post*, June 22, 1925, and the *New York Herald-Tribune*, June 21, 1925. A mining party, it is reported, found skeletons measuring 10 to 12 feet, with feet 18 to 20 inches long, near Sisoguiche, Mexico. The *Los Angeles Times*, October 2, 1927, says that explorers in Mexico located large human bones near Tapextla, indicating a race of "gigantic size."

All this, if unfounded, would be straining coincidence or imagination pretty far. Press accounts say that the skeleton of a gigantic man, with head missing, has been unearthed at El Boquin, on the Mico River, in the Chontales district. The ribs are a yard long and four inches wide and the shin bone is too heavy for one man to carry. "Chontales" is an Indian word, meaning "wild men."

FIRE FROM HEAVEN

In 1543, Juan de Olmos, lieutenant governor of Port Viejo, Guayaquil, in Ecuador, ordered excavations be made in the valley at the place where the natives claimed giants were destroyed by fire from heaven.

According to *Strange Artifacts: A Source Book On Ancient Man,* compiled by William R. Corliss in 1973, in reference to Ecuador's Giants:

At first, the Spaniards thought that the natives of Guayaquil, Ecuador were fabricating a tale concerning a tribe of giants who once invaded their land and terrified them for some years. But they spoke so convincingly about such a time that, in 1543 Juan de Olmos, lieutenant governor of Porto Viejo, finally ordered excavations to be made in the valley at the place where the natives claim these giants were destroyed by fire from heaven. In his account of these archaeological diggings, Zarate reports that:

> Olmos' party "...found such large ribs and other bones that, if the skulls had not appeared at the same time, it would not have been credible they were of human persons.... Teeth then found were sent to different parts of Peru; they were three fingers broad and four in length." The giants had "...come by sea in rafts of reeds after the manner of large boats, some men who were so tall that from the knee down they were as big as the full length of an ordinary fair-sized man." They also found marks from thunderbolts in the rocks there, giving further credibility to the story the natives told.

Pedro Cieza de Leon, whose report on the Guayaquil giants was published in 1553, says that the "natives tell, from what they had heard through their forefathers, who heard and had it from far back, that three came by sea in rafts of reeds after the manner of large boats, some men who were so tall that, from the knee down, they were as big as full length of an ordinary fair-sized man; and the limbs were in proportion to their bodies, so misshapen that it was monstrous to look at their heads, as large as they were, and with the hair that came down to the shoulders. The eyes they give to understand, were of the size of small plates. They affirm that they had no beards and that some were clad in skins of animals, while others came as nature made them, and there were no women along."

American Anthropological Association, Volume 8, from 1906, carries this intriguing story:

> *American Anthropologist Volume 8* from 1906, tells the story of Juan de Olmos. In 1543, Juan de Olmos was lieutenant governor of Port Viejo Guayaquil, in Ecuador. He ordered excavations to be made in the valley of the place where the natives claimed giants were destroyed by fire from heaven. Olmos's party "found such large ribs and other bones that, skulls had not appeared at the same time, it would not have been credible that they were human beings. Teeth, then found, were sent to different parts of Peru; they were three fingers broad and four in length." The Giants had "come by sea in rafts of reeds after the manner of large boats, some men who were so tall that from the knee down they were as big as the full length of an ordinary fair-sized man."

After their landing near Punta Santa Elena, according to Cieza, the Giants constructed themselves a village – but in a place that lacked a sufficient water supply. When this became evident, they simply dug themselves deep wells, using their great strength to break through the rock formation.

Having established themselves, continues Cieza, "these tall men or giants....ate and wasted all the food they could find in this land, for each one of them consumed more than 50 of the natives of the country. And, as the supply was not sufficient for them, they killed much fish in the sea by means of their nets and contrivances which, it stands to reason, they must have had. The natives abhorred them for they killed their women in making use of them; and, the man, they killed for other reasons. The Indians did not feel strong enough to kill these few people that had come to take their country and domain. Although great meetings were held to confer about it, they dared not attack them. After a few years, the Giants, being in the country and having no women, and those of the Indians not suiting their great size—or because it may have been by advice and inducement of the demon—they resorted to an unnatural vice of God and had little shame of themselves."

Cieza then writes that, according to the account handed down by the natives, an Angel in a massive fire descended from heaven and killed the Giants. Some scholars theorize that this unusual destruction that the natives witness, was caused by the fall of "some meteorite of unusual size and brilliancy," or that it could possibly "have been one of those electrical phenomena, such as ball lightning." *[It also sounds like a nuclear attack from above.]*

Besides the enormous human bones in the thunderbolt marks, the "wells mentioned above, which were attributed to the Giants, are also found in this locality," says T.A. Joyce. "They are deep circular excavations cut into the solid rock or lined with rough stones. One of the former class is 42 feet deep, exclusive of the earth which has been washed into it; many of them are now filled up, but the water reappears as soon as they are cleared."

392

In his *Cronica del Peru,* Cieza de Leon also informs us that, in Peru, Ecuador's southern neighbor, "they make great mention of certain giants, which have been in those parts, whose bones are yet seen at Manta and Puerto Viejo, of a huge greatness; and by their proportion, they should be thrice as big as the Indians."

It should also not be forgotten that the above Indian stories, even if pre-Colombian originally, might have been "myths of observation." Comparison of the remarkable cleft of the Tequendama with the effects of earthquakes experienced elsewhere, may have led to an explanatory tale in which the seismic forces become personified.

Translation of these stories from Colombia to Ecuador is through Pasto, situated near the confines of both countries. Of one of its well-known volcanoes, Pedro de Cieza relates, in 1550, after having visited it in 1539: "Farther on (south of Popayan) is a tall range; on its summit is a volcano, from which sometimes much smoke arises. And, in times past, according to what the natives say, it broke out once and threw out a great quantity of stones."

This evidently refers to the eruption previous to the arrival of the Spaniards; for, had it occurred subsequently, Cieza would have recorded the fact. The term "stones" refers to lapilli.* **

Lapilli is rock thrown from a volcano.

**It seems that Pedro de Cieza is trying to explain the destruction of the giants by "fire from heaven" and "the marks of the thunderbolt seen in the rocks." Back in the time of Spanish explorations in South America, things like nuclear weapons were not imagined. But they do fit the descriptions given. In the Bible, Revelation 13:11-13 states: "....another beast coming out of the earth....two horns....spoke like a dragon....he maketh fire come down*

Ancient Sumerian carved relief in stone of Gilgamesh and the "Bull of Heaven."

from heaven on the earth in the sight of men." This could be reference to the Anunnaki weapon that chased Gilgamesh the Giant, used by Inanna after he spurned her advances. The weapon was called the "bull of heaven" and had "two horns, out of which powerful lightning bolts shot, destroying all in the airborne weapon's path."

The tale of giants having landed in pre-Colombian times at Punta Santa Elena, west of Guayaquil, has been discussed in a paper previously published in this journal. I returned to the subject because of the report of Agustin de Zarate on the matter in which the story became confirmed in the eyes of the Spaniards; and for the reason that a somewhat different version of the tale has been obtained subsequent to its publication. Zarate, who was an administrative officer of high rank, went to Peru in 1543. My translation of his statements not being literal, I give the original text in a note. He says:

"Withal, what the Indians told about these giants was not fully believed until, in the year 1543, when the captain Juan de Olmos, a native of Trujillo, was lieutenant governor at Puerto Viejo, he caused excavations to be made in the valley, having heard of these matters. They found ribs and bones so large that, if the heads had not appeared at the same time, it would not have seemed credible [i.e., that the remains were] of human beings. And so, after the investigations were finished; and the marks of the thunderbolt seen in the rocks; what the Indians said was held to be true. And, of the teeth found there, some were sent to various parts of Peru and found to measure each, three fingers and four in length." There is hardly any doubt concerning the pre-Columbian origin of the tradition, for it cannot be a distorted account of the first appearance of Spaniards on the coast of Ecuador in 1525.

VIRACOCHA

The god Viracocha Pachayachachi, which translates to "Creator Of All Things" was the Creator god to many Mesoamerican tribes. He was Kukulkan to the Mayas; Quetzalcoatl by the Aztecs; Gucumatz in Central America; Votan in Palenque; and Zamna in Izamal. He is described by the Incas as being a bearded man with white skin, having hair on his face and green eyes, usually wearing long white robes. He was also described as being very tall, a giant.

It was believed that human beings were actually Viracocha's second attempt at living creatures. The Incas believed that Viracocha originally created a world without sun, stars or the moon; everything was dark. He then created giant beings made out of stone. He gave them the specific rule that there shall be no quarrelling on the earth. But, these giants were so unruly and uncontrollable, that it was necessary for Viracocha to punish them by sending a great flood. In the legend, all these giants were returned to their original stone form. Some were swallowed by the earth; some were swallowed by the sea; and some were turned into stone. Several of the latter can still be seen in modern times hovering over sites such as Tiahuanaco Pukará.

After the great flood wiped out all remnants of the giants, out from the dark depths of Lake Titicaca, Viracocha bought eternal light to the new earth summoning the sun, moon and the stars. He then created two human beings out of clay. Viracocha then sent one of his servants to the east to a region called 'Andesuyo' and the other to the west to a region called 'Condesuyo' to awaken the people of this region Viracocha disguised as an old man and set out for the city of 'Cuzco.' Along the way, he came across a province of Cacha, where he awoke the Canas people, who didn't recognize Viracocha and attacked him. In response to this, Viracocha made a nearby mountain erupt. In seeing this, the Canas bowed down at his feet and he forgave them.

When Viracocha founded the city of Cuzco he called forth those who would be the lords of Cuzco. Once that was done, he walked across the sea, awakening people along his journey. When he reached the ocean, he was greeted by his two human servants. Together, they walked across the ocean and gave his inhabitants one last word of advice "Beware of the false men who would come and claim that they were the returned Viracocha".

PYRAMIDS OF TEOTIHUACAN

Mexico is a country that is rich in ancient artifacts and legends. Some of these legends are about giants. By tradition, it is said that the largest of the pyramids in the ancient city of Teotihuacan, the Pyramid of the Sun and the Pyramid of the Moon, were built by the giants that existed in ancient days. Legend contends that Teotihuacan was built by giants; its purpose was to transform men into gods.

Hernán Cortés (1485–1547) led the Spanish conquest of Mexico in 1518. Cortés wrote a series of five letters to the King of Spain to chronicle the events that took place during this conquest of Mexico. The first letter, dated July 1519, has never been found. The second and third letters were published in Seville (1522 and 1523 respectively). The fourth letter was published in Toledo in 1525. The fifth letter remained unpublished until 1842.

In his second narrative letter to the King of Spain, published in Seville in 1522, Hernan Cortes describes the province of Culua, with its great cities, especially "Tenustitlan" (Tenochtitlán) built on Lake Texcoco. Cortés speaks with great admiration about the Aztec king, Moctezuma (Montezuma), about how his people serve him, and about their rites and ceremonies. The letter relates the most noteworthy events concerning the entry into New Spain. One of these events was the meeting with the Aztec chief in Tenochtitlán. When Hernan Cortes asked who had built such a colossal city, the Aztecs replied, "We were not the builders of Teotihuacan. This city was built by the Quinanatzin, a race of giants who came from the heavens in the times of the Second Sun." Cortes and his companions were awestruck at the impressive pyramids at the center of this city, with the Pyramid of the Sun looming above all.

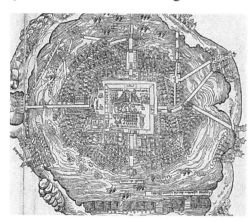

At Left: MAP ACCOMPANYING ONE OF HERNAN CORTES' LETTERS FROM "NEW SPAIN" TO THE KING OF SPAIN, 1520.

The Full Title of This Letter Translates to:

The Splendid Narrative of Ferdinand Cortes About the New Spain of the Sea and Ocean Transmitted to the Most Sacred and Invincible, Always August Charles Emperor of the Romans, King of the Spaniards in the Year of the Lord 1520: In Which is Contained Many Things Worthy of Knowledge and Admiration About the Excellent Cities of Their Provinces... Above All About the Famous City Temixtitan and Its Diverse Wonders, Which Will Wondrously Please the Reader.

Built some time between 1 A.D. and 250 A.D., during the height of the Teotihuacan culture, this massive structure measures approximately 720 feet by 760 feet by 200 feet high. It is the largest in the ancient city, and third largest pyramid in the world. It was made of earth and rubble, adobe bricks, and covered with limestone, believed to be quarried, and delivered by foot, from about 37 miles away, in Tula, as there were no limestone quarries in the surrounding area. 129,166,925 square feet of architectural surface was covered with lime plaster throughout the entire city. Large quantities of mica have also been discovered throughout every building in the city, including the pyramid, in layers up to one-foot-thick. The mica is believed to have originated from Brazil, more than 3000 miles away. Mica is not only shiny and decorative, but it is it is an excellent insulator. According to the Minerals Education Coalition website mineralseducationcoalition.org, today, we know that mica is stable when exposed to light, moisture, extreme temperatures, and electricity; it can support an electrostatic field while dissipating minimal energy in the form of heat, and is thermally stable to 932 °F (500 °C). Mica has not been found in any other archaeological site in the vicinity, or the Americas. Did these people understand mica's properties? Did this primitive culture have the mathematical and astronomical understanding required to construct the city, which is laid out with what appears to be an understanding of our solar system. The great Pyramid of the Sun is at the center of this complex of pyramids, each aligned with a planet in the solar system.

BERNAL DIAZ & THE GIANTS OF MEXICO

When the Spanish first explored and conquered Mexico they heard of mythical races of giants wherever they went, from the Baja Peninsula in the northwest part of the country to the Maya areas of southern and eastern Mexico. The Spanish heard the myths and legends from the natives that seemed to correlate with their own Biblical stories about giants as found in the Book of Genesis, which told them that, some time in the distant past, giants roamed the earth alongside humans.

According to local legends of the ancient civilization of the Olmecs, giants lived in the plains of Tlaxcala. These giants came there before another more ancient people, called the Toltecs. The legends said that giants were responsible for much of what was left behind by previous civilizations and the giant explanation was common in many parts of the New World. To the people of central Mexico at the time of the Spanish contact, giants featured so prominently in their belief system that they even named their capital city, Tenochtitlán, after a man called Tenoch, who belonged to an ancient race of giants called the *Quinametzin,* which translates to "The Old Ones" or "Giant People."

At the time of the Spanish Conquest, Bernal Diaz, one of the chief chroniclers of the conquest of Mexico by the Spaniards, was told of the huge stature of these giants as well as their crimes. And, to show him how big they were, the storytellers brought him a bone of one of them, which he measured himself against. The bone was as tall as the narrator, who was a man of reasonable stature. Diaz and his companions were astonished to see those bones, and held it for certain that there had been giants in that land.

FIFTH SUN OF THE AZTECS

According to Aztec legends, in the beginning of the Aztec "Fifth Sun," or the epoch of time in which we currently live, there were four giants who held up the sky. Their names were Cuahtémoc, Izcóatl, Ixcaqlli and Tenexuche.

The Mixteca people, referred to as "Mixtecs" by modern anthropologists and historians, were supposedly fathered by a member of the Quinametzin, a giant by the name of Mixtécatl. Giants were often used by the ancient Mesoamericans to explain colossal ruins. According to the Aztecs, the Toltecs had help from giants in building their capital city of Tula. The ancient central Mexican city of Teotihuacán, with its large pyramids and broad avenues, had giants as its initial builders. Finally, the great pyramid at Cholula, the largest pyramid in the world, was said to have been built by Xelhua, a 20-foot-tall member of the Quinametzin tribe. Xelhua was also credited with founding seven cities in central Mexico in the times before the coming of the Aztecs.

MAYAN CHAAC & CHAACOB

Unlike the Aztecs, the Maya did not believe that a race of giant humans existed before them, but giants were part of the ancient Mayan religious belief system in the form of Chaacob, a group of demigods who would serve the god Chaac, and who take human form in the shape of dwarves or giants. Some researchers cite a Maya belief in giants as evidenced by larger human figures being depicted in murals, carvings and other works of art.

Mainstream archaeologists claim that these depictions of larger humans speak more to class and societal position than belief in a race of actual giants, as there is very little in Maya oral tradition that would indicate such a belief. As recently as the 1690s, almost two centuries after the Spanish Conquest, Jesuit missionaries to the remote desert areas of Baja California were still being told by the local Cochimi people that the large rock wall art, carved so high up in the cliff surfaces in the rugged mountains of Baja, was done by a race of giants who were tall enough to paint so high on the wall.

DIEGO DE ORDAZ

One of the writings from the 16th century, a book by Peter Martyr d'Anghiera, called *De Orbe Novo: The Eight Decades of Peter Martyr,* is a history of New Spain. The count had been commissioned by Charles the Fifth to produce the work, which was published in the 1520s. There is a section that references conquistador, Diego de Ordaz, and his discovery of what appears to be the remains of giants:

"I wish to end this chapter with a gigantic story, which, like the formidable Atlas, comes to support my claims. Diego de Ordaz, whom I have before mentioned, knew many hidden places in those lands, especially in the land of cacao, where I learned to plant and grow the tree of money, as I have explained on that occasion." Ordaz found "in the vault of a temple, the thighbone of a giant. The bone was worn and almost destroyed by age. The licentiate Ayllón, one of the most learned jurists in Hispaniola, brought this bone to the city of Victoria a short time after Your Holiness left for Rome. For some days I had that bone in my home; it measured five palms in length, and its width in proportion. Those who were afterwards sent by Cortés into the mountains if the south returned, saying that they had discovered a country inhabited by giants; in proof of this claim it is said that they brought back many ribs of the dead."

Following, is the actual text of *De Orbe Novo, The Eight Decades of Peter Martyr d'Anghera* on this subject:

I wish to terminate this narrative by a story of a giant who, similar to the formidable Atlas, will serve me as an ending and confirm what I have told. Diego Ordaz, whom I have before mentioned, explored several unknown parts of that region and conquered a number of caciques, amongst whom was one in whose country the fruits used as money grow. He it was who taught the

Spaniards how to cultivate that tree, as I have already told. Ordaz found in the sanctuary of a temple the hip-bone of a giant, which was half worn away by age. A short time after Your Holiness had left for Rome, the bone was brought to Victoria by the licentiate Ayllion, one of the most learned jurists in the Senate of Hispaniola. For some days I had that bone in my possession; it measured five cubits in length, and its thickness is in proportion. Some of the men sent by Cortes into the southern mountains afterwards discovered a country inhabited by these giants; in proof of their discovery they have brought back several ribs taken from bodies.

All the other events we have witnessed are known precisely and at first hand, to Your Holiness, thanks to the Emperor's envoys. You will not, therefore, exact that I should describe the misfortunes which wait upon the Christian princes now occupied in driving out the Mohammedans and in mutually rending one another for motives of religious hatred. Permit me, therefore, to wish good health to Your Holiness, at whose feet I prostrate myself, offering my most humble homage.

JESUS DEL MONTE'S BIG TOOTH

Another story of the remains of giants being found in Mexico comes from a Spanish source from the late 16th Century, a book titled *The Natural and Moral History of the Indies* by José de Acosta. Acosta writes:

"When I was in Mexico, in the year of our Lord one thousand five hundred eighty six, they found one of those giants buried in one of our farms, which we call Jesus del Monte, of whom they brought a tooth to be seen, which (without augmenting) was as big as the fist of a man, and, according to this, all the rest was proportionate, which I saw and admired at his deformed greatness."

JESUS DEL MONTE'S BIG TOOTH

There is another account of an encounter with a giant by Spaniards documented. During the siege of Tenochtitlán around 1521, in the final stages of the takeover of the Aztec Empire by Spaniards, forces commanded by Pedro de Alvarado arrived at Tlatelolco, just north of the main city of Tenochtitlan, which was in the Aztec home island in the middle of Lake Texcoco. No people came to fight the Spanish except for a warrior named Tzilcatzin. According to eyewitness accounts, "Tzilcatzin stood over 10 feet tall" and "repelled the Spanish by throwing at them rocks the size of watermelons." Tzilcatzin's bravery motivated other men of Tlatelolco to fight. As a consequence, the standoff with the Spanish lasted several days. In the twelfth book of Franciscan friar Bernardino de Sahagún's *Florentine Codex* (originally titled *La Historia Universal de las Cosas de Nueva España; or,* in English, *The Universal History of the Things of New Spain*), the friar writes:

Tzilacatzin as depicted in the
Florentine Codex, **1590.**

"The brigantines came to the neighborhood called Xocotitlán; as they came ashore, they jumped ashore and joined in the battle that was occurring. And when that Indian captain, by the name of Tzilacatzin, saw them fighting, he came to them with other people who followed him; and they fought them out of that neighborhood. They made them return to the brigantines."

This grainy photo, taken in Peru's Gold Museum, is of an actual mummified head of a crowned king. The head is twice the size of a normal human's head. This museum has other gold-clad giant kings, but it is private and not open to the public, so it is hard to get photos. There is a tunic hung on the wall made of spun gold. It is over eight feet tall, and tailored in such a way as to suggest that it was not intended to drag on the floor behind a king, but rather to hang straight down to the floor.

The New York Times

New York, New York   May 4, 1908

GIANTS' SKELETONS FOUND.

Cave in Mexico Gives Up the Bones of an Ancient Race.

Special to THE NEW YORK TIMES.

BOSTON, May 3.—Charles C. Clapp, who has recently returned from Mexico, where he has been in charge of Thomas W. Lawson's mining interests, has called the attention of Prof. Agassiz to a remarkable discovery made by him.

He found in Mexico a cave containing some 200 skeletons of men each above eight feet in height. The cave was evidently the burial place of a race of giants who antedated the Aztecs. Mr. Clapp arranged the bones of one of these skeletons and found the total length to be 8 feet 11 inches. The femur reached up to his thigh, and the molars were big enough to crack a cocoanut. The head measured eighteen inches from front to back.

NORTHERN STAR
Lismore, NSW, Australia
May 15, 1926

10-FOOT GIANT'S BONES
FOUND IN MEXICO

TEPIC (Mexico), Thursday.—The discovery of the bones of a race of giants who towered more than 10 feet in height is reported, by Capt. Page, an American, and Capt. Devalda; an Englishman, who returned from an unsuccessful search of legendary Spanish gold mines. The discovery was made of great burial mounds in the mountains south-west of here. They state that the preservation indicated that the race lived more than 500 years ago. The reported discovery finds some substantiation in the tales handed down for generations of Indian tribes of the coast of Mexico.

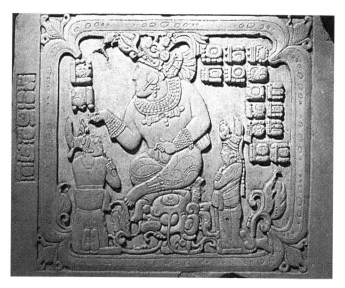

Stone relief of a South American Giant sur-rounded by average size humans.

A group of natives in the central highlands of Mexico, capturing and putting to death, a giant.

(From the *Codex Vaticano A)*

In this Mayan relief, giants are depicted standing on the backs of smaller beings.

Around 900 A.D., six tribes of people came to Mexico from a place near the present-day state of Florida, which they called Aztlán. Some have speculated that these tribes were remnants of survivors of the legendary continent of Atlantis. Around 300 years later, in the early 1200s, a seventh related tribe, the Aztecs, arrived in Central Mexico. According to the history of these seven tribes (including the Aztecs), when they arrived Mexico was already inhabited by two distinctly different groups of people. In the western mountains, which the Spanish named the Sierra Madre Occidentál, were a people called Chichimecs or Chichimecas. In the east, in the areas of present-day Puebla and Cholula were the Quiname, which meant "men of great stature." Both the Chichimecas and the Quiname were said to have been at least 7 to 8 feet tall.

When the newer tribes arrived, they set out to rid the land of the people already living there. They killed thousands, but many fled high into the Sierra, hiding themselves in isolated areas. The Quiname refused to give up their homeland and fought valiantly to defend it. But they were greatly outnumbered, especially when the tribes allied against them. Many were slaughtered through trickery. Others flung themselves from cliffs and precipices, rather than be con-quered. They were harassed and pursued until almost all were destroyed. It is believed some may have migrated to other parts of Mexico, farther north.

For example, the Seri, a giant tribe of Indians found by Coronado, were living on the island the Spanish named Tiburón and the adjacent coast of Sonora on the Gulf of California. Coronado's men described the Seri as being so huge that the tallest of the Spaniards only came to their waists or lower chests.

Farther north, in what is now the state of Arizona, Coronado encountered the Cocopa, a Yuman tribe. All were reported to be over 8 feet tall and incredibly strong. Coronado's historian noted that six of the Spaniards tried to carry a large log to the fire and were unable to move it. A Cocopa man lifted it easily onto his head and carried it to the fire.

Others obviously survived, as well. Bernardino de Sahagan, who arrived in Mexico in 1523, and was considered to be the foremost authority of his time on the pre-conquest Aztec culture, wrote of the "giants of Quinametzin" and even asserted that they built both Teotihuacán and Cholula.

MOHAN

The Mohan (moo-ahn), sometimes also known as *Poira* is a name applied to several mythological or otherwise supernatural creatures in South and Central American folklore. These huge creatures are connected with the souls of the dead and the indigenous ancestors of old. The word is also used for shamans or witch doctors in some Colombian in-digenous cultures, like the Panches.

Various legends exist about the Mohan. Many of these have come from Colom-bia. In Colombia, Mohan can also mean a forest or barren land kind of supernatural being that is assoc-iated with natural forces such as the great rivers and the mysteries lying within the forests, beyond human reach and comprehension. In some legends, the Mohan is a satyr-like (a man with a horse's ears and tail) being who steals and rapes young women and lives in a cave or grotto at the bottom of the great jungle rivers; this is where he keeps his female captives. In others tales, the Mohan is depicted as the spirit of an old Indian, strong and stout, with a terrifying grin and stare; he has a larger than human stature and proportions, and steals fishermen's bait, catch or nets. In his giant form, he has the power to change shape into a cat-like beast. Writer Alvaro Botero, in his 1999 book, *Fable & Disaster: Critical Studies On The Colombian Novel, 1650-1931*, describes the Mohan as a "big-headed Indian, with short legs and fish fins on his back, and very brown. He is an extremely hairy being with a very treacherous personality who dwells in the backwaters and is feared by many people. He also causes mischief for young girls who come to wash clothes in the water."

According to John Roth in his 1997 book, *American Elves: An Encyclopedia of Little People from the Lore of 380 Ethnic Groups of the Western Hemisphere,* the Poira, whose name is interchangeable with the Mohan, is described as "an Indian warlock who lives on the Cerro del Pacandé in Tolima, Colombia. The Poira is also believed to be a small, naked invisible boy or adult who can also appear formless or as a black bear."

THE GIANT CHILD OF PERU

A mummy skeleton of a giant toddler, found in Cuzco, Peru. "It is currently housed at the Ritos Andinos Museum, which is located far southeast of Lima. A hole in the mummy's skull indicates that it had a fontanel, which is an area of connective tissue atop a baby's head that later fills in with bone.

Like modern babies, the skull is larger than the rest of the body. But the strangest feature is that the skull is 20 inches long, which is larger than normal adult skulls. And it has molars that usually appears between approximately 13 and 19 months. So we are looking at a child under two years old with an enormous head."

So what? The Giants once walked on this earth. If we do not find more trace of them, it is because we don't look for them. Some traces do exist. Not much, because the giants came away from where they came: home, up in the stars.

Now, a mummy skeleton found in Peru looks like a giant toddler. If that is indeed what it is, then it adds more weight to the idea that giants were real.

Researchers found the mummy near Cuzco, Peru. It is currently housed at the Ritos Andinos Museum, which is located far southeast of Lima. A hole in the mummy's skull indicates that it had a fontanel, which is an area of connective tissue atop a baby's head that later fills in with bone. Like modern babies, the skull is larger than the rest of the body. But the strangest feature is that the skull is 20 inches long, which is larger than normal adult skulls. Lima anthropologist Pablo Bayabar examined the mummy and told the Chinese news source New Tang Dynasty Television:

> Children's heads are proportionally bigger than their bodies. Here we have two points. First, the fontanelle is open, which usually closes at 31 months. And it has molars that usually appears [sic] between approximately 13 and 19 months. So we are looking at a child under two years old with an enormous head.

> If the youngster had fully matured, he would have qualified as a giant. The skeleton has other unique features, including large eye sockets, a unique molar structure, and an unusual shelf on its chin. Ritos Andinos Museum Director Renato Davila said, "It's 20 inches tall, which doesn't coincide with the stereotypes of humans." Some anthropologists are reluctant to call it human.

DAILY MAIL
United Kingdom
July 21, 2018

A mummified elongated skull found in Peru could finally prove the existence of aliens. The strangely shaped head – almost as big as its 50 cm. (20 in.) body – has baffled anthropologists. It was one of two sets of remains found in the city of Andahuaylillas in the southern province of Quispicanchi. The skeletal sets were discovered by Renato Davila Riquelme, who works for the Privado Ritos Andinos museum in Cusco in south-eastern Peru. He said that the eye cavities are far larger than normally seen in humans. There is a soft spot in the skull - called an open fontanelle - which is a characteristic of children in their first year of life, yet the skull also has two large molars, only found in much older humans. Davila Riquelme said three anthropologists, from Spain and Russia, arrived at the museum last week to investigate the findings and agreed it was 'not a human being' and would conduct further studies. He added: 'Although the assessment was superficial, it is obvious that its features do not correspond to any ethnic group in the world. The remains of an eyeball

The unidentified creature has a strangely shaped skull nearly as large as its 20-inch-tall body.

in the right socket will help determine its genetic DNA

and clear up the controversy of whether it is human or not.

The second mummy is incomplete and is only 30 cm. (12 in.). It lacks a face and seems to be wrapped in a layer as a placenta, fetal position. The remains bear a striking resemblance to the triangular crystal skull in the 2008 Indiana Jones film *Kingdom of the Crystal Skull* - which turned out to be of alien origin and have supernatural powers.

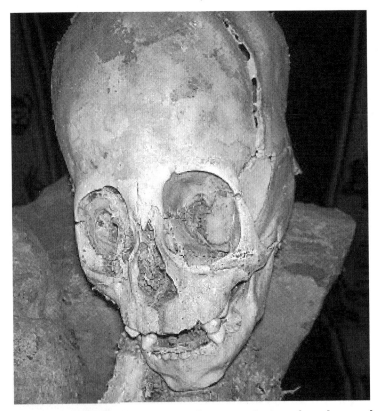

The unidentified creature has a strangely shaped skull nearly as large as its 20-inch-tall body. Skull has soft spot, found in infants, yet also two large molars, found in older humans.

There are many cultures around the world that have myths of magical Little People who live their lives outside of the view of normal humans. Gnomes, fairies, elves, leprechauns, and pixies are some of the European versions of this phenomenon. In South American lore, such Little People go by many names.

The concept of actual races of Little People in Mexico and the continent of South America, dates back thousands of years. The Olmec culture, considered the "mother civilization" in ancient Mexico, flourished from around 1600 BC to 300 BC. Although the Olmecs had no written record, they left behind much in the form of sculpture, pottery and architecture. Among the artifacts of this civilization we see depictions of dwarflike humans serving the elites or as court entertainers. Just who these dwarves were, is the subject of debate. Some investigators believe that actual human dwarves held special status in Olmec society. Others see ancient depictions of smaller humanoids in the archaeological record as proof that a mythical race of Little People existed, dating back thousands of years.

In the Mayan culture there are similar depictions. Are they evidence of smaller humanoids, a race of supernatural beings, or human dwarves who held special status in the ancient Maya world? When the Spanish encountered the living cultures of the New World, they found that the people of the Aztec and Maya lands had a powerful belief in Little People called Aluxes and Chaneques. This belief lingers today in these areas.

People who have reported seeing such wee folk generally describe them as fully human but smaller, sometimes standing no more than two feet tall. Sometimes they wear clothes, other times not. When they are dressed, the tiny beings are said to wear straw hats and cloth shoes. They tend to have larger eyes, sometimes described as glowing red, and their noses are larger than a normal human's. Their ears are pointed like those of European elves. They carry bags made of cloth or cactus fiber, their "bag of tricks." In some legends, the Little People carry around slingshots to use in hunting or to shoot stones at disagreeable humans. There are some stories of these creatures painting them as unfriendly and have a more diabolical appearance.

In some modern sightings in Mexico, little humanoids have been depicted hairless, with a large forehead, big black eyes, and claws on their feet and hands. In some legends, the creature is said to have backwards-facing feet and is covered in fur. According to some accounts, these creatures have been known to shape-shift from their diminutive humanlike form into the form of animals.

A brief summary of some the Southern hemisphere's little folk follows:

CHANEQUE

There are legendary creatures in Mexican and Aztec folklore called Chaneque, which means "those who inhabit dangerous places." They are small, sprite-like beings who live in harmony with elemental forces and guardians of nature. Traditions tells that these beings would attack intruders, frightening them so much that their soul would abandon their body. The Chaneques would capture the soul and conceal it. If the victim did not recover their soul through a specific ritual, he or she would become ill and die soon after.

Chaneques are described as children with the face of old men or women; that make people go stray for days, after which the victims cannot recall anything that happened. They just have a vague impression that they were taken by the Chaneques to their home in the Underworld, of which the entrance is a dry kapok tree.

In Catholic beliefs, the Chaneque are the souls of the children who died without Christian baptism, and that they are a sort of violent child demon who prey on people who wander in the forest or jungles of Mexico. They confuse people to make them lost, then prey on them at night, eating them. To get rid of a Cheneque, a person has to turn their shirt inside out or yell "Juan" three times to break their spell.

Similar mythical beings are common in Mesoamerican and other Latin American folkloric traditions generally, referred to in Spanish as Duende. In the folkloric tradition of the Yucatán Peninsula, these elementals are known as Alux in Yucatec Maya.

ALUX

P.T. Barnum, was an American promoter who ran the Barnum American Museum, which featured human oddities. Mayan dwarves traveled with P.T. Barnum's freak shows from 1841 to 1868. These Mayan dwarves told of the Alux, who were described as a small race of magical, feral, humanlike beings who lived in the mountains and forests of Mexico and Central America.

Besides the possibility of shape-shifting, Aluxes and Chaneques possess many powers that either help or serve to confound humans. According to Maya legend, Aluxes were on this planet before humans. Some myths even place them here before the arrival of the sun to the earth; therefore, they are accustomed to working in darkness. They sometimes work together with local spirits and gods to affect changes in their environments, like making it rain, for example. These beings are seen as caretakers of the wild areas in which they live; they look after the animals and the plants in their area. Certain Aluxes and Chaneques inhabit forests, mountains, rivers and beaches. In the Maya culture, wherever there is a distinct natural formation, a Chaneque or Alux is usually living nearby. If their peaceful coexistence with nature is upset by humans, there will be hell to pay.

They will take revenge on anyone disrespecting them and their habitat; so, great respect must be shown to these magical beings.
For example, if a farmer plants a new field of corn in a forest-ed area, he should ask permission of the local spirit, or give up offerings before he starts digging. A farmer may leave behind food or tobacco in thanks for permission to use the land.

ALUXES IN CANCUN

There are modern-day stories in the Yucatan that demonstrate belief in the Little People myths, and care was taken by authorities to appease the local Aluxes. One has to do with the construction of the Cancun-Nizuc Bridge near the Cancún International Airport located in Cancún, on the Caribbean coast of Mexico's Yucatán Peninsula. Several times during the construction of the bridge, workers would return in the morning to the site to find the bridge mysteriously destroyed. Some locals suggested that the recurring destruction of the bridge was caused by a mischievous Alux who did not want the bridge built. The government then contacted a local Maya shaman to perform a ceremony at the construction site to acknowledge the Alux and to ask its permission to carry on with the construction.

After the shamanic ceremony, no further incidents occurred. Today, you can see a small stone house constructed under the Cancun-Nizuc Bridge as a sign of respect for the Alux; offerings are periodically left by locals who believe.

Mayan Aluxes

THE YUCATAN TIMES
Yucatan, Mexico
April 9, 2015

DO YOU KNOW THE MOST FAMOUS LEGEND OF ALUXES IN CANCUN?

CANCUN.—Aluxes in the Mayan culture are known as small supernatural beings (elf sort of creatures), with whom the peasants had to pact, in order to protect the cornfields, that over the years reached urban development.

The Cancun-Nizuc bridge, which is in the route to the international airport of the city, work that was carried out by the Secretariat of Communications and Transportation (SCT) has been one of the most famous and representative legends in Cancun involving Aluxes.

The chronicler of the city, Francisco Verdayes said that this is a story that has passed from generation to generation, has changed its versions, but the essence of the legend about the history of Aluxes and the bridge to the airport yet remains.

"People passing the bridge sees the Aluxes house and tell the story of how these beings protected their land so much from construction on the site where the bridge stands now." he said.

ALUX VANDALISM TO THE BRIDGE

The popular story says that Aluxes knocked down, on more than one occasion, the construction of the Cancun-Nizuc bridge, which perplexed the architects, engineers and construction workers. According to the account of the communicator and opinion leader of the town, Juan Pablo Torres-Limón "The construction of the bridge leading to the airport from the city was prepared during the days work to arrive the next day, engineers and

418

workers to find that early works were destroyed without explanation."

According to Torres Limón, the bridge fell more than three times before finally the engineers accepted—with skepticism—to resort to a Mayan priest to negotiate with the Aluxes and finish the work.

SUPERNATURAL PACT

Aluxes are made of mud and "given breath" according to Mayan belief and people pact with these beings to protect some ground and keep out intruders, so despite the years, they continued taking care of the earth. The Mayan priest noted that Aluxes did not mean to hurt, but they were guarding their land, that happened to be the construction site. The priest contacted them through a ritual to make a new covenant, which allowed them to continue with the construction of the bridge.

In a survey conducted through social networks, it was asked to users of Facebook, if they knew the story. And, in accordance with the results, for half of them the story was unknown; the other half, most of them roughly know the story; and just a few actually did know it.

On the underside of the bridge, which was opened in 1991 by former President of Mexico, Carlos Salinas de Gortari, you can see a small house in the typical style of the region, both tourists and some residents believe it is a tourist attraction, but actually that was the new agreement to curb the dispute between the Aluxes and the construction engineers.

The Aluxes allowed the construction under the condition that they be given a space and not be moved away from their home, place where, according to the beliefs, they still live.

THE PLAYATIMES
June 8, 2016

THE LEGEND OF THE ALUXES

Do You Dare To Ignore A Mystical Creatures´ Demand For Respect?

A FAIRYTALE OR NOT, LEGENDS SAY IT MAY BE BEST TO HONOR THE ALUXES

Born in a ceremony conducted by a Mayan priest, Aluxes are believed to protect their owners and their owners' property.

How many of you have traveled on the bridge from the Cancun airport to the hotel zone? Or driven beneath it on your way to Cancun? How many of you know that during construction, the bridge collapsed…twice. Was it from faulty construction techniques? Engineering issues? Or was it something more mischievous and dangerous – an Alux!

Similar to Irish leprechauns or European gnomes and fairies, Aluxes (pronounced ah-loosh-es) are mysterious and mythical creatures in the Maya culture. Born in a ceremony conducted by a Maya priest, Aluxes are believed to protect their owners and their owners' property. When treated well, through offerings of food, honey, corn, and tobacco, Aluxes protect fields and property from thieves or others wishing to do harm. These light and agile creatures are rarely seen and when not treated well, can wreak havoc.

Stories of Aluxes terrorizing children, harassing neglectful owners, and even leading people into the jungle where they become lost for days can be heard all over the Yucatan Peninsula. When property is sold or passed down, it is important for the new owners to continue to make offerings. You may even see small houses or shelters built out of respect for Aluxes in some of resorts, hotels and even roads throughout the Yucatan.

Prior to concerts given by Luciano Pavarotti and Sarah Brightman at Chichen Itza, sacred ceremonies and offerings were conducted by Maya priests to please the Aluxes. Both concerts went off without a hitch. Then, during preparation for the Elton John concert (also held at Chichen Itza) the stage collapsed and three workers were injured. Later, it was admitted that a ceremonial offering was not made to the Aluxes. Some believe the Aluxes were to blame for the stage collapse.

As for the Cancun bridge problems, rumor has it, following the second incident with the bridge, a Maya priest was brought in to conduct a sacred ceremony and workers constructed a small house to honor the Aluxes, which still stands. The bridge was finished without incident and millions of travelers use the bridge every year, unaware of the mischievous Aluxes in their presence.

As seen in the two examples and in many others, the changing temperaments of Aluxes or Chaneques are legendary. The creature may be playful and joyful like a child, and then be quick to anger. Because they are somewhat childlike, these creatures are said to have an affinity for children. Sightings of Aluxes or Chaneques are more common by children than by adults. But, most sightings by children are often dismissed as imaginary friends or made up stories; but, parents who believe in these creatures often tell their children to be careful while playing in the wilder areas because of the reputation for kidnapping children that is attached to Aluxes or Chaneques.

Although many believe that the Aluxes and Chaneques have been around long before humans, some people in various regions of the Mayan area believe that Aluxes can actually be created by humans through shamanic ceremonies. Property owners will fashion an Alux out of clay with a heart made of honey. The effigy must also include 9 drops of blood from the landowner. When finished, the creator takes the clay figure to a shaman or priest, who calls upon the wind, sun, rain and earth for the proper alignment to create the perfect guardian spirit that will enter the clay figure. After the ceremony, the small Alux statue is placed somewhere on the person's property. At night, it is said, the Alux comes to life.

It is the responsibility of the person who created the clay figure to maintain the statue, to leave offerings, and to ask the Alux for permission or forgiveness. The shaman who animates the Alux also has the power to counteract the being's malevolent power. If an Alux is up to bad tricks – like breaking windows, or stealing keys, for example – the shaman may intervene on behalf of the landowner by making special offerings in a ceremony. In extreme cases, especially when the Alux has been blamed for diseases or pestilence, the shaman will conduct a ceremony in which the clay figurine is shattered by a big rock, thus releasing any curses of the Alux or obligations to it.

For those who are skeptical of such beings, because they are elusive and temperamental by nature, it will be difficult to capture a creatures that does not want to be found. For those who believe in these beings, no proof is needed. All that needs to be done is to give it proper respect and take precautions to ensure the creatures are not upset. Leave them to their own little worlds.

DUENDE

A Duende is a creature from Latin American folklore. The Spanish term means "possessor of a house." The Duende originated as a mischievous spirit inhabiting a house. n the Hispanic folklore of Mexico and the American Southwest, duendes are known as gnome-like creatures who live inside the walls of homes, especially in the bedroom walls of young children. They attempt to clip the toenails of unkempt children, often leading to the mistaken removal of entire toes. In some Latin American cultures, Duendes are described as being helpers of people who get lost in the forest; they guide the traveler back home. In the folklore of the Central American country of Belize, Duendes are thought of as forest spirits called "Tata Duende," a form of this being who lacks thumbs. They are most commonly found in the mossy cloud forests of the mountain ranges.

A mummified skeleton from the Atacama Desert in Chile has been described as "alien." But genetic analysis shows that she was human and may have had a previously unknown bone disorder.

Photo Credit: Bhattacharya S et al. 2018.

NEW YORK TIMES
New York, New York
March 22, 2018

By CARL ZIMMER

Nearly two decades ago, the rumors began: In the Atacama Desert of northern Chile, someone had discovered a tiny mummified alien. An amateur collector exploring a ghost town was said to have come across a white cloth in a leather pouch. Unwrapping it, he found a six-inch-long skeleton. Despite its size, the skeleton was remarkably complete. It even had hardened teeth. And yet there were striking anomalies: it had 10 ribs instead of the usual 12, giant eye sockets and a long skull that ended in a point. Ata, as the remains came to be known, ended up in a private collection, but the rumors continued, fueled in part by a U.F.O. documentary in 2013 that featured the skeleton. On Thursday, a team of scientists presented a very different explanation for Ata — one without aliens, but intriguing in its own way.

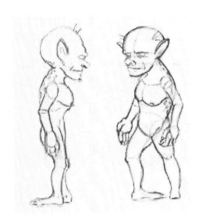

CURUPIRA

The Curupira is a mythological creature of Brazilian folklore. The name means "covered in blisters." This creature was most often regarded as a demon. The Curupira has bright red/orange hair, and resembles a man or a dwarf; but its feet are turned backwards. The Curupira lives in the forests of Brazil. It uses its backward feet to create footprints that lead to its starting point, rather than where it went. This confuses hunters and travelers. The Curupira can also create illusions and produce a sound that's like a high pitched whistle. It does these things in order to intimidate its victim and drive it to madness. A common portrayal is of a Curupira riding a collared peccary, which resembles a boar, much like another Brazilian creature called Caipora. A Curupira will prey on poachers and hunters that take more than they need of the forest; he also attacks people who hunt animals that were tending to their offspring. There are many different versions of the legend, so the creature's appearance and habits may vary between regions in Brazil.

CAIPORA

An entity of the Tupi-Guarani mythology in Brazil, the word "Caipora" means "inhabitant of the forest." Depicted as a dark-skinned, small Indian, naked with a very long black mane, smoking a cigar and very mischievous, the Caipora can be a boy or a girl. Like the Curupira, representations of the creature varies among the different regions of Brazil. Some indigenous tribes believed that the Caipora was afraid of light. For this reason, they would walk around the forest protecting themselves using firebrands. Some say, the Caipora rides a great peccary (a type of swine), holding a stick. In some other areas, the Caipora is considered to be a cannibal who would eat anything, even the smallest insects.

Known as a forest dweller, and a king of the animals there, the Caipora is very vengeful of hunters who do not respect the rules of fair play when hunting. Legends say that it scares away prey and hides animal tracks or makes hunters lose their way in the jungle. It disorients the hunters by simulating animal noises and by leaving fake tracks.

According to a popular belief, Caipora activity increases on days in which hunting is forbidden: Fridays, Sundays, and the religious holidays. It is claimed that there are ways to trick this protector of the forest. It is known that the Caipora likes smoke; so, on Thursday nights, the hunters would leave smoke by the trunk of a tree and say in their native language,

"Here you go, Caipora, let me leave." Good luck is bestowed by Caipora on hunters who leave them gifts.

IKALS

The legends of small humanoid creatures in Central America include the small, dwarflike beings known as Ikals. The Ikals were known to the Tzeltal Indians, who described them as being about three feet tall, quite hairy, and living in caves like bats. Black, ugly, hairy, the Ikal is half-human, with human hands, but the hooves of a horse. Some reports say that these beings are protectors, guarding a patron's house at night, and frightening people away at dusk. Some of the Tzeltal Indian accounts portray these beings as demons. In his volume, *Passport to Magonia* (1969), scientific researcher Jacques Vallee writes of Ikals. He states:

> ....Let us follow the (reports of the) 'strong beings' across the world now, to Mexico, where the American anthropologist, Brian Stross, from Berkeley, reports that the Tzeltal Indians have strange legends of their own. One night, Stross and his Indian assistant discussed these legends, of the Ihk'als or Ikals, the little black beings that appeared after seeing a strange light wandering about in the Mexican sky.

> The Ikals are three-foot tall, hairy, black humanoids whom natives encounter frequently; and, Stross learned: "About twenty years ago, or less, there were many sightings of this creature or creatures, and several people tried to fight it with machetes. One man also saw a sphere following him from about five feet. After many attempts he finally hit it with his machete and it disintegrated, leaving only an ash-like substance."

> These beings were observed in ancient times. They fly; they attack people; and, in the modern reports, they carry a kind of rocket on their backs and kidnap Indians. Occasionally, Stross was told, people have been 'paralyzed' when they came upon the Ikals, who are said to live in caves, which the natives are careful to not enter.

426

INEXPLICATA - THE JOURNAL
OF HISPANIC UFOLOGY
July 18, 2007

STRANGE CREATURES SEEN IN SAN LUIS, ARGENTINA

RESIDENTS OF MERLO CLAIM HAVING SEEN IMPS NEAR A HUNDRED YEAR OLD EUCALYPTUS TREE.

A Strange Story From Valle de Conlara.

[From Scott Corrales]

The Municipality trimmed the tree because its large branches were jeopardizing motorists traveling along Avenida del Inca. After work, some residents reportedly saw little men coming out [of the tree] in single file from that location.

The landscapes described by the prolific South African (sic) writer John Ronald Reuel Tolkien, author of The Lord of the Rings, as the habitat of imps, elves, trolls and fairies that appear in his works do not vary all that much. These creatures enjoy living in forests, trees, small rivers and clean environments. They tend to dwell within trees or openings in the surface.

Described thus, an infinite number of similar landscapes can be described in a number of points throughout the country, and Merlo is no exception, even though humans may be accused of making these places fewer and fewer.

Days ago, the Municipality of Merlo, at the request of local residents, trimmed a hundred-year old eucalyptus that is next to the Leopoldo Lugones Library in Piedra Blanca, on a tight curve by Avenida de los Incas. The large branches obscured visibility for motorists and jeopardized light and telephone wires on windy days.

While the trimming operations took place on the avenue, adjacent to a stream, traffic was interrupted and once restored, locals driving through the area, lighting it with their car headlights, claimed to have seen the strange figures. They reportedly saw some little men coming out of the amputated tree and walking single file toward the library. Most witnesses did not offer details, but one woman described their clothing as having a brownish hue, said Cecillia de Gabrele, an employee at the library who fielded several phone calls at her workplace from locals who sought confirmation for what they had seen nearby. However, neither the employee nor her coworkers noticed anything unusual.

Cecilia added that for many years there have been stories of sightings in that district. "That's where Aguaribay Street begins, which has abundant native flora, and many claim having seen tiny beings between the branches and shadows.

Once the trimming operation was over in what some believe may have been the dwelling of these little people, the landscape was devastating, according to De Gabriele. The eucalyptus has a reddish wood and after being trimmed, this shade became visible. Faced with the bizarre scene, some have gone as far as to suggest that the strong coloring gave the impression that the tree was bleeding.

HEXA-
DACTYLS

The word *hexadactyl* literally means "six digits." Many giants that have been described through all of history and folklore, have six fingers on each hand; or six fingers on each toe; or both. Ancient man, although sometimes thought to be not too intelligent, showed that he could count fingers and toes. Petroglyphs, cave paintings, and other ancient carvings include occasional depictions of people who had extra digits.

It is related in the Bible, that some members of giant races had six fingers and six toes. In ancient times, in the Levant, polydactylism was considered to be a mark of the Rephaim, a race of giants. In the Old Testament, the book of Samuel describes such giants (II Samuel 21:20): "Yet again there was war at Gath, where there was a man of great stature, who had six fingers on each hand and six toes on each foot, twenty-four in number; and he also was born to the giant."

Archaeologists have uncovered bones from the earth proving that such conditions did exist. This pheno-menon could be found all over the earth. Long before our time, impressions were made in the art work of native peoples everywhere. The same goes for ancient religious texts. Bigfoot researchers have reported coming across six-toed tracks.

One example of this can be found online:

"I live in Penticton British Columbia. I usually don't tell this story because everyone laughs at me, here it is, take it or leave it. About 5 years ago, I was mountain biking with friends NE of Penticton, B.C., when I came across footprints that were about 18" long, a left foot and a right. They were about 4 inches in the ground, which was very hard (an old railway bed). They had 6 toes, yes 6 toes on each foot and the prints had grain and lines to them like your hand does. I left them and went to get my friends. When I came back with my friends they all laughed, they thought I did it as a trick. Honestly, I could not reproduce what I found even if I wanted to, I have thought about how a forgery could have been made but the details on the print itself, and the fact they were 4" in the old train tracks, truck tire tracks only sink in maybe 1 inch. The prints were heading west down a very steep bank, to the east was a cliff about 35-40' straight up.

Assuming the tracks were real, it appeared the bigfoot had jumped down the cliff onto the tracks and continued down the embankment, explaining the depth of the prints.

Of course, not all giants ever reported in oral and written accounts, or illustrated through some artwork, had more than the usual five fingers on each hand; and five toes on each foot, depictions like those that follow cannot be ignored:

THREE RIVERS, NM

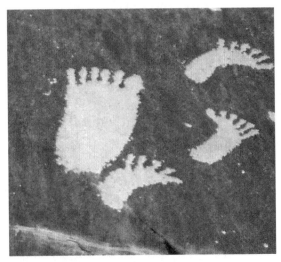

NEWSPAPER ROCK, UTAH

CHACO CANYON, NM

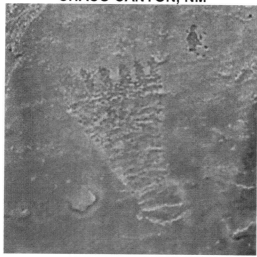

MOGOLLON RIM, AZ

FRANCE

THREE RIVERS, MEXICO

SUMERIA

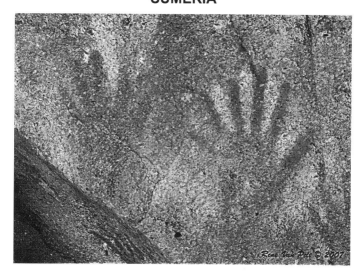

CHILE

MEXICO

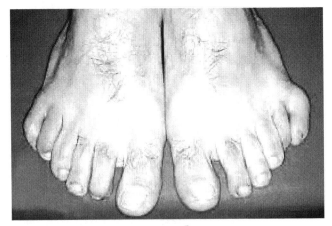

ACTUAL MODERN HUMAN

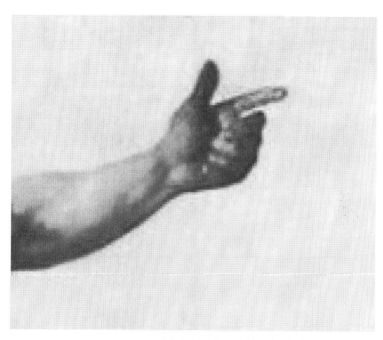

DETAIL FROM OLD OIL PAINTING

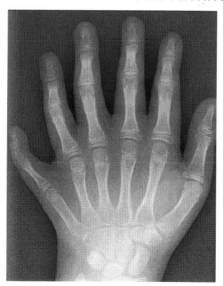

X-RAY OF MODERN HUMAN

THEY WERE HERE BEFORE US....

THEY ONCE WALKED THIS EARTH

THE EVIDENCE EXISTS

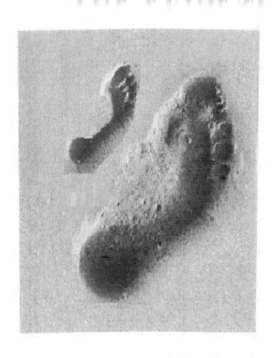

THEIR FEET TOO TOUCHED THE GROUND

FOOTPRINTS BIG & SMALL UPON THE EARTH

HOW LONG WAS THEIR STRIDE?

HOW TALL WAS THE SHADOW?

FROM MAMMOTH TO MINISCULE....

Author Peter Netzel brings you –

HERE BEFORE US....
GIANTS and LITTLE PEOPLE
Volume 2

Printed in Great Britain
by Amazon